The Consultant's Guide to Results-Driven Business Proposals

The Consultant's Guide to Results-Driven Business Proposals

How to Write Proposals That Forecast Impact and ROI

JACK PHILLIPS AND PATRICIA PULLIAM PHILLIPS

New York   Chicago   San Francisco   Lisbon
London   Madrid   Mexico City   Milan   New Delhi
San Juan   Seoul   Singapore   Sydney   Toronto

1   2   3   4   5   6   7   8   9   0   DOC/DOC   0   1   0   9

ISBN: 978-0-07-163880-7
MHID: 0-07-163880-6

This publication is designed to provide accurate and authoritative information in regard to the subject matter covered. It is sold with the understanding that the publisher is not engaged in rendering legal, accounting, or other professional service. If legal advice or other expert assistance is required, the services of a competent professional person should be sought.
—*From a Declaration of Principles Jointly Adopted by a Committee of the American Bar Association and a Committee of Publishers and Associations*

McGraw-Hill books are available at special quantity discounts to use as premiums and sales promotions, or for use in corporate training programs. To contact a representative, please visit the Contact Us pages at www.mhprofessional.com.

This book is printed on acid-free paper.

♦ ♦ ♦

Contents

♦ ♦ ♦

Acknowledgments

Every author will quickly admit that a book is not solely his or her work, but a myriad of influences from others. This idea is particularly true for a book on consulting. We have been fortunate to be involved in hundreds of consulting projects, and as we approach almost two decades of consulting, the future looks even brighter. We have learned from many sources; first and foremost are the clients that we work with, who are some of the largest and most prestigious organizations and include four of the top five consulting firms. We are honored that they would invite us into their organizations to seek our advice as we implement projects and conduct studies. In turn, our involvement with them garnered many learning opportunities—some mentioned in this book.

We have also learned from other impressive consultants, who focus on results, such as Alan Weiss and Robert H. Shaffer. These two consultants are admirable in their drive to communicate and deliver value up front in terms of clear expectations from the client. We have also learned from consultants who are not positive role models, avoid accountability, and are disinterested in delivering value. Obviously, we cannot mention them, but their numbers are more than they should be. Although we've been disappointed with the accountability of some consulting firms, particularly the larger ones, the current and most recent economic climate is unfortunately taking its toll on those who do not deliver quality value for their clients.

In this book's development, we also appreciate the great efforts of McGraw-Hill. This book is our fourth with them, and our third involving consulting. With them, we hope to offer a full range of products and services to the consulting professional, particularly those who are embarking on this profession as a change in career. We thank Knox Huston, particularly, for his interest in our work as well as his patience in getting the work done.

We also thank our staff at the ROI Institute. Always a charm to work with, they are helpful in so many ways. We are particularly indebted to our managing editor, Alison Frenzel, who is, without a doubt in our almost three decades of writing books, the best editor on our staff, past and present. Her outstanding work shines in every phase of this book, and through her efforts, this is a much better book.

And now for our own guarantee of success: If you have purchased this book and are disappointed that it did not deliver value for you, we will be happy to refund the entire purchase price. If this is the case, send us a note detailing your concerns with a receipt for your purchase, and we'll send you a refund. You can keep the book. This policy is our standard guarantee with all of our books, and so far, we've never had to make a refund. Please also let us know your thoughts about the book. We appreciate your feedback.

From Jack:

I am delighted to co-author a book with my friend, spouse, and colleague, Patti, who is an outstanding consultant, researcher, writer, and facilitator. She is a perfectionist who ensures that our work is always proper and that we deliver what we promise. To her, I owe a great appreciation for her continued support for what I do, and particularly, for the projects that we tackle together.

From Patti:

As always, much love and thanks go to Jack. You invest in others more than you get in return. What a contribution you make! Thank you for your inspiration and the fun you bring to my life.

1

The Value Evolution

Before you gather your courage for your presentation, you must know the project's value. Before you put the finishing touches on your project's estimated costs, you must understand the project's value. And before you even think of approaching your executive, you must be able to identify the project's value.

The bottom line is value. Projects need to deliver value, and proposals need to show the promise of value. Of course, this statement is somewhat obvious and isn't new, especially in business settings. Executives of all types and in all kinds of organizations want value for their investments. What is new, however, is the method used to obtain this value. While "showing the money" is the ultimate report of value, executives recognize that value lies in the eye of the beholder; therefore, the method used to show the money must also show the value as perceived by all stakeholders. Just as important is a methodology that provides data to help improve investment decisions for organizations.

This chapter presents the evolution of value for projects—moving from activity-focused data to the ultimate value, return on investment (ROI). This chapter also describes issues and challenges involved in including these types of data in proposals.

VALUE REDEFINED

The phrase "show me the money" represents the newest value statement. In the past project success was measured by activity: number of people involved, money spent, days to complete, system implemented, equipment installed. Little consideration was given to what was derived from these activities. Today, the meaning of value has shifted: Value is defined by results instead of activity. More frequently, value is shown as monetary gains compared with costs. From Six-Sigma quality improvement processes in technology to public policy, project leaders are showing value by using a comprehensive evaluation process. The following organizations have used this paradigm shift in their projects:

- The U.S. Air Force developed the ROI for data security to prevent intrusion into its databases.
- Apple Computer calculated the ROI for investing in process improvement teams.
- Sprint/NEXTEL developed the ROI on its diversity program.
- The Australian Capital Territory Community Care agency forecast the ROI for the implementation of a client relationship management (CRM) system.
- Accenture calculated the ROI on a new sales platform for its consultants.
- A major hotel chain calculated the financial value and ROI of its coaching program.
- The cities of New York, San Francisco, and Phoenix showed the monetary value of investing in projects to reduce the number of homeless citizens on the streets.
- Cisco Systems is measuring the ROI for its key meetings and events.
- A major U.S. Defense Department agency developed the ROI for a master's degree program offered by a major university.

Suppose that in each of the above scenarios, a forecast was made to predict the value in advance. Is it possible? Is it reliable? Does it even matter? If a client asked for this forecast, how would you react? What would be your approach? If you could forecast and do it credibly with a reasonable amount of resources, what advantage would it give your proposal? Would it help win the project?

The answers to these questions and more are fully explored in this book to give you an important strategic advantage in getting your proposal approved. It is possible to forecast values on these types of projects credibly and with a reasonable amount of resources before they are implemented. This ability is even more desired as many clients are asking, hinting, or at least bringing up the possibility as an option. This methodology to show the money has become the most comprehensive and broad-reaching approach to demonstrating—and forecasting—the value of project investment.

Types of values

Value is determined by the stakeholders' perspectives, which may include organizational, spiritual, personal, and social values. Value is defined by consumers, taxpayers, and shareholders. In the capitalist system value is defined as the economic contribution to shareholders.

However, even as projects are implemented to improve the social, environmental, and economic climates, the monetary value is often sought to ensure that resources are allocated appropriately and that investments reap a return. No longer is it enough to report the number of projects completed, the number of participants or volunteers involved, or the money generated through a fund-raising effort. Stakeholders at all levels—including executives, shareholders, managers and supervisors, taxpayers, project designers, and participants—are searching for outcomes, and in many cases, the monetary values of those outcomes.

The importance of monetary values

While some are concerned that too much focus is placed on economic value, it is actually economics, or money, that allows organizations and individuals to contribute to the greater good. Monetary resources are limited, and they can be put to best use—or underuse and overuse. Organizations and individuals have choices about where they invest these resources. To ensure that monetary resources are put to best use, they must be allocated to projects that yield the greatest return.

For example, if a process-improvement project is begun to improve efficiencies and it does indeed improve them, one might assume that the project was successful. But if the project costs more than the efficiency gains are worth, has value been added to the organization? Could a less expensive process have yielded similar or even better results, possibly reaping a positive ROI? Is it possible to know these issues before the project is approved? Questions like these are, or should be, asked on a routine basis. No longer will activity suffice as a measure of results. A new generation of decision makers is defining value in a new way, and they want it before the project is approved.

The "Show-me generation"

Figure 1.1 illustrates the requirements of the new show-me generation (Phillips and Phillips 2007). Early attempts to show value in projects implied that stakeholders wanted to see data (i.e., numbers and measures), but this early attempt to show value in projects evolved into "show me the money," a direct call for financial results. However, this alone did not provide the evidence to ensure that projects add value. Often a connection between projects and value is assumed, but that assumption must give way to the need to show an actual connection. Hence "show me the real money" is an attempt at

Figure 1.1. How "Show me the money" evolved.

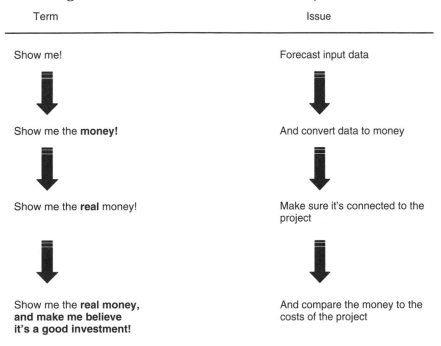

Term	Issue
Show me!	Forecast input data
Show me the **money!**	And convert data to money
Show me the **real** money!	Make sure it's connected to the project
Show me the **real money, and make me believe it's a good investment!**	And compare the money to the costs of the project

establishing credibility. This phase, though critical, still leaves stakeholders with an unanswered question: Do the proposed monetary benefits linked to the project outweigh the costs? This question is the mantra for the new show-me generation: Show me the real money, and make me believe it is a good investment. Additionally, this new generation of project sponsors recognizes that value is more than just a single number: Value is what makes the entire organizational system tick—hence, the need to report value based on the stakeholders' various definitions.

The new definition of value

The changing perspectives on value and the shifts that are occurring in organizations have all led to a new definition of value. Value is not defined as a single number. Rather, its definition includes a variety of data points. Value must be balanced with quantitative and qualitative data, as well as financial and nonfinancial perspectives. The data sometimes reflect tactical issues, such as activity, as well as strategic issues, such as ROI. Value must be derived using different time frames and not necessarily represent a single point in time. It must reflect the value systems that are important to different stakeholders. The data composing value must be collected from credible sources, using cost-effective methods; and value must be action-oriented, compelling individuals to make adjustments and changes. Under the new, balanced definitions of value, value for projects must:

- Be balanced, with qualitative and quantitative data
- Contain financial and nonfinancial perspectives
- Reflect strategic and tactical issues
- Represent different time frames
- Satisfy all key stakeholders
- Be consistent in collection and analysis
- Be grounded in conservative standards
- Come from credible sources
- Reflect efficiency in its development
- Create a call for action

The processes used to forecast value must be consistent from one project to another. Standards must be in place so that forecast and follow-up results can be compared. These standards must support conservative outcomes when communicating to decision makers. The ROI methodology presented in this book meets all these criteria. It forecasts or captures eight types of outcome data that reflect the issues contained in the new definition of value: reaction, learning, application, impact, monetary benefits, costs, return on investment, and intangible benefits.

WHY NOW?

In the past decade a variety of forces have demanded additional focus on forecasting the impact of projects in the proposal stage, including the financial contribution and ROI. These forces have challenged old ways of defining project success.

Project failures

Almost every organization encounters unsuccessful projects—projects that go astray, costing far too much and failing to deliver on promises. Project disasters occur in business organizations as well as in government and nonprofit organizations. Some project disasters are legendary. Some are swept under rugs and covered up, but they are there, and the numbers are far too large to tolerate (Nickson and Siddons 2005). The endless string of failures has generated increased concerns about measuring project and program success—before, during, and after implementation. Many critics of these projects suggest that the failure could be avoided if: (1) the project is based on a legitimate need from the beginning; (2) adequate planning is in place at the outset; (3) a forecast of value is made before the project is developed; (4) data are collected throughout the project to confirm that the implementation is on track; and (5) an impact study is conducted to detail the project's contribution. Unfortunately, these steps are sometimes unintentionally omitted, not fully understood, or purposely ignored; thus greater emphasis is being placed on the processes of accountability. This book shows how needs, planning, and forecast are developed as a part of the proposal to create winning, value-adding projects.

Project costs

The costs of projects continue to grow. As costs rise, the budgets for these projects become targets for others who would like to have the money for their projects. What was once considered a mere cost of doing business is now considered an investment, and one to be wisely allocated. For example, consider the field of learning and development in business. Learning and development is, of course, necessary, particularly to introduce new skills and technology to employees, but 20 years ago it was regarded by some company executives as a frivolous expense. These days, the annual direct cost of organizational learning and development is estimated to be more than $100 billion in the United States. A few large organizations spend as much as $1 billion every year on corporate learning and development. With numbers like these, learning and development is no longer considered a frivolous expense; rather, it is regarded as an investment, and many executives expect a return on that investment.

The same is true for information technology (IT). Years ago, it seemed a necessary, but minor, part of most organizational expenses. This is not the case today. For example, Federal Express considers IT to be a major investment. Casual observers may not regard FedEx with trucks and airplanes moving packages as a high-tech company. However, IT is essential for FedEx to keep track of more than six million packages per day and to coordinate the work of two hundred thousand employees operating 677 airplanes and more than ninety thousand vehicles in 220 countries. Seconds and minutes count with FedEx. A technology glitch could amount to a public relations disaster (Colvin 2006). Because of the importance of IT, the company allocates an annual budget of $1 billion for information technology, a significant amount that attracts the attention of many executives.

Considerable pressure is placed on various governments today to do more with less money. As economic turmoil impacts big businesses, governments are often left with less to provide a variety of needed services. To reduce budgets, administrators must ensure that every dollar spent has a return. If there are programs that are not adding value, they should be eliminated or modified so that they can add value. These pressures force all administrators to manage costs and to undertake projects with the value projected. Here is what President Obama (2009) said about this in his inauguration speech.

> The question we ask today is not whether our government is too big or too small, but whether it works—whether it helps families find jobs at a decent wage, care they can afford, a retirement that is dignified. Where the answer is yes, we intend to move forward. Where the answer is no, programs will end. And those of us who manage the public's dollars will be held to account—to spend wisely, reform bad habits, and do our business in the light of day—because only then can we restore the vital trust between a people and their government.

Accountability trend

A consistent and lasting trend in accountability is evident in organizations across the globe: Almost every function, process, project, or initiative is judged based on higher standards than in the past. Various functions in organizations attempt to show their worth by capturing and demonstrating the value they add to the organization. They compete for funds; therefore, they have to show value. For example, the research and development function must show its value in monetary terms to compete with mainstream processes, such as sales and production, which have shown their value in direct monetary terms for more than a century.

ROI as a proposal tool

Some project sponsors are requesting that proposals address the issue of forecasting value, and they are including this information in their decision-making process. Choosing not to forecast, suggesting that it's not credible or an exercise in futility, could weigh heavily in the evaluation criteria. Because many sponsors recognize the difficulty and the newness of forecasting value, they are exploring what approaches are followed. They are quickly evaluating the credibility of the approaches. In this scenario, it is important to have a process that is credible, will stand the test of time, and meets the requirements of senior executives and administrators. More importantly, it must be and should be a reliable tool to suggest the value on a preproject basis. The approach presented in this book meets these criteria.

A business approach to projects

In the past, executives in governments, nonprofit organizations, and institutions had little or no business experience. Today, things have changed. Many of these managers have a business background, a formal business education, or a business focus. These new, enlightened executives are more aware of bottom-line issues in the organization and more knowledgeable of operational and financial concerns. They often take a business approach to their processes, with ROI being a part of that strategy. Because of their background, ROI is a familiar term. They have studied the use of ROI in their academic preparation, where the ROI methodology was used to evaluate projects for purchasing equipment, building new facilities, or buying a new building. Consequently, they understand and appreciate ROI and are eager to apply it in other areas as well as use it as a tool for project approval and project management.

The growth of project management

Few processes in organizations have grown as much as project management. Just two decades ago, attempting to bring organizational and management structure to projects was a lonely process. Today the Project Management Institute, for example, offers three levels of certification for professional project managers and has more than two hundred thousand members in 125 countries. Jobs are being restructured and designed to focus on projects. With the growing use of project management solutions, tools, and processes, a corresponding need to show the accountability for investing so heavily in this process has developed. This includes ROI forecasting for new projects.

Evidence-based or fact-based management

Recently there has been an important trend to move to fact-based or evidence-based management. Although many key decisions have been made using instinctive input and gut feelings, more managers are now using sophisticated and detailed processes to show value. Quality decisions must be based on more than gut feelings. With a comprehensive set of measures, including financial ROI, better organizational decisions regarding people, products, projects, and processes are possible. When taken seriously, evidence-based management can change how every manager thinks and acts. It is a way of seeing the world and thinking about the craft of management. Evidence-based management proceeds from the premise that using better, deeper logic and facts to the maximum extent possible helps leaders do their jobs better. It is based on the belief that facing the hard facts about what works and what doesn't work, and understanding and rejecting the nonsense that often passes for sound advice, will help organizations perform better (Pfeffer and Sutton 2006). This move to fact-based management makes expanding measurement to include ROI easier.

The executive appetite for monetary value

Monetary contribution and ROI is receiving increased interest in the executive suite. Executives, directors, and administrators have seen budgets continue to grow without appropriate accountability measures. They are responding to the situation by turning to ROI.

Top executives now demand ROI calculations and monetary contributions from departments and functions where they were not previously required. For years, functional managers and department heads convinced executives that their processes could not be measured and that the value of their projects should be taken on faith. Executives no longer buy that argument; they demand the same accountability from these functions as they do from the sales and production areas of the organization, and sometimes this includes a forecast of value before a project is approved. These major forces are requiring organizations to shift their measurement processes to include the financial impact and ROI.

CHALLENGES ALONG THE WAY

The journey to increased accountability and the quest to show monetary value, including ROI, are not going unchallenged. This movement represents a tremendous cultural shift for proposal writers, and often a complete rethinking of the initiation of projects in organizations is required.

The commitment dilemma

Commitment is key to successful implementation of the ROI methodology. While there are immediate benefits for using ROI forecasting, there is more to it than a simple calculation, as previously mentioned. Forecasting involves up to nine types of data that show the success of the proposed project (see the discussion below). To achieve success, commitment to making changes is imperative when the data reveal that the change is needed, as is commitment to using the information the process provides.

Preparation and skills

Although interest in forecasting ROI is now heightened and much progress has been made, these are still issues that challenge even the most sophisticated and progressive proposal writers. The problem often lies in the lack of preparation and skills that are needed to conduct these types of analyses. Rarely do the curricula in degree programs or the courses in a professional development program include processes and techniques to forecast value in proposals. Consequently, these skills must be developed using a variety of resources.

Fear of ROI

Few topics stir up emotions to the degree that ROI does. For a few executives, the conclusion behind the ROI forecast is simple: If it is negative, they kill the project; if it is extremely positive, they do not believe it. The potential for this response from clients causes some professionals to avoid the issue altogether. A familiar reaction emerges: "If my project is not delivering value, the last thing I want to do is publish ROI in my proposal for my sponsor." Unfortunately, if the project cannot deliver value, the sponsor will already know it, or at least someone in the organization will. Even without the forecast, the sponsor will know something about the value. The best thing to do is to show the value using a systematic, credible process. Then, adjust the project design and scope to ensure that it adds value. The fear of the ROI forecast can be minimized when the individuals involved understand the process, how it is designed and delivered, and the value that it can bring from a positive perspective.

Time to respond

Thorough analysis takes time. An ROI forecast will add time to the proposal process. Many proposal writers are overly eager and do not want to take the time to do the appropriate analyses. In a fast-paced work environment where decisions are often made quickly and with too little data, some bidders question the time and the effort involved in this type of analysis. What must be shown, however, is that this effort is necessary and appropriate and that it will ultimately pay off.

When the process is implemented, the successful bidders usually see that the value of the increased effort and activity far outweighs the cost of the time.

Power and politics

Having appropriate data represents power to many individuals, and how that power is used is important. If used for constructive purposes or to improve processes, data are perceived as valuable. If data are used for destructive or political purposes, they may be seen as less valuable. The important issue is that if the information is based on credible facts, then it generates power. If it is based on opinions or gut feelings, then the person who provides those opinions is more influential than the opinions themselves. Essentially, facts create a level playing field for decision making. As one executive from a high-technology company said, "If a decision is based on facts, then anyone's facts are equal as long as they are relevant; however, if it must be based on opinions, then my opinion counts a lot more." This underscores the power of having credible data for making decisions (Pfeffer and Sutton 2006).

Misleading hype

Claims abound about success and the use of data to support an idea or project. When the facts are examined, however, they often reveal something completely different. Tremendous claims and success stories are presented to promote a concept or idea. Exaggerated statements in marketing campaigns add to the confusion. For example, SAP, the world's largest business software company, ran a series of ads claiming that companies that use their software are more profitable than those that do not. An independent research unit found the opposite to be true. SAP then failed to show how they arrived at the conclusion. Projects are evaluated in a variety of ways, and few accepted standards, rules, and processes exist with which to validate those assumptions and claims. A systematic process with conservative, accepted standards can create a credible story of program success. This book offers a systematic process with conservative standards.

Sustainability

The final challenge is sustaining such a radical shift in accountability in projects and proposals. The use of the ROI methodology must consist of more than just developing one proposal to show the value of the project. It must represent a complete change in processes so that future projects and their proposals focus on results. This change will require building capability, developing consistent and compelling communication, involving stakeholders, building more process into proposals, creating expectations, and using data for process improvements. This is the only way to sustain any change for the long term; otherwise, it becomes a one-shot project opportunity.

FORECASTING VALUE AND GUARANTEEING SUCCESS

Now for the difficulties. Is it possible to forecast success, and if so, what does this success look like? Is it rational or feasible to even guarantee success? Obviously, this book makes a strong case for a strong yes for both of those issues, forecasting and guaranteeing success.

Forecasting value

As will be described in later chapters, it is possible to forecast value for the project. Some forecasting is a part of every proposal. When a project proposal suggests who will be involved, the areas that are covered, and the date when something will be delivered, these are forecasting promises. However, that's not enough. Forecasting must consist of a range of values. Here are the nine types of data that we suggest should be considered for the forecast:

1. **Inputs.** The inputs are what go into the project and involve individuals, resources, and time. Sometimes the inputs include equipment and technology.

2. **Costs.** The budget or price of the project is a forecast of what the fully loaded costs will be. It's a necessary issue when the ROI is calculated.

3. **Reaction to the project.** Predicting the reaction is important, especially because an adverse reaction can translate into the early demise of the project.

4. **Learning.** Sometimes projects fail because the project participants did not learn what was needed to make it successful. A forecast of what individuals will learn is necessary and involves estimating the extent of learning of knowledge, skills, and tasks to make the project successful.

5. **Application.** This is a forecast of what project participants will be doing and how they will be using the action items to make the project successful. The definition of these also includes behavior, actions, tasks, and procedures—all necessary for project success.

6. **Business impact.** What will drive the project? Will it be quality, accidents, revenue, productivity, cycle time, teen pregnancies, patient satisfaction, or citizen complaints? These measures are influenced by the project.

7. **Monetary benefits.** The monetary value of the business impact allows executives to see the conversion, meeting their request to show the money.

8. **The ROI.** A comparison of the monetary benefits to the cost of the program is the ultimate accountability of your project success and is the goal of many project proposals.

9. **Intangibles.** A forecast of what intangibles will be influenced by the project is made. Intangible benefits are an impact measure

not converted to money. This is often as important as the ROI forecast, if not more important than the ROI forecast.

The forecast addresses project disappointments

The forecast is an early attempt to avoid the disappointments of projects. Here are some of the common disappointments expressed as a comment and the specific forecast measure that addresses that disappointment.

1. "The wrong people were involved." The **input** forecast defines exactly who's involved and for how long.
2. "The project costs too much." The **cost** forecast describes exactly what will occur and how much money would be spent and when.
3. "From the beginning the participants never found the project to be relevant." **Reaction** data can bring attention to the desired reaction early so it can be adjusted in the process.
4. "They didn't have a clue how to make it work." **Learning** forecasts, based on learning objectives, will focus on what must be learned to be successful.
5. "They never used it." The **application** forecast defines what must be done (i.e., specific actions) and under what conditions and what accuracy.
6. "It was never connected to the business." The **impact** forecast shows the specific business measures driven by the project. They represent the connection to the business, even in the public and nonprofit sectors.
7. "We never got enough money out of the project." The **monetary value** of the business impact is a critical part of the forecast. This shows the expected money from the project.
8. "It was a bad investment." The **ROI** forecast is a realistic indication of what should be expected, adjusted for the uncertainty of the situation and the error in the estimate.
9. "We saw no other benefits." The **intangibles** are probably the most important legacies of the success of the project and must

be detailed in advance so that they can be monitored and connected to the project.

As you can see, projects that don't begin with addressing these vital issues can go astray. Plus, when a forecast is combined with detailed objectives, the project focus intensifies to a level that's needed to make it successful. Finally, the follow-up evaluation, which is always recommended, will ensure that the success has been delivered as promised.

Guarantee

Speaking of promises, is it possible to guarantee success? Is it possible to suggest that a certain level of performance in any or all of the nine types of data can be guaranteed? If not, then perhaps the cost of the project is reduced or diminished or even eliminated. For some proposal writers, this is a frightening scenario. They have visions that the project could go astray, through no fault of theirs, and then they have to assume the complete cost of the project.

On the other extreme, some individuals argue this point, "This is a great way for me to show the value of what we can do. Let's put some incentives beyond the forecast. If we can achieve and succeed, we can share some of the rewards." This challenge may not be appropriate for everyone, but it is feasible. To tackle the issues out of the control of the project team, conditions are placed on the project to ensure that the circumstances for success are clearly defined. If there are deviations from these conditions, then they serve as a way to avoid the guarantee. Thus, as this book will show, this is possible, feasible, and being done now by some progressive organizations, providing the ultimate strategic advantage.

KEY DEFINITIONS

As we begin the book, it's helpful to define some of the specific stakeholders and terms used.

• **Project.** In this book the term *project* is used to describe a variety of processes that may be approved through the proposal process. This is an important issue, because readers may vary widely in their perspective. Individuals involved in technology applications may use the terms *system, software,* and *technology* rather than *program.* In public policy, on the other hand, the word *program* is prominent. For a professional meetings and events planner, programs may not be very pertinent. In human resources, program fits the need quite well. Finding one term that fits all these situations would be difficult. Consequently, the term *project* is used. Table 1.1 lists these and other terms that may be used depending on the context.

Table 1.1. Variations in project terminology.

TERM	EXAMPLE
Policy	A new preschool policy for disadvantaged citizens
Project	A re-engineering project for the plastics division
Program	Leadership development skills enhancement for senior executives
System	A fully interconnected network for all branches
Initiative	A faith-based effort to reduce recidivism
Procedure	A new scheduling arrangement for truck drivers
Event	A golf outing for customers
Meeting	U.S. Coast Guard innovations conference
Process	A quality sampling process for the production plan
People	Staff additions in the customer care center
Tool	A new means of selection for the hotel staff

- **Request for Proposal (RFP).** When organizations have a need to fulfill or a problem to be solved, they will request proposals for bids from qualified vendors, agencies, or project teams.
- **Stakeholders.** Many stakeholders are involved in the proposal and project approval process. A stakeholder is defined as any individual or group interested or involved in the project and project approval. Stakeholders may include the individuals where the project is located, proposal team, and key clients, among others. Descriptions of these stakeholders are presented next, and they will be referred to routinely throughout the book.
- **Sponsor/Clients.** The individuals who fund, initiate, request, or support a particular project. Sometimes referred to as the sponsor, this is the key group—usually at the senior management level—that cares about the project's success and is in a position to approve the project.
- **Participants.** The individuals who are directly involved in the project. These are the individuals who make the project successful. The term *citizen, associate, user, stakeholder,* or *employee* may represent these individuals. For most projects, the term *participant* appropriately reflects this group.
- **Immediate Managers.** The individuals who are one level above the participants involved in the project. For some projects inside organizations, these are the team leaders who have supervisory authority over the participants in the projects. They are very important to project success, as their support (or lack of support) influences participants' progress.
- **The Organizations.** The entity within which the particular project is implemented. Organizations may be companies (either privately held or publicly held); government organizations at the local, state, federal, and international levels; nonprofits;

or nongovernmental organizations. They may also include educational institutions, associations, networks, citizens, and other loosely organized bodies of individuals.

- **CEO/Managing Director/Agency Executive.** The top executive in an organization. The top executive could be a company president, division manager, regional executive, association CEO, nonprofit administrator, mayor, or agency head. This is the top administrator or executive in the operating entity where the project is implemented.

- **Project Leader.** The individual responsible for project implementation. This is the individual who manages the project and is interested in showing the value of the project before it is implemented, during its implementation, and after it is implemented. The project leader can be a consultant, an internal project manager or any other functional expert responsible for project implementation.

- **Project Team.** The individuals involved in the project, helping to analyze and implement it. For larger-scale projects, these individuals are often assigned full-time on a temporary basis or, sometimes, on a permanent basis. For small projects, these may be part-time duties.

- **Proposal Writer.** The individual who prepares the proposal. This person is responsible for all the processes outlined in this book. If this is a member of the project team, measures must be taken to ensure this person remains objective. It may also be a person who is completely independent of the project, who performs these duties full- or part-time.

- **Proposal Team.** The entire team involved in developing the proposal. For large proposals, this is a group of individuals that will be involved and must work cohesively to produce a top-quality, winning proposal.

- **Finance and Accounting Staff.** These individuals are concerned about the cost and impact of the project from a financial perspective. They provide valuable support. Their approval of processes, assumptions, and methodologies is important. Sometimes, they are involved in the project evaluation; at other times they are involved in the approval of the project. For major projects, this could include the organization's finance director or chief financial officer.
- **Analysts.** The individuals who collect the data to determine whether the project is needed. They may be involved in analyzing various parts of the project. Analysts are usually more important in the beginning phases of the projects.
- **Subject-Matter Experts.** The individuals who are the resources to the proposal team. They are individuals who can provide expertise and input to the forecast and may be part of the client organization, possibly experts involved in the field, or those who are most knowledgeable about the process. As for their primary function, they can provide estimates of how things will change if this project is implemented.
- **Audience.** Those individuals who will review the proposal. They are essentially part of the client or the decision-making team, but may not have an actual vote. They are perhaps reviewing parts of it and providing their assessment of how well the proposal meets the requirements. An important group, they must be impressed with the success factors outlined in the next chapter.
- **Bystanders.** The individuals who observe the project, sometimes at a distance. They are not actively involved as stakeholders, but are concerned about the outcomes, including the money. These bystanders are important because they can become cheerleaders or critics of the project.

FINAL THOUGHTS

As the concept of value has changed over the past few years, defining and forecasting value has grown in importance when creating and considering future projects. This chapter addresses the fact that today value means very different things, particularly in the context of key stakeholders. Sometimes value means to show me the money, such as the actual cost or return on an investment. At other times, value is defined in terms of impact. Or, in other times, value reflects the intangibles.

Proposals are evaluated differently now than they were in the past due to various issues and forces. Two important additions are the concept of value added, which is now an important ingredient in almost all proposals, and the forecast of ROI, a requirement for many executives.

It is possible to forecast value and guarantee success, as this chapter briefly introduces and subsequent chapters will explore in more detail. The next chapter focuses on the proposal process.

2

The Proposal Process

Homework is never convenient, but if it works the way it's supposed to, the next day goes much smoother than without it. This lesson is undoubtedly elementary, but it still applies in a myriad of situations—especially when considering a business proposal. Before developing a detailed and informative proposal that will win over your client or executive, you must understand the process for the proposal's approval or denial. This chapter discusses the proposal within a decision-making process and the importance of the various factors that influence the proposal's success as well as the reasoning behind those factors. A considerable amount of preparation and analysis is needed before the proposal is developed. This chapter addresses pertinent questions many project leaders have, such as, "How do we actually position ourselves to have the opportunity to submit a proposal for a project?" It also examines the significance of the audience's influence and how to judge that influence, as well as issues that arise before proposal development that may make or break its approval.

IMPORTANCE OF THE PROPOSAL

A proposal is essential to securing a project; however, it is just as important to know the reasoning behind the request for the proposal. How necessary a proposal is varies with contexts, issues, and types of proposals.

Types of proposals

For informal projects where the project is requested and only a brief proposal is necessary to secure the contract and get the funding, the actual proposal process may not be crucial to the decision. Essentially, the decision to approve the project has been made; the proposal is just a formality in order to document this understanding. However, some decisions concerning major projects are based on the content of the proposal. In the past, the lead author has had the opportunity to work on proposals and projects for Lockheed-Martin as a functional manager. The proposal became the sole reason for awarding the contract. The proposals responded to requests for proposals (RFPs) and were very formal and structured, consisting of thousands of pages.

Figure 2.1 displays the connection between the types of proposals, their formality, and the importance of the proposal. Informal projects, whether internal or external, may hold little importance, and hence the proposal is of low importance. However, when external consultants, bidders, or government grants are involved with many possible candidates and large consulting projects and billions of dollars are at stake, the proposal is the key "decision maker," or the key factor in the decision-making process. The first consideration for these types of proposals is understanding the project in terms of its context, scope, and formality.

In reality, most project proposal writers are concerned with developing a proposal to win a business, knowing that the proposal is the key decision maker—the make-or-break factor for their project. Thus, because so much is riding on it, the proposal must have all of the team's attention, resources, and expertise. Unfortunately, many bidders are presenting proposals, and the competition for approval is intense. The upfront costs are expensive, and therefore, the odds for winning must be evaluated. At the same time, the proposal itself may be the greatest determinant of that win.

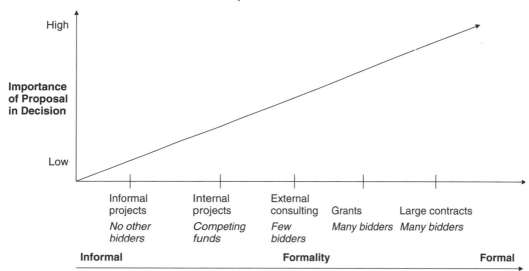

Figure 2.1. The importance of a proposal depends on its formality.

Not only steak, but sizzle

Some proposal developers base the sale of the proposal on the facts or the content. Thoughts on this presumption tend to hold capability, expertise, and know-how as the keys in winning the contract. This is not necessarily the case. The emotional part of the process must be considered along with the value proposition, and the creation of a compelling story of why a contract should be awarded to you and not someone else. In short, the proposal must have a balance of very creative content, a unique experience, and an emotional, soft side.

Proposals must convince and sell

An old saying rings true when it states that the client is not buying an item or a thing, but a promise—a promise to deliver. So, when the contract is awarded, a promise is expected. As illustrated in Chapter 1, a promise must be clearly spelled out and may be the most important part of the proposal process. This promise is, in sum, a forecast of value in a credible, feasible way.

HOW THE DECISION IS MADE

A key to a successful proposal is understanding how the decision will be made. Most clients will tell you the basis for their decision making upfront; others will include this information in the proposal request. Still others will offer this information at preproposal conferences. There are official statements and documents. The decision usually comes down to three issues: feasibility, experience, and advantage.

Feasibility

The client will examine the proposal from all facets of feasibility, considering questions such as, "Is it feasible to accomplish what I'm promised?" "Are the project's terms appropriate and consistent with what's required and necessary, particularly with those spelled out in the RFP?" "Is the pricing fair and appropriate?" (In some cases, the client must choose the lowest bidder.) "Is the schedule consistent with what can be achieved practically?" "Is it rational, logical, and achievable?" If the client can answer yes to all of these questions, the assumption is that it is a feasible project that can meet all the requirements of the RFP.

Experience

Typically, a client will not put a project in the hands of a novice, based on the thought that an inexperienced person or team cannot deliver desired success. Current experience, capability, track record, and reputation are all a fundamental part of the process. Questions that a client may ponder when considering experience include, "To what extent has the consultant or the team demonstrated that they could deliver this?" "Do they have the capability and the proven success to deliver?" Ignoring this important issue or failing to address it when developing the proposal is too risky in terms of client expectations and project delivery realities.

Advantage

When choosing one bidder instead of another, a client is looking for advantages. Early in the process, the client attempts to identify the worst bidders to be eliminated first. Then the potential winners are those that surface to the top and stand out among the rest of the candidates. Therefore, a proposal must show an advantage—a uniqueness—in order to be considered among the potential winners and show that a promise of value can be delivered. The advantage may be a credible forecast of value, including the impact and ROI.

For a proposal that captures a client's attention and respect, considering and addressing these three key decision-making factors is vital for project approval.

SUCCESS FACTORS

When the above project decision issues are considered, success factors begin to emerge. Those who win successful projects will soon understand why they won. Moreover, a client may mention informally while working together which factors made a difference to why their project was chosen. Combined with the trend of project accountability, recent economic turmoil has influenced new success factors that, a decade ago, were not seriously considered at all. In all, 10 success factors are crucial for proposal success. Their initial letters spell out "successful."

Specific Needs
Unwavering Passion
Customer Focus

<u>C</u>redibility

<u>E</u>motional Connection

<u>S</u>tory Approach

<u>S</u>uccess Guarantee

<u>F</u>orecast of Value

<u>U</u>nique Selling Proposition

<u>L</u>ess, Not More

At the ROI Institute, we've continually witnessed the power of a successful track record in those individuals who adhere to all 10 of these issues and not some smaller subset. These success factors are devised from recent awarded projects, reports in various publications, and discussions with our clients. Examining these factors in more detail is beneficial for everyone in the troughs of proposal development.

Specific needs

An important task before writing your proposal is to ensure that the specific need identified for the project, program, solution, system, or initiative is actually proper for the client. Doing this extra step with tact is important because the initial assumption on many projects is that someone has defined the actual need. The proposal describes how the project meets that need. However, if the need is not appropriate, the project will be unsuccessful through no fault of the project team (i.e., we're working on the wrong solution).

Some projects identify solely a problem, and then the need must be clearly defined and the solution implemented. For those projects, the proposal may be in two parts, depending on what is actually requested. The first part is to solve the problem (define the need). The second part is to implement the solution.

Another situation, which is typical of most, involves discussing with the client the need that has been identified to ensure that it is proper. Some may choose a sloppy path of research by assuming the need is appropriate and implementing the project only to discover later that something else was actually needed. The proper approach to identifying a need is to raise enough questions to ensure your proposal is solving a problem. These kinds of questions will be covered in Chapter 4.

When the project requires that a needs analysis be conducted, then the materials in Chapter 4 would have to be expanded to include more assessment and analysis to derive a proper solution. The important issue is to ensure there is a legitimate connection to a specific need that has been identified appropriately.

Unwavering passion

Passion exhibited in the proposal and, in some cases, during its presentation, has a tremendous effect on success. The client can spot a passionate response and desire for the project, because the client wants the creators of proposals to be enthusiastic and interested in the project. Excitement is ideal in that it can be translated into confidence that the work can be done. Enthusiasm is contagious, and often gets others excited. Though it's not always apparent, enthusiasm should be generated easily, especially for a project in one's expertise. For a consulting firm, the consults are usually enthused about the consulting process, where they can see the results from their hard work. When a firm takes on a particular project, it should be based on the firm's enthusiasm for that project. However, too often, enthusiasm does not exist in a project. It's perceived as "just another project," "just another proposal." Consequently, the proposal team must take the extra step to generate enthusiasm for the project and show the advantage for the firm itself, as well as the client, to be involved in this particular project.

Customer focus

Clients want to believe that the world and its issues revolve around them. Clients want the proposal to be personally written for them and their situation, and doing this will require fully customizing the proposal and its details for the client. The proposal should also reflect that the project team fully understands the background and all of the RFP details. This customization means that boilerplate proposals are not appropriate anymore. However, some noncustomized parts may be appropriate. For example, capability statements, definitions of a particular trademark process, and testimonials from other satisfied clients may be appropriate boilerplate items. Most of the proposal should be written from the point of view of the client, customized specifically to the situation, environment, and context.

Credibility

Credibility is vital in the success of the proposal process, and few would disagree with this statement. Credibility is reflected in the experience of the team and track record of the organization. It is defined in the team's reputation, clients' satisfaction, and the knowledge of the team. Credibility is revealed in the honest statements, insights, and conclusions. It is displayed in the behavior of the team and firm. Credibility is not something that comes quickly; it must be earned and, therefore, comes with experience. Beginners who have nothing but the personal credibility of the proposal (or perhaps, the presenter) are challenged by this factor. Credibility is high in a client's considerations of proposals.

Emotional connection

The proposal should also connect emotionally to the client and audience, producing that "warm, fuzzy feeling" that convinces them that this is the right proposal for their particular need. The client (and the audience reviewing the proposal) must identify with, and find value in, what's presented. This emotional part is often reflected in intangibles, which are measures that cannot be converted to money but are critical for success. By definition in this book, intangibles are a measure that cannot be converted to money with minimum resources. Typical intangibles include measures such as:

- Adaptability
- Brand
- Caring
- Cooperation
- Creativity
- Culture
- Decisiveness

- Engagement
- Execution
- Image
- Innovation
- Reputation
- Resilience
- Social Responsibility

Every project has intangibles. Some of them are very important to the client and audience, and therefore, should be addressed in the proposal and perhaps in the forecast of value.

Story approach

People relate to stories. Some people relate to stories more than numbers. As a proposal is presented, the project team's goal is to wrap the client and audience up in a compelling story. This story could be about a similar success that created a very satisfied client, or perhaps it's showing how the actual value delivered exceeded the forecast, much to the surprise of the client. At other times, the story might be about how the consultant (or the supplier) got started in the business. It could be about the basis for the interest in this topic and how it evolved. Perhaps the story involves how similar projects were addressed, providing specific examples and their impact.

These stories often make the client feel comfortable with the proposal and that the project team is on track. Compelling stories help paint the picture of success and challenges, and for some, the story may be the most important part of the proposal.

Success guarantee

Perhaps the newest addition to the success factor is a guarantee of success, which means that the project will deliver a defined level of success. Otherwise, there will be penalties for the project team, up to and including the possibility of no charge for the project. Though this is not for every project, guaranteeing that the project will deliver success is of particular interest to clients. For some projects, guaranteeing success may be the difference in securing the project or not. At times, this is frightening for some and not applicable for others. The greatest fear of using this approach is that success could be out of the control of those who are involved in the project. These issues can be controlled and managed by placing some conditions on the success guarantee. This will be discussed in more detail in Chapter 11.

Forecast of value

The best way to express the value proposition is to show details about what will occur when the project is implemented. The more detailed the forecast, the better, and the more credible the basis for the forecast, the better. In an ideal situation, forecasts would include a variety of different types of measures, providing a balanced profile of success. They may include how various stakeholders will react to the project, what they would actually learn from it, and what they will be doing to make it successful. It should include a forecast of the impact, and even the ROI. Additionally, a forecast or the connection to certain intangibles may be presented. Doing this in a credible, feasible way is the heart of this book. In the future, this could be the most important success factor, as some clients are already requiring a forecast as a part of the proposal.

Unique selling proposition

A unique selling proposition shows the advantages of this proposal over others and is often the basis of the proposal. A unique selling proposition clearly makes the distinction of providing something that is different, innovative, and very successful. Three words come together in describing this factor. The "unique" means that it's very different from others or what is expected. "Selling" refers to a persuasive aspect so that the proposal will create an interest in its implementation. "Proposition" means that it's something proposed that must present value. A forecast of value with an exceptional creative solution forms the basis of this unique selling proposition.

Less, not more

Proposals need to be efficient; the thicker the proposal is does not necessarily mean that it's better. Some proposals will require enormous documentation, and the size and thickness may be a plus. For example, Lockheed-Martin delivered a military aircraft system project proposal to the Pentagon in a large truck because of the proposal's tremendous size. In that situation, having extensive paperwork was probably a plus. However, today's environment demands streamlined, efficient proposals for an advantage. Some proposal requests suggest that the proposal should be only one page, although this requirement is often not possible for most formal proposal processes. A notable point is not to bloat the proposal with unnecessary information, but instead provide precise, concrete, on-target information that satisfies the success factors with the minimum amount of paper, words, charts, and appendices.

Scoring yourself

The 10 success factors form the basis of proposal success, and the acronym "SUCCESSFUL" naturally serves as an easy, quick review format to be used before proposal development. Table 2.1 shows a template that can be used to score the success of a proposal. Completed early in the process, perhaps even before the proposal is developed, this score can help decipher where the project falls in

Table 2.1. Success factors checklist: How did you score?

SUCCESS FACTORS	VERY LOW	LOW	OK	HIGH	VERY HIGH
	1	2	3	4	5
Specific Needs					
Unwavering Passion					
Customer Focus					
Credibility					
Emotional Connection					
Story Approach					
Success Guarantee					
Forecast of Value					
Unique Selling Proposition					
Less, Not More					
				Total Score: _____	

Score Interpretation

Over 40 = Great chance for success.

31–40 = Possibility for success.

21–30 = It would take a miracle.

Less than 20 = Forget it.

terms of success. This is a useful tool throughout the process, even right before the proposal is to be delivered. This will be explained more in Chapter 6, which addresses managing the proposal process.

KEY STEPS IN THE PROPOSAL PROCESS

Several factors should be addressed to make the proposal process work, and Figure 2.2 shows some of the major steps in the proposal process. Purposely modified to reflect this vital part of preproposal issues, the first four parts of the process must be addressed before the

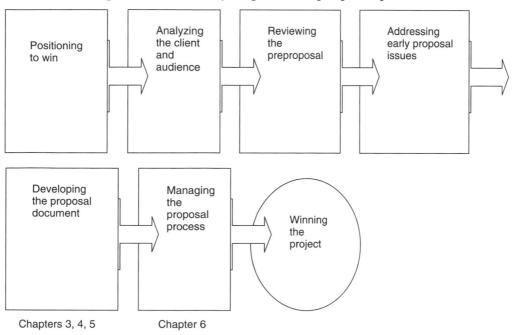

Figure 2.2. The key steps in the proposal process.

actual proposal is written. These parts are discussed in more detail in this chapter. The content of the proposal is possibly the most critical and definitely the most time-consuming part of the process. These issues are presented in Chapters 3, 4, and 5. Chapter 6 focuses on managing the proposal process, addressing the issues necessary to organize and manage the process throughout the complete cycle to the point where the award is made. Beyond this process, the remainder of this book focuses on how to develop the forecast and a success guarantee, both of which are included in the proposal. Here's more detail on the first four steps in the proposal process.

Positioning to win

One of the first and early goals for winning projects is to become a key player in the particular field or arena where the project is located.

When a client is considering a team or project leader for the project, does your name make the list? How do you get to this point? This goal is often met with several deliberate efforts, the first being your history with similar projects. At some point during a project—either in the past or currently—you must make the decision to become a key player in other types of future projects. This decision may stem from your thoughts on your organization's possibilities in other project areas. To become a key player, you must become actively involved in project proposals, such as participating in projects even when the chance of success is low. Your presence as an individual or that of your organization is then established in a specific area. You can also benefit from recruiting individuals who understand more about that particular field or process.

Relationships need to be made, whether they are with professional associations or general networking, as these contacts can be very valuable. This includes relationships with key players in the field. Developing key ties with these individuals, attending pertinent conferences, serving on panel discussions, and making presentations are all aimed at achieving visibility in your designated area. Networking can make a difference.

For example, the ROI Institute provides expertise to several different fields, and when exploring a new one, we find it beneficial to get involved in professional associations, subscribe to various magazines, and attend particular events and activities (usually as a speaker). After some time, we see clearly the key issues in the field, the important contacts and players, and where the opportunities lie. Collectively, this approach is the best way to understand a new area and, in turn, win a new project.

The new task is to build expert capability. This can easily be done by hiring someone with the particular talent for the team. Studying or learning about this area yourself is another approach to attain expertise. All the members of the team may benefit from learning more about what's involved. Without expert capability, your chance at acquiring a project is extremely low. Usually, this goal is not met until you are able to gradually build the capability over time.

The next task is to build a track record as a project leader in this field of interest. Achieving this is difficult if you're working in an area as a novice. When developing a proposal for a client, your experience should be in alignment with your correct interest.

Finally, your attitude makes a significant difference to becoming a key player in a new area. A "can-do attitude" can often overcome deficiencies. A client may be motivated to choose a project leader who is willing to go the extra mile to provide excellent service. A results guarantee is an example of an approach to a can-do attitude.

Analyzing the client and audience

Understanding your client is imperative, especially understanding the client from different dimensions. The first dimension is the background. The client's previous history can be very revealing. Knowing the sequence of events helps understand why this is an important issue for the client and why its resolution is necessary.

The second dimension is understanding the motives for a request for proposal. For the most part, a client or funder seeks a proposal to find the best person or team to the do the job. For most proposals, the client wants a problem solved or a solution implemented in the best way. In some cases, the client wants to see if anything unique is available. Others may try to understand the different ways the issue can be addressed; it's an educational process for them. For example, our firm submitted a proposal for a project with Verizon Communications in the Dominican Republic. After a very lengthy proposal to implement the ROI methodology for the human resources function, no bid was actually awarded to any of the proposal submissions. Basically, the company just wanted to examine the issues involved in implementing ROI. Others may even ask for proposals just to satisfy the requirement that they must have a certain number of proposals. Knowing this upfront can make a difference in your efforts to have your proposal chosen. Of course, it can be difficult to understand a client's motives. Asking the client about its motives directly may not unveil any issues. Here having key contacts and inside information about the client could be helpful in revealing any actual motives.

The third dimension is politics, which always is an issue. Sometimes the decision maker is not actually the person who is securing the proposals. In other cases, the decision is a team effort. Even in team decision making, someone in the organization has veto power to kill the project. Understanding the political ramifications and challenges can make a difference in success or failure.

The fourth dimension is understanding hidden agendas, which are common. Hidden agendas involve issues the client may want to explore or achieve that are not revealed. For example, one of our associates discovered before bidding on a project with Chevron that they had an interest in ROI and how it could be forecasted. Therefore, Chevron was looking for an approach to ROI, although this issue was not identified in the RFP. While reviewing each of the proposals, bidders were asked in the proposal presentation, "How would you show ROI on this project?" Their response was a key determinant for their success in securing the proposal.

The fifth dimension is knowing the role of different individuals involved. Understanding who's going to make the decision, who's involved in the process, who has the most (and least) decision-making authority, what can you expect from them, and what can you not expect from them are all important issues to be addressed. Clearly, understanding the role of the client and those in the audience is just as important before the proposal is developed as it is when the final proposal is submitted and defended.

Reviewing the preproposal process

Before a proposal's inception, the proposal bidder must consider whether or not to submit a bid. Having a strategy for which projects are appropriate for the success of the business is helpful, as well as knowing how a "no-bid decision" can positively or negatively affect your organization. Sometimes, a firm will only bid on certain types of projects or only participate if they know exactly what is involved. Others are open to almost anything that might fit their capability. The key is to have this understanding clearly developed and defined before proposal development.

Attending a preproposal conference to learn more about the project's requirements is extremely educational, as you, as a potential bidder, may pick up on the client's signals about any other issues that may affect the project. Even your presence alone alerts the client of your interest, even if you decide not to submit a proposal.

Analyzing the RFP in detail is another helpful task to understanding the client issue. Reading the proposal more than once and having other people read it is beneficial, as well as developing a checklist. Table 2.2 shows a checklist that was developed to uncover certain key elements of an RFP.

The final concern about the preproposal process is to collect project information about the issues described in this chapter. Relationships are vital here, as others often can tell you more about a client or potential projects.

Addressing early proposal issues

Before the proposal is developed, various issues can surface. Each of these unique issues can cause serious problems if not addressed early in the preproposal process. The first issue is the vague request for proposal from a client, whether in terms of delivery or a solution. A project leader must examine a vague request in detail and consult

Table 2.2. RFP checklist referenced to RFP paragraphs.*

PROJECT REQUIREMENTS	PROPOSAL REQUIREMENTS	EVALUATION CRITERIA
Turnkey Operation 3.2	Schedule 5.2	Delivery 6.2
Technology Provisions 3.4	Detail Pricing 5.4	Pricing 6.4
Pilot Group 4.2	List of Deliverables 5.7	Experience 6.7
Training of Teams 4.6	Résumé of Project Team 5.8	Capability 6.9
Intellectual Property 4.7	Specific Approach 5.9	Advantage 6.11
Specific Experience 4.9	Forecasting Value 5.11	Value Proposal 6.4
Operating Manuals 5.1		

*Adapted in part from Holtz (2008).

with the client, whether in a preproposal conference or indirect contact. If communication is not possible, the proposal may need to be developed with several variations, one for each interpretation of the vague language.

Another issue is the "wired" proposal, or wired RFP. Here the client has preselected an organization for a project, but the system requires that other bids must be submitted regardless. Unfortunately, this is one of the most unproductive areas of writing proposals. Questions such as, "How can we tell if this is wired?" or "What has happened in the past with this type of project?" or "Does this client have a preference for someone else?" or "Why is it now put out for bid?" all need to be addressed. Usually, a straight answer will not be forthcoming. ROI Institute experienced a wired proposal when a bid was requested by the U.S. Navy for a proposal that referenced our methodology and books. Essentially, the project required the use of our methodology to evaluate a master's degree program. Unfortunately, we lost the proposal and then realized that it was wired to someone else. The winner was an individual who had retired from this office and developed a one-person consulting shop. The lesson here? Don't assume that because the RFP appears to be customized for you, it's going to be awarded to you. The best advice with this issue? If you think it may be wired, avoid it, unless you want to practice.

Sometimes the client doesn't fully know what he or she wants, which is revealed in confusion and vague answers to questions during a preproposal conference. This kind of behavior reflects a client who's unsure and doesn't understand fully or appreciate what solutions are forthcoming. An unknowing client is, at times, a red flag for misguided expectations. The project may not be awarded on the basis of the best solution.

The opposite situation occurs when the client "knows it all." This issue arises when the client is well informed or has experts involved to shape the client's expectations. On one hand, this is helpful because, the client can sort what can be and what cannot be accomplished with the project. However, this "knowledge" is often a facade. In this situation, you must tread lightly, tackling the issue very diplomatically, and being careful not to bruise any egos.

An RFP evolution can also occur, where the RFP has many new additions and requirements. A constantly evolving RFP can be a problem because not everyone may know the changes. This kind of project also indicates that the client does not know what he or she wants, and until the RFP is more secure, it is prudent not to get involved.

Walking away from the project is always an option, but this decision should be evaluated carefully. Walking away can mean repercussions or damages to future projects, even if the project was wired for someone else. However, the client may really desire your participation. For one major Fortune 500 company, we were a top player among potential bidders, even before the proposal process although we were not aware of this. When the RFP was delivered, we considered opting out of participating. Yet, a phone conversation with an involved individual clarified their desire for our participation. With that encouragement, we moved forward.

Finally, another preproposal issue to examine closely is protesting a project. Protesting may occur after the project is awarded, but could also happen in the early phases of the process. A protest should be considered very carefully, because it can keep you from being involved in the future as a potential bidder for the project at hand or others. For example, we at the ROI Institute submitted a bid on a project for a large broadcasting company outside the United States. When the bid was awarded to us, one of the competing bidders protested to the board of governors of this organization. The criticism was not focused on our methodology but on the fact that we were not citizens of that country. Incidentally, the requirement wasn't that we had to be citizens of that country. The protest was overruled, and this person got very upset and belligerent with the client. Privately, we were told later that this person had sealed his fate in terms of participating in any other future projects. Protesting must be considered carefully.

FINAL THOUGHTS

We'll be honest—excuses that worked elsewhere won't work here. If your dog did indeed eat your assignment, no one cares, especially your client. What he or she does care about is a promising proposal, and doing your homework increases the chance for success as a potential project winner. Highlighting the significance of the preproposal process, this chapter specifically encourages examination of those issues necessary for the actual proposal before it is developed. The most important issue is analyzing what makes for proposal success. These days, success factors have changed and evolved, and therefore, much needs to be considered before the proposal is written. The next three chapters are focused on guiding the content and developing the written proposal.

3

How to Develop Objectives Your Clients Will Love

Just as a team huddle is needed before the play is put into place, conveying objectives is essential to a project's progression. But for many project initiators, the value of objectives and the role they play are much broader than they may appear. In this chapter, we cover why we need specific, measurable project objectives categorized at different levels. More importantly, we will examine the benefits of objectives from many perspectives.

FUNDAMENTAL ISSUES

Before describing the benefits of objectives, a few basic concepts are addressed to provide a better understanding for this chapter.

Principles of objectives

Objectives described in this book are based on research, application, and practice. They are logical, credible, and sequential. An objective is a statement describing the intended outcome, rather than a process of the project. Objectives rest on a foundation of important principles.

Levels of objectives. There are six levels of objectives (0 to 5: input, reaction, learning, application, impact, and ROI), as described in Table 3.1. Each level produces an additional category of data, representing a different definition of value. Data are sometimes considered more valuable at the higher levels—by a senior executive, for example. This perspective, however, should not discount the importance of data generated at lower levels, which represent value to other stakeholders, such as members of the project team, who value learning data, or managers, who value application data, or project participants, who value reaction data, especially when it's their reaction. Objectives should reflect measures of value important to all stakeholders.

The data categories could be subdivided into different groups. For example, costs are a part of Level 0, input, but could be listed separately, as will be reported in this book. Intangible benefits are

Table 3.1. Levels of objectives.

LEVEL OF OBJECTIVES	MEASUREMENT FOCUS	TYPICAL MEASURES
Level 0: Inputs	The input into the project in terms of scope, volume, efficiencies, and costs	Participants Hours Costs Duration
Level 1: Reaction and Perceived Value	Reaction to the project, including the perceived value	Relevance Importance Usefulness Appropriateness Intent to use Motivation to take action

Table 3.1. Levels of objectives *(continued).*

LEVEL OF OBJECTIVES	MEASUREMENT FOCUS	TYPICAL MEASURES
Level 2: Learning and Confidence	Learning to use the project content and materials, including the confidence to use what was learned	Skills Knowledge Capacity Competencies Confidence Contacts
Level 3: Application and Implementation	Use of project content, materials, and system in the work environment including progress with implementation	Extent of use Task completion Frequency of use Actions completed Success with use Barriers to use Enablers to use
Level 4: Impact	The consequences of the use of the content and materials expressed as business impact measures	Productivity HIV infections Revenue Teen pregnancies Quality Literary roles Time Accidents Customer satisfaction Employee engagement

continued

Table 3.1. Levels of objectives *(continued).*

LEVEL OF OBJECTIVES	MEASUREMENT FOCUS	TYPICAL MEASURES
Level 5: ROI	Comparison of monetary benefits from project to project costs	Benefit-cost ratio (BCR) ROI (%) Payback period

impact measures not converted to money. They are preserved as a different category of objectives in this book.

Chain of impact. For a project to add value and result in a positive ROI, a multilevel chain of impact must occur. The project is initiated, and people are involved (Level 0 objectives are met). Participants who react to the project in the desired way may see value in it (Level 1 objectives are met). Participants acquire information and learn how to make the project successful (Level 2 objectives are met). Participants apply what they learned to make the project successful (Level 3 objectives are met). The project has a positive consequence in one or more impact measures (Level 4 objectives are met). Project leaders determine whether the monetary benefits of the impact measures exceed the costs at an acceptable rate of return (Level 5 objectives are met). For the ROI to be positive, the chain of impact must exist and remain intact.

Conditions. An objective might depend on a condition. For example, a participant might use software, given a variety of operational situations. Performance is described based on that condition. For example, an objective might be "When a customer becomes angry, the following five steps will be taken." The condition for performance is the customer's behavior. A condition could also be based on something tangible, such as a job aid, operating manual, or Internet access. An example of an objective in this case could be "Identify the cause of the complaint, given the customer's transaction history."

Criterion. Objectives need to be specific, defining precise amounts, such as "A 10 percent decrease in HIV infections" or "Ninety-five percent of action items are complete." Most objectives are time-based. Application and impact objectives, for example, set deadlines for actions to be completed and impact measures to be improved. A time-based objective might be "Ninety-five percent of approval forms will be completed by June 16" or "Lost time accidents are reduced by 30 percent in nine months."

Collectively, these principles define objectives by level, their connection to each other, certain conditions on which they rest, and a desired level of precision.

Projects without objectives

Although it's hard to imagine, some projects are implemented without objectives. They might have descriptions—or schedules—but no objectives. The information might be in someone's mind, yet nothing is committed to paper. These situations are certainly undesirable. Objectives give direction, focus, and attention to a project. They clarify the reasons for a project, spell out expectations of those involved, and specify incremental deadlines. Objectives position the project for success. These days, objectives also include the amount of money to be made, costs to be reduced, or expense to be avoided. In addition, they must be defined at different levels, be powerful and attention-grabbing, and communicate a strong message.

Issues with objectives

At the ROI Institute, we have had the opportunity to examine and evaluate hundreds of projects in all types of settings. When conducting a project evaluation at the ROI Institute, we first examine the objectives. In the majority of situations, the project leader begins the initial meeting by apologizing for the objectives, which are often ill-defined. Here are the most common problems with objectives.

Unclear objectives. An unclear objective might read, "The objective of this project is to develop a diverse, multifaceted, interdisciplinary team that can function in a competitive, challenging, and dynamically changing environment to produce extraordinary and sophisticated outcomes that will dramatically enhance results." What does this mean? Obviously, clarity is needed.

Incomplete objectives. Sometimes objectives are incomplete in that they lack definition. Consider the statement, "The objective of this project is to improve the sales force." Immediately, the question becomes, "So, what?" What is lacking about the sales force that would cause it to need improvement? Is the objective to change behavior or actions? Or is it to improve sales, market share, profits, customer loyalty, customer satisfaction, or some other measure? Without sufficient detail, the objective is left to interpretation.

Nonspecific objectives. Specificity can be defined at the project level or the individual level. A new compliance project had the objective to reduce compliance discrepancies. More details are needed. Which discrepancies? By what date? By how much? A more specific project objective would be, "Reduce compliance discrepancies from $2 million in fines per year to no more than $100,000 by the end of the second year following project implementation." If the compliance discrepancies are at an individual level, then specificity needs to be applied there as well. Conditions for success can add further specificity. For example, the objective might be, "Fines will not increase as business volume increases." The increase in business volume is the condition that makes the objective more specific than if it were written, "Fines will not increase."

Missing objectives. Certain levels of objectives are sometimes omitted, particularly those at higher levels. For example, business impact and ROI objectives are sometimes excluded. If the goal is to add business value, then the objectives should be defined at the business impact level. When a specific return on investment is needed, an ROI objective is needed. These objectives are developed along with objectives at the lower levels.

Objectives vs. forecasts. Because much of this book's content is focused on how to forecast value for a variety of measures, it is important to understand the difference between a forecast and an objective. Many similarities exist between the two because, to a certain extent, the level of an objective matches the forecasting. One difference is that the forecast will have other categories, such as costs, monetary value, and intangibles. The objective is sometimes the forecast because they are constructive and generally very specific in suggesting what will occur. However, we make this distinction: An objective is an acceptable level of value for the measure described in the objectives. The forecast is that best estimate of what the value will be.

For some projects, this objective and the forecast will be the same value, but for others, it may vary significantly. For example, the most interesting and emotionally fueled forecast data is the ROI value. The ROI is also the forecast that's sought by the sponsors or clients. An ROI objective is set using one of four strategies. One is to set the value to what's expected from capital investments (these are investments in buildings, equipment, or other companies, etc.). The second strategy is to set the value using a little higher standard, usually around 20 to 30 percent. The third strategy is to set the value at zero, the break-even point. The fourth strategy lets the client set the objective. Any one of these strategies yields a number, usually in the range of 0 to 30 percent. The key question to ask about an ROI objective is "What is the acceptable level?" Anything less and we're disappointed; anything more and we declare a success.

However, a forecast can be much larger than that. At the ROI Institute, we have seen forecasts that go up to 300 or 400 percent because the project team anticipated a result that is much more than the acceptable amount. Decision makers must understand this difference. This difference will be underscored in other chapters, where the forecast will be developed for these different types of data.

THE POWER OF OBJECTIVES

Objectives are powerful because they provide direction, focus, and guidance. They create interest, commitment, expectations, and satisfaction. Their effect on different stakeholders varies; they are a necessity, not a luxury. Additional detail is offered here.

Objectives drive projects

Objectives are routinely omitted from projects, although they are the most powerful elements of the process. They focus on the organization's needs, drive project success, and define the outcomes. More specifically, here's how these higher levels of objectives fuel a project.

Provide focus and meaning to the project. Objectives often present the rationale for a project's existence. They explain the beginning point—the original business need—which translates into a business impact objective. The behavior or performance issues causing the business need to translate directly into application objectives.

Provide direction to stakeholders. Specific objectives at different levels let everyone involved know what must be done to achieve success and what the consequences of that success will be. Actions and consequences represent the important outcomes from almost every project. When these objectives are clearly stated, stakeholders can define the actions they need to take to succeed in their role in program implementation.

Define success. Objectives, clearly expressed with specific criteria and indicators, take the mystery out of the definition of success.

Objectives enhance design and development

A risk not worth taking is to send vague objectives to a project designer or developer. Designers are creative and use their imaginations to build project content. Without clear, specific direction, they will insert their own assumptions regarding the ultimate use of the project and the impact to the organization. Objectives have several effects on project design and development.

Define content issues. The content essentially moves from what participants must learn to make the project successful to what they must do to make it successful. In addition, the application of the content leads to how that success will ultimately be defined. The content shifts from concept and theory to a practical application intended to drive important business outcomes. Although the general principles and facts might remain the same, the situational aspect of the content changes.

Help with design of support tools. When the objectives are known, the tools, activities, problems, guides, and checklists in a project can focus on learning, application, and impact. The scenarios described in the content form the basis of these items. When exercises and activities are focused on application in the work setting, participants can then envision what they must do to be successful.

Facilitate action plans. One of the most effective ways to measure project success is through action planning, in which participants plan what they must do to succeed with the project. When objectives exist, the action planning becomes easier, more specific, and carefully connected to the intended outcomes. Action plans often flow directly from application objectives, removing the temptation to stray from the intended purpose of the project.

Objectives improve project leadership

Objectives are the first information reviewed prior to leading a project and define the project leader's approach in leading the project. They provide guidance for the project leader, and more specifically, objectives provide project leaders with the information to do the following.

Show the end result and provide the focus to achieve it. An objective-based approach to project leadership allows the leader to show individuals how to make the project successful and define the impact it will have.

Focus the discussions on application and impact. The dialogue with the project participants consists of what they will do and how they will do it on the job, including the challenges and enablers that will either inhibit or help them achieve success. Group discussions and examples presented by the project leader help focus on application and impact. The leader can describe actual experiences in the setting.

Objectives help participants understand what is expected

Participants in a project implementation need clear direction as to why they are involved in the project and what they are expected to do. Essentially, the role of a participant changes with higher levels of objectives. Of course, participants are expected to attend meetings, become involved and engaged, and learn. When application and impact objectives are communicated to them, they will realize there is an expectation for them to apply what they learn to make the project successful. Again, application and impact objectives remove the mystery from the project and their roles within it. Here are a few specific ways these higher-level objectives help participants understand expectations.

Clarify expectations by detailing what the participant must do. Application objectives define expectations in terms of action—the detail needed when participants use the tools, skills, or knowledge on the job.

Application objectives also define tasks that must be completed, software that must be used, meetings that must be held, or forms to be delivered. The action required or expected of the participants is made clear.

Set clear expectations about what the participant must ultimately accomplish. Impact objectives connect the project to the business measures and the participants' performance. When participants apply what is learned in a project, there is a consequence. Often, that consequence is the immediate measure that represents their performance, such as measures of productivity, quality, time, or costs. Participants control or influence these measures.

Define "what's in it for me?" Participants must engage and commit to achieving results and providing data. They need to know their reward, and impact objectives clearly show them. For example, when participants are involved in a project implementation of new sales software, the impact objectives clearly indicate the ultimate outcome. These objectives are typically stated in terms of increasing sales, enhancing customer satisfaction, improving market share, increasing customer loyalty, and other important measures. These objectives clarify what's in it for participants. They want to improve these measures, so such objectives provide incentive to participate.

Explain why the project is being implemented. Individuals may participate in a particular project without a clear understanding of why the project exists. Typical questions include, "How would this help this organization?" or "How will this help my unit?" Application and impact objectives clearly explain the project's purpose and the expected outcome, in addition to what participants must do and ultimately accomplish.

Objectives excite clients and sponsors

The sponsors (those who actually fund the project) often request data showing how well the program achieved its goal. Impact measures resonate with executives and sponsors. Executives rarely get excited about reaction and learning objectives. Rather, their interest lies in what participants do with what they learn and the ultimate impact on the organization. Impact objectives grab the attention of executives for several reasons.

Connect the project to the business. Impact objectives connect the project directly to business goals. This linkage piques executive interest and builds project support.

Connect the project to key performance indicators (KPI). Important scorecard measures are goals for the client or sponsor. Impact objectives often contain executive KPIs, scorecard performance measures, dashboard indicators, or operating results. A deficiency in one or more of these measures often precipitates the need for the project.

Show business value. This is the first opportunity for the sponsor to see value that he or she can appreciate. Business value and attempts to "show the money" make sponsors happy.

Objectives simplify evaluation

Objectives pave the way for project evaluation by providing the focus and details needed for the evaluator to collect and analyze results. Here, objectives aid evaluation by:

- Identifying data to be collected in the organization.
- Suggesting the appropriate data collection method to be used. In some cases, the measure itself, when clearly defined, suggests how it might be collected.
- Suggesting the source of data by identifying where it is and who has it.
- Suggesting the timing of data collection. The objectives provide hints as to when action is needed and when change will occur, which influence the timing of when data will be collected.

- Suggesting responsibilities to collect data. The definition of data suggests who may be the best person to collect the data.

In summary, objectives are extremely valuable for the evaluator. They provide the information necessary to complete the data collection plan and the ROI analysis plan, ultimately making for a more effective, sound evaluation.

Objectives inform the stakeholders

Collectively, all levels of objectives help stakeholders understand the project more clearly. All stakeholders need to know not only why the project is being implemented, but also about participant reaction, what the participants have learned, what actions they will take, and, ultimately, what they will accomplish.

That knowledge is particularly critical for managers of participants directly involved in the project. They may not be supportive because they see neither value to which they can relate nor objectives that reflect their interests. These managers must be able to see how the project connects to key measures. The good news is projects often show value that can make a manager take an interest in and ultimately support the process. Project objectives provide a preview of what is to come.

CASE STUDIES

Three examples underscore the types and nature of the objectives described in this chapter. They illustrate how the different levels of objectives are used and how they are stacked to form a chain of impact that should occur as a project is implemented.

Business coaching

Table 3.2 shows the objectives from a business-coaching project for a global hotel chain. The project team was challenged to identify

Table 3.2. Objectives of coaching for business impact.

Level 1: Reaction Objectives

After participating in this coaching project, the executive will:

1. Perceive coaching to be relevant to the job
2. Perceive coaching to be important to job performance at the present time
3. Perceive coaching to be value added in terms of time and funds invested
4. Rate the coach as effective
5. Recommend this program to other executives

Level 2: Learning Objectives

After completing this coaching project, the executives should improve their understanding of or skills for:

1. Uncovering individual strengths and weaknesses
2. Translating feedback into action plans
3. Involving team members in projects and goals
4. Communicating effectively
5. Collaborating with colleagues
6. Improving personal effectiveness
7. Enhancing leadership skills

Level 3: Application Objectives

Six months after completing this coaching project, executives should:

1. Complete an action plan
2. Adjust the plan accordingly as needed for changes in the environment
3. Show improvements in the following areas:
   a   Uncovering individual strengths and weaknesses
   b. Translating feedback into action plans
   c. Involving team members in projects and goals
   d. Communicating effectively

Table 3.2. Objectives of coaching for business impact *(continued)*.

e. Collaborating with colleagues
    f. Improving personal effectiveness
    g. Enhancing leadership skills
  4. Identify barriers and enablers to application of knowledge acquired

Level 4: Impact Objectives
Six months after completing this coaching project, executives should improve at least three specific measures from the following areas:
  1. Sales growth
  2. Productivity/operational efficiency
  3. Direct cost reduction
  4. Retention of key staff members
  5. Customer satisfaction

Level 5: ROI Objective The ROI value of the coaching project should be 25%

needs to help executives find ways to improve efficiency, customer satisfaction, and revenue growth in the company. A key component of the project was a formal, structured coaching plan for executives, with specific objectives at each level. These objectives provided the framework to achieve and report success. Corporate executives were interested in seeing the actual ROI for the coaching project.

Each person receiving coaching was required to select three out of the five measures listed in the impact objectives, providing flexibility for focus and concentration. The objectives provided the immediate focus throughout the coaching process. The challenge is to develop very specific objectives, sometimes even more specific than those in this example.

Software implementation

Global Financial Services Inc. (GFS) is a large international firm that offers a variety of financial services to clients. After analyzing its current sales practices and results, the firm identified the need to manage sales relationships more effectively. A task force comprising representatives from field sales, marketing, financial consulting, information technology, and education and training examined several solutions for improving relationships, including customer-contact software packages.

The firm chose to implement a software package designed to turn contacts into relationships and relationships into increased sales. The software contained a flexible customer database, easy contact entry, a calendar, and a to-do list. The software enables quick, effective customer communication and is designed for use with customized reports. It also has built-in contact and calendar sharing and is Internet-ready.

Instead of purchasing software and training for each of the 4,000 relationship managers, GFS planned to evaluate the success of the software on a pilot basis using three groups, each comprising of 20 relationship managers. A one-day workshop was required to teach these relationship managers to use the software. If the project proved successful, yielding the appropriate return on investment, GFS planned to implement the program for all its relationship managers. With a focus on results, detailed project objectives were developed for the implementation that provided the appropriate direction and information for the project. These objectives are shown in Table 3.3.

Absenteeism control

The Metro Transit Authority (MTA) operates a comprehensive transportation system in a large metropolitan area. More than 1,000 buses operate regularly and provide citizens with essential transportation.

Table 3.3. Objectives for software implementation.

Level 1: Reaction Objectives

After reviewing the software, the participants will:

1. Provide a rating of 4 out of 5 on the relevance for specific job applications
2. Indicate an intention to use the software within two weeks of the workshop (90% target)

Level 2: Learning Objectives

After participating in the workshop, participants will:

1. Score 75 or better on a software test (80% target)
2. Successfully demonstrate 4 of the 5 key features of ACT!™ listed below:
   a. Enter a new contact
   b. Create a mail-merge document
   c. Create a query
   d. Send an e-mail
   e. Create a call report

Level 3: Application Objectives

Following the workshop, the participants will:

1. Enter data for 80% of new customer prospects within 10 days of workshop completion
2. Increase the number of planned follow-up contacts with customers within three months of workshop completion
3. Use the software daily as reflected by an 80% score on an unscheduled audit of use after one month of workshop completion

---

Level 4: Impact Objectives

Three months after implementation, the following impact should occur:

1. Reduced number of customer complaints regarding missed deadlines, late responses, and failure to complete transactions

---

continued

Table 3.3. Objectives for software implementation *(continued).*

2. Reduced time to respond to customer inquiries and requests 3. Increased sales for existing customers 4. Increased customer satisfaction composite survey index by 20% on the next survey
Level 5: ROI Objective Implementation of the new software to achieve a 25% return on investment using first-year benefits

Many passengers depend on the bus system for their commute to and from work, as well as other travel. MTA employs more than 2,900 drivers to operate the bus system around the clock.

As with many transit systems, MTA experienced excessive driver absenteeism, and the problem continued to grow. Three years prior

Table 3.4. Objectives for absenteeism-reduction program.

Level 1: Reaction Objectives After announcing the project: 1. Supervisors will see the need tor this particular project 2. Supervisors will see the project as important to their own success 3. The current employees will experience little or no adverse reaction as the No-Fault absenteeism policy is implemented
Level 2: Learning Objectives After implementing this new policy, employees and supervisors should be able to: 1. Describe the No-Fault process 2. Identify the features and benefits of the No-Fault policy 3. Explain the rationale for the absenteeism-reduction solutions

Table 3.4. Objectives for absenteeism-reduction program *(continued)*.

Level 3: Application Objectives Immediately after the project is implemented: 1. Supervisors will communicate the new No-Fault policy to all employees and explain how the policy is applied in a rational format 2. The human resources staff should utilize the new screening process for each selection decision so that a systematic and consistent selection process is in place 3. Supervisors should implement and enforce the No-Fault policy consistently throughout all operating units
Level 4: Impact Objectives Within the first year, when this project is completely implemented: 1. Driver absenteeism should be reduced at least 2% 2. The present level of job satisfaction is maintained as the absenteeism initiatives are implemented and applied 3. Customer service and satisfaction should improve with a reduction in schedule delays caused by absenteeism
Level 5: ROI Objective Implementation of the project to achieve at least a 25% ROI

to the decision to implement a solution, MTA's absenteeism was 7 percent, compared to 8.7 percent in the three-month period prior to implementation—too excessive to keep the transit system operating consistently. Two solutions, along with objectives for both, were developed to correct the problem. The first solution, a low-cost absenteeism policy, allowed a fixed number of absences before termination. The second solution changed the selection process to screen individuals with a history of absenteeism problems. Table 3.4 shows the proposed objectives for these solutions.

FINAL THOUGHTS

Your stakeholder wants the glory, and you have the winning play. Pressing into the huddle, everyone looks to you for his or her next move. How will you win? How will you ensure that their investment in you and your project is worthy?

Objectives are a necessary part of a promising project, but this chapter emphasizes and explains the importance of objectives for project success. They help drive the results of projects, clarify expectations, secure commitment, and make for a much more effective program or project. Objectives must be developed with as much specificity as possible, along with a clear description of the desired outcomes at all levels. If business results are desired, a project should have application, impact, and, in some cases, ROI objectives. The next chapter will show how objectives are derived, which are based on specific needs.

4

Project Needs: The Basis for Objectives

Missions are not without a cause. Journeys are not without the hope of enlightenment. Projects are always based on unfulfilled needs. This fact is explored in the content of the proposal, and if these needs are not clearly defined early in the process, the result may be a flawed project that creates inefficiencies and other problems. When a forecast of the value of the project is required by the client or is pursued to gain a strategic advantage, additional analysis of needs is usually necessary. In this chapter, we explore assessment of the various levels of needs, which leads to the levels of objectives described in the previous chapter. Specifically, we will address ROI needs, business needs, performance needs, learning needs, and preference needs. We'll also examine input needs.

The model presented in Figure 4.1 will prove helpful as analysis begins. In the following pages, we will examine the process of detailing the needs at six levels (0 to 5), beginning with payoff needs and progressing to input needs. The objectives derived directly from these needs are defined, making a case for multiple levels of objectives that correspond with specific needs. The objectives serve as the transition from needs assessment to evaluation, and they form the basis for forecasting value.

Figure 4.1. From project needs to project objectives and evaluation.

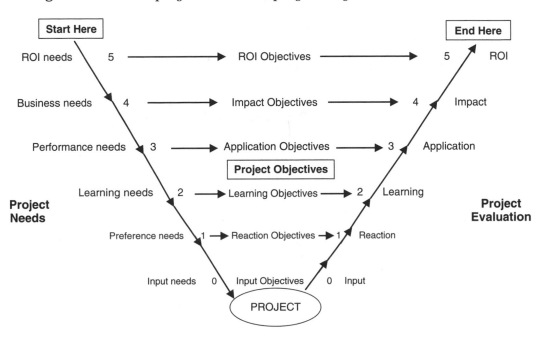

For some projects, this analysis is completed before the RFP is released. Hence, much of this analysis is not needed. In others, the analysis is required as part of the project (i.e., uncover the precise solution and implement it). In still others, this analysis may be an additional step to validate or fully understand the proposed solution.

ROI NEEDS

The highest level of needs, return on investment, comes from a financial analysis of the need for the project. This initial step begins with a few crucial questions:

- Is this project worth pursuing?
- Does this project address a critical issue?
- Is there an opportunity to add value with the project?

- Is it a feasible project?
- What is the likelihood of a positive ROI?

The answers to these questions are obvious for proposed projects that address significant problems or opportunities with potentially high rewards. The questions might take longer to answer for lower-profile projects or those for which the possible payoff is less apparent. In any case, these are legitimate questions, and the analysis can be simple or comprehensive. Figure 4.2 shows the potential payoff in monetary terms. A project's payoff comes in the form of either profit increases or cost savings (derived from cost reduction or cost avoidance).

Profit increases (sales and revenue) are generated with projects that improve sales, increase market share, introduce new products, open new markets, enhance customer service, or increase customer loyalty. Other revenue-generating measures include increasing memberships, increasing donations, obtaining grants, and generating tuition from new and returning students—all of which, after accounting for the cost, yield a profit or operating margin.

However, most programs pay off with cost savings. Savings are generated through cost reduction or cost avoidance. For example, projects that reduce HIV infections improve quality, reduce cycle time, lower downtime, decrease complaints, prevent employee

Figure 4.2. The payoff opportunity.

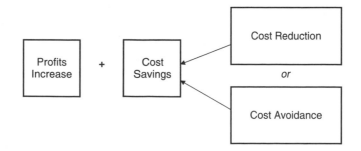

turnover, and minimize delays, which are all examples of cost savings. When the goal is solving a problem, monetary value is often based on cost reduction.

Cost-avoidance programs aim to reduce risks, avoid problems, or prevent unwanted events. Some may view cost avoidance as an inappropriate measure for developing monetary benefits and calculating ROI. However, if the assumptions are correct, an avoided cost (for example, compliance fines) can yield a higher reward than an actual cost reduction. Preventing a problem is more cost-effective than waiting for it to occur and then having to resolve it.

Determining potential payoff is the first step in the needs-analysis process. Closely related is the next step, determining impact need, as the potential payoff is often based on improvements or changes in business measures.

Determining the payoff involves two factors: (1) the potential monetary value derived from the business measure's improvement and (2) the approximate cost of the project. Calculating these monetary values usually yields a credible ROI forecast for the project. However, this step may be omitted in situations where the business need must be resolved regardless of the project cost or when resolution of the business need has an obviously high payoff. For example, if the problem involves a serious quality concern, a regulatory compliance issue, or the protection of human life, then a detailed analysis of the payoff may not be unnecessary.

Key questions

A needs analysis should begin with several questions. Some possible questions to ask about a proposed project are listed here.
- Why is this needed?
- Who will support the project?
- Who will not support the project?
- Are there important intangible benefits?

- How is the project funded?
- Is this issue critical?
- Is it possible to solve the problem?
- How much is it costing?
- Can we find a solution?
- Are there multiple solutions?
- What happens if we do nothing?
- How much should the project cost?
- Is a forecast needed?
- Is there a potential for a positive ROI?
- Is this a strategic issue?
- Is it feasible to improve it?

The answers to these questions might make the case for proceeding without analysis or indicate the need for additional analysis. The answers could also show that the project is not needed. Understanding the implications of moving forward (or not) can reveal the legitimacy of the proposed project. For many potential projects, the good news is that answers to these questions are readily available. The needs may have already been developed and validated and the project is ready to go.

Obvious versus not-so-obvious payoff

The potential payoff is obvious for some proposed projects, but not as obvious for others. Some situations with obvious opportunities for payoffs are listed here.

- The annual cost for one homeless person is $75,000.
- Excessive turnover of critical talent: 35 percent above benchmark data.
- Crime rates for categories are increasing at 20 percent or more.
- Very low market share (8 percent) in a market with few players.
- Inadequate customer service: 3.89 on a 10-point customer satisfaction scale.

- Safety record is among the worst in the industry.
- Teenage pregnancy rates are two times the national average.
- Out-of-compliance fines total $1.2 million, up 82 percent from last year.
- Excessive product returns: 30 percent higher than previous year.
- Citizen complaints doubled last year.
- Excessive absenteeism in call centers: 12.3 percent, compared to 5.4 percent industry average.
- Sexual harassment complaints per 1,000 employees are the highest in the industry.
- Grievances are up 38 percent from last year.

Each item is a serious problem that needs attention from executives, administrators, or politicians. For these situations, it would be safe to move ahead to the business needs level rather than invest too much time and resources in analysis of the potential ROI. After the solution (project) is defined, an ROI forecast may be appropriate.

In other proposed projects, however, the issues might be unclear and arise from political motives, or biases, or improper assumptions. Project objectives or opportunities for which the payoff isn't as obvious might include the following:

- Provide job training for unemployed workers
- Improve leadership competencies for all administrators
- Organize an innovations conference
- Establish a green organization
- Develop highly effective employees
- Implement a work-life balance program
- Improve literacy for young adults
- Train all team leaders on crucial conversations
- Provide rangers on horses for each city park
- Provide sexual harassment awareness program
- Develop an "open-book" company

- Improve the image of the agency
- Become a technology leader
- Create a great place to work
- Implement a career advancement program
- Create a wellness and fitness center
- Build capability for future growth
- Create an empowerment program for women

These not-so-obvious opportunities call for more detail. Some requests are common, as executives and administrators suggest a process change. The requests appear to have the project identified, but without a clear reason as to why. These types of requests could deliver substantial value, but only if they are focused and clearly defined from the start. In our work at the ROI Institute, we have seen many vague requests turn into valuable projects. Sometimes overlooking the vague request is a mistake; these requests can result in valuable contributions, as they can lead to critical analysis that ensures an appropriate focus on success.

The cost of a problem

Problems often are expensive. To determine the cost of a problem, its potential consequences must be examined and converted to monetary values. A few potentially costly problems include the following:

- Excessive crime
- Time savings
- Excessive employee turnover
- Errors/mistakes
- Carbon emissions
- Employee withdrawal
- Waste
- Accidents
- Delays
- Chemical spills

- Employee dissatisfaction
- Productivity problems
- Customer dissatisfaction
- Inefficiencies
- Excessive conflicts
- Excessive direct costs
- Tarnished image
- Equipment damage
- Fatalities
- Equipment underused
- Excessive stress
- Excessive illnesses

Some can easily be converted to money, and some already are. Those that cannot be converted within the resource and time constraints under which you are working are left as intangibles.

Examining costs means examining *all* the costs and their implications. For example, the full costs of accidents include not only the cost of lost workdays and medical expenses, but also their effect on insurance premiums, the time required for investigations, damages to equipment, and the time of all employees who are involved in the accident. The cost of a customer complaint includes the cost of the time to resolve the complaint, as well as the value of the item or fee that is adjusted due to the complaint. The most important cost is the loss of future business and goodwill from the complaining customer, plus potential customers who become aware of the issue.

The value of opportunity

Just as the cost of a problem can be tabulated in most situations, the value of an opportunity can also be determined. Examples of opportunities include:

- Implementing a new preventive process
- Installing a system for data security

- Upgrading the workforce for a more competitive environment
- Automating a manual process

In these situations, a problem might not exist, but a tremendous opportunity exists for taking immediate action. Properly placing a value on this opportunity requires considering possible consequences if the project is not pursued or taking into account the windfall that might be realized by seizing the opportunity. The monetary value is derived by following the different scenarios to convert specific business impact measures to money. The challenge lies in ensuring a credible analysis. Forecasting the value of an opportunity involves many assumptions, whereas calculating the value of a known outcome is often grounded in a more credible analysis.

BUSINESS NEEDS

Most projects are based on business needs. It's difficult to imagine a project that's not driven by a business need. Determining specific business needs is linked to the previous step in the needs analysis, developing the potential ROI. To determine business needs, specific measures must be pinpointed so the business situation is clearly assessed. Here, the term *business* is applied to projects in governments, nonprofits, educational institutions, and private-sector organizations. Projects in all types of organizations can show a business contribution by improving output, quality, and efficiency, as well as by saving time and reducing costs.

Business measures

A business need is represented by a business measure. Any process, item, or perception can be measured, and the measurement is critical to this level of analysis. When the project focuses on solving a problem, clients and project leaders have a clear understanding of that problem and the measures that define the problem. Measures might also be obvious if the project prevents a problem. If the project takes advantage of a potential opportunity, the measures are usually still apparent. If not, a clear, detailed description of the opportunity will help clarify the measure.

The key issue is that measures are in the system, ready to be captured for this level of analysis. The challenge is to define and find them economically and swiftly.

Business measures represented by hard data

Business measures are represented by hard data and soft data. Distinguishing between the two types of data helps in the process of defining specific business measures. Hard data are primary measures of improvement presented in rational, undisputed facts that are usually accumulated. They are the most desired type of data because they're easy to measure and quantify and relatively easy to convert to monetary values. The ultimate criteria for measuring the effectiveness of an organization are hard data, such as revenue, productivity, profitability, cost control, and quality assurance.

Hard data are objectively based and represent common, credible measures of performance. Hard data usually are sorted into four categories, as shown in Table 4.1. These categories—output, quality, costs, and time—are typical performance measures in organizations, including private-sector firms, governments, nongovernment agencies, nonprofits, and educational institutions.

Business measures represented by soft data

Hard data might lag behind changes and conditions in human performance within an organization by many months; therefore, it is useful to supplement hard data with soft data such as attitude, motivation, and satisfaction. Often more difficult to collect and analyze, soft data are used when hard data are unavailable. Soft data are also more difficult to convert to monetary values and often based on subjective input. They are less credible as a performance measurement and

Table 4.1. Examples of hard data.

OUTPUT	TIME
Sales	Cycle Time
Completion Rate	Equipment Downtime
Food Produced	Overtime
Units Manufactured	Delivery Time
Items Assembled	Time to Project Completion
Money Collected	Processing Time
Items Sold	Employee Time
New Accounts Generated	Time to Proficiency
Forms Processed	Response Time
Loans Approved	Meeting Time
Inventory Turnover	Repair Time
Patients Discharged	Efficiency
Applications Processed	Recruiting Time
Students Graduated	Average Delay Time
Projects Completed	Late Reporting
Productivity	Lost Time Days
Work Backlog	
Shipments	
COSTS	**QUALITY**
Shelter Costs	Failure Rates
Treatment Costs	Dropout Rates
Budget Variances	Scrap
Unit Costs	Waste
Cost by Account	Rejects
Variable Costs	Reject Rates
Fixed Costs	Error Rates

Continued

Table 4.1. Examples of hard data *(continued)*.

COSTS	QUALITY
Overhead Cost	Rework
Operating Costs	Shortages
Project Cost Savings	Product Defects
Accident Costs	Deviation from Standard
Sales Expense	Product Failures
Participant Costs	Inventory Adjustments
Administrative Costs	Infections
	Incidents
	Compliance Discrepancies
	Accidents

tend to be behavior-oriented, but represent important measures just the same. Table 4.2 lists common examples of soft data.

Sources of impact data

Sources of impact data, whether hard or soft, are plentiful. They come from routine reporting systems within the organization. In many situations, these items have led to the need for the program or project. Here is a sampling of the vast array of documents, systems, databases, and reports that can be used to select the specific measure or measures to monitor throughout the program:

- Agency records
- Websites
- Government reports
- Human capital databases
- Payroll records
- Quality reports
- Design documents

Table 4.2. Examples of soft data.

WORK CLIMATE/SATISFACTION	CUSTOMER SERVICE
Job Satisfaction	Customer Complaints
Organization Commitment	Customer Satisfaction
Employee Engagement	Customer Dissatisfaction
Employee Loyalty	Customer Impressions
Tardiness	Customer Loyalty
Grievances	Customer Retention
Discrimination Charges	Customer Value
Complaints	Lost Customers
Intent to Leave	**EMPLOYEE DEVELOPMENT/**
Stress	**ADVANCEMENT**
Teamwork	Promotions
Communication	Capability
Cooperation	Intellectual Capital
Conflicts	Requests for Transfer
INITIATIVE/INNOVATION	Performance Appraisal Ratings
	Readiness
Creativity	Networking
Innovation	**IMAGE**
New Ideas	
Suggestions	Brand Awareness
New Products	Reputation
New Services	Leadership
Trademarks	Social Responsibility
Copyrights	Environmental Friendliness
Patents	Social Consciousness
Process Improvements	Diversity
Partnerships	External Awards
Alliances	

- Manufacturing reports
- Test data
- Compliance reports
- Marketing data
- Sales records
- Trend reports
- Service records
- Annual reports
- Safety and health reports
- Census data
- Research data
- Legal data
- Benchmarking data
- Industry/trade association data
- R&D status reports
- Suggestion system data
- Customer satisfaction data
- Project management data
- Cost data statements
- Financial records
- Scorecards
- Dashboards
- Productivity records
- Employee engagement data

Some project planners believe corporate data sources are scarce because the data are not readily available to them, near their workplace, or within easy reach through database systems. With a little determination and searching, however, the data can usually be identified. In our experience, more than 90 percent of the impact measures that matter to a specific project have already been developed and are readily available in databases or systems. Rarely do new data collection systems or processes have to be developed.

Collateral measures

When searching for the proper measures to connect to the project and pinpoint business needs, it's helpful to consider all the possible measures that could be influenced. Sometimes, collateral measures move in harmony with the project. For example, efforts to improve safety might also improve productivity and increase job satisfaction. Thinking about the adverse impact on certain measures also helps. For example, when cycle times are reduced, quality could suffer; or when sales increase, customer satisfaction could deteriorate. Finally, project team members must prepare for unintended consequences and capture them as relevant data items.

PERFORMANCE NEEDS

Some projects are based on performance needs. All projects will at least contain one link to a performance need. In the needs analysis, this step explores reasons the business measure is where it is rather than at the desired level of performance. If the proposed project addresses a problem, this step focuses on the cause of the problem. If the program takes advantage of an opportunity, this step focuses on what is inhibiting the organization from taking advantage of that opportunity.

Analysis techniques

This step might require a variety of analytical techniques to uncover the causes of the problem or the inhibitors to success. A brief listing of these analysis techniques follows.

- Statistical process control
- Brainstorming
- Problem analysis
- Cause-and-effect diagram
- Force-field analysis

- Mind mapping
- Affinity diagrams
- Simulations
- Diagnostic instruments
- Focus groups
- Probing interviews
- Job satisfaction surveys
- Engagement surveys
- Exit interviews
- Exit surveys
- Nominal group technique

It is important to relate the issue to the organizational setting, behavior of the individuals involved, and functioning of various systems. These analytical techniques often use tools from reengineering, quality management, and performance improvement fields. Searching for multiple solutions is also important, because measures are often inhibited for several reasons. Keep in mind the implementation of multiple solutions—whether they should be explored in total or tackled in priority order. The detailed approaches of all the techniques are contained in many references.

A sensible approach

The resources needed to examine records, research databases, and observe situations and individuals must be taken into account. Analysis takes time, and the use of expert input, both internally and externally, can add to the cost and duration of the evaluation. The needs at this level can vary considerably and might include:

- Ineffective behavior
- Dysfunctional work climate
- Inadequate systems
- Disconnected process flow
- Improper procedures

- Unsupportive culture
- Insufficient technology

These needs have to be uncovered using many of the analysis techniques we've listed above. When needs vary and techniques abound, the risk exists for excessive analysis and cost. Consequently, a sensible approach must be taken. Balance must exist between the level of analysis and availability of resources and time.

LEARNING NEEDS

All projects have learning needs. Addressing the job performance needs revealed in the previous step often requires a knowledge or information component, such as participants and team members learning how to perform a task differently or how to use a new process. In some cases, learning is the principal solution, as in competency development, process improvements, capability development, and compliance projects. In these situations, the learning becomes the actual solution.

For other projects, learning is a minor solution and involves simply understanding the process, procedure, or policy. For example, when a new ethics policy is implemented, the learning component requires understanding how the policy works and the participants' role in the policy. In short, a learning solution is not always needed, but all solutions have a learning component.

A variety of approaches measure specific learning needs. Multiple tasks and jobs are usually in a program, and each should be addressed separately.

Subject matter experts

One of the most important approaches to determining learning needs is to ask those who understand the process. They can best determine what skills and knowledge are necessary to address the job performance issues defined above. Then it might be possible to understand how much knowledge and how many skills already exist.

Job and task analysis

A job and task analysis offers a systematic analysis when a new job is created or when tasks within an existing job description change significantly. Essentially, the analysis collects and evaluates work-related information, determining specific knowledge, skills, tools, and conditions necessary to perform a particular job. The primary objective of the analysis is to collect information about the scope, responsibilities, and tasks related to a particular job or new set of responsibilities. In the context of developing learning needs, this information helps in preparing job profiles and job descriptions. These descriptions, in turn, serve as a platform for linking project requirements to specific learning needs.

Performing a job and task analysis not only helps individuals who will use the project content develop a clear picture of their responsibilities, but it will also indicate what is expected of them. The amount of time needed to complete a job and task analysis varies from a few days to several months, depending on the complexity of the solution. Steps in the analysis include identifying high performers, preparing a job analysis questionnaire, and developing data-collection tools. During the job analysis, responsibilities are defined, tasks are detailed, and specific learning requirements are identified.

Observations

Current practices within an organization might have to be observed to understand the context in which the project is implemented. This technique can provide insight into the level of capability, as well as appropriate procedures. Observation is an established and respected data-collection method that can examine work flow and interpersonal interactions.

Sometimes, the observer is unknown (invisible) to those being observed (placed in the environment specifically to observe the current processes). Another possibility is that the observer is unnoticeable to those being observed. Examples include retail mystery shopping, video or audio observation, and built-in observation with software. It is important to remember that observation can uncover what individuals need to know or do as a program changes.

Demonstrations

In some situations, having employees demonstrate their abilities to perform a certain task or procedure provides valuable insight. The demonstration can be as simple as skill practice or role playing, or as complex as an extensive mechanical or electronic simulation. From this determination of job knowledge, specific learning needs can evolve.

Tests

Testing is not used as frequently as other needs assessment methods, but it can prove highly useful. Employees are tested to find out what they know about a particular project situation. Test results help guide learning issues. For example, in one hospital chain, management was concerned that employees were unaware of the company's policy on sexual harassment or what actions constitute sexual harassment. In the early stages of the program analysis, a group of supervisors and managers, the target audience for the proposed project, took a 20-item test about their knowledge of the sexual harassment policy (10 items) and knowledge about sexual harassment actions (10 items). The test scores revealed where insufficient knowledge existed and formed the basis of a project to reduce the number of sexual harassment complaints.

Management Assessment

When implementing projects in organizations with existing managers or team leaders, input from the management team may be used to assess the current situation and the knowledge and skills that the new situation requires. This input can be collected through surveys, interviews, or focus groups. It can be a rich source of information about what the users of a new program would need to know to make it a success.

Keep it simple

Where the learning component is minor, learning needs are simple. Determining specific learning needs can be time-consuming for a major project for which new procedures, technologies, and processes are developed. As in the previous step, it is important not to spend excessive time analyzing at this early stage in the process, but collecting as much data as possible with minimal resources.

PREFERENCE NEEDS

Projects have preference needs. This level of needs analysis drives the project's features and requirements. Essentially, individuals prefer certain processes, schedules, or activities for the project. Those preferences define how the project will be implemented and how it will be perceived.

Typical preference needs define the parameters of the project in terms of convenience, value, location, and utility. Although everyone involved has certain needs or preferences for the project, implementation is based on the input of several stakeholders rather than that of an individual. For example, participants involved in the project (those who must make it work) might have a particular preference, but their preference could exceed resources, time, and budget requirements. The immediate manager's input may help minimize the amount of disruption and maximize resources. For the most part, performance focuses on project content issues, such as relevance, importance, appropriateness, usefulness, value, and challenges. Because this is a Level 1 need, the project structure and solution will directly relate to the reaction objectives and to the initial reaction to the project.

INPUT NEEDS

Every project has input needs. This level of analysis is similar to the preference analysis and defines the basic input requirements. If the project is derived from analysis, this analysis would define various parameters and input requirements. If the project is addressing compliance, the compliance regulation could define the requirements in terms of timing, content, audience, and even location. Because resources are limited, some constraints might surround budget. Because some projects are urgent, timing issues could come into play. Some projects need to be conveniently located, calling for location requirements. Input needs are often straightforward and come directly from the request for the project. Understand clearly that the basis of these requirements captures all the needs, and they quickly and straightforwardly translate into input objectives.

FINAL THOUGHTS

Projects are based on clearly defined needs that are derived from careful analysis of the problem, opportunity, or requirement that led to the request for the project. By considering the needs stacked on different levels, ranging from ROI needs to input needs, the complete profile is developed, which leads to a profile of objectives. Objectives form the basis for forecasts.

Not every project should be subjected to all of these analyses. Some are based solely on learning needs. Others might be based strictly on preference needs, which is the case for many projects in the meetings and events arena, for example. The important issue is to take a rational, logical approach when determining needs and, ultimately, objectives. For the majority of this book, we will focus on how to construct the objectives and forecasts that evolve from these needs.

5

Developing the Proposal

After introductions, handshakes, initial meetings, and other formalities are behind you, all eyes and ears—especially the major decision makers'—are on you and your proposal. When developing your proposal, what should you include that will set you apart from the competition? What should you address in your proposal so that clients can identify their need for it? How can you develop their trust for the project's implementation? This chapter focuses on the flow of the proposal and the specific elements that must be contained in the proposal. While these can vary, there are key components that must be addressed, which are highlighted here.

PROPOSAL ELEMENTS

The proposal can have a wide variety of complexity and length. For the very simplest issues with one-on-one contracting between the client and consultant, a very simple proposal is needed. The more formal the process, the more detailed the proposal needs to be, up to and including a comprehensive process.

For a very simple proposal, it's important to convey the basic understanding of the project and present what is planned. A one- or two-page proposal, or perhaps even just a long letter, may suffice. Table 5.1 shows the bare essentials using the logic methodology (Freed, Freed, and Romano 2003). This approach has helped consultants and their clients think about the logic flowing from the

Table 5.1. The essentials of a brief proposal.

ISSUE	COMMENT
Situation	This is our understanding of your problem or opportunity.
Objectives	Given that problem or opportunity, these are our objectives for solving or realizing it.
Methods	Given those objectives, these are the methods we will use to achieve them.
Qualifications	Given those methods, these are qualifications for performing them.
Costs	Given those qualifications and methods, this is how much it will cost.
Benefits	Given our efforts and their associated costs, these are the benefits or value that you will receive.

bottom up, essentially telling the client: "Here are the *benefits* you will receive from our project, considering the *costs* that will be involved, given our *qualifications* to complete the project, and using our *methods* to achieve the project's *objectives*. This should all improve your basic *situation*." These are the bare essentials of telling the client what is expected, which is a good practice to put in a letter, even if it is not requested.

Building from the simple process, the proposals become more complex to include more detail, parts, and requirements. Obviously, every proposal must address all the issues in the RFP. However, a comprehensive proposal usually should include these topics or components:

1. Title Page
2. Executive Summary
3. Situation Analysis
4. Project Inputs and Scope

5. Objectives and Forecasts
6. Project Timing/Schedule
7. Project Budget and Costs
8. Methodology and Approach
9. Resources
10. Responsibilities
11. Deliverables
12. Experience/Unique Advantages
13. Qualifications
14. Results Guarantee
15. Terms and Conditions
16. Acceptance
17. Back Matter

This comprehensive approach is a useful framework to explore any proposal, even if the amount of detail is not desired or needed. It helps clarify all critical issues.

SITUATION ANALYSIS

Here is a list of questions for a situation analysis.

- What created the need?
- What motivated the client to pursue this now?
- How thoroughly has the need been described?
- What is the client's experience with this topic?
- Do all of the stakeholders see the need the same way?
- Has the commitment for implementation been secured?
- Is the needs assessment accurate?
- Can we shape the client's requirement?
- What is the scope of the project?
- Have the funds been secured?
- Are there underlying assumptions?
- Are there any hidden agendas?
- What deliverables are expected?

- How much detail is expected?
- What are the expected outcomes?
- Is there a specific protocol?
- Will the culture support this?
- What procedures must be followed?
- Is there a proposal conference?
- What are the proposal evaluation criteria?
- Why is the client interested in us?
- Is there a history of effective consultant-client relationships?

Ideally, all these questions should be addressed to thoroughly understand the situation. Each of the questions delves in detail into the reasons for the proposal and the client's experience with this issue. Collectively, these issues provide a wealth of information about the current situation and the viability of the project. A clear understanding of all of these issues provides the backdrop for developing an effective and successful proposal.

Situational analysis is used in the proposal to summarize for the client a specific understanding of the situation. Presenting this analysis is important because many clients want to make sure that the consultant fully understands the issue. A complete description of the solution in a nonchallenging and nonthreatening way can keep the client's interest in the proposal and help ensure that he or she reads the rest of the proposal.

The situation analysis proceeds in a logical progression. It starts by stating and validating the proposal team's understanding of the background, relationships, and key stakeholders that are most important. Next it moves to analyzing the issue, problem, or opportunity, ensuring that the team clearly understands the challenge at hand. This analysis is sometimes presented in terms of the consequences of the project, the impact it can have, or the cost of problems that are created if it's not resolved. It should also focus on the challenges of the project, recognizing that there may be some difficult issues, uncharted waters, or other obstacles that may make the project difficult, but yet manageable. Also included is the discussion of any previous efforts to address the issue, particularly if they've failed, and what the team must learn from these efforts. Here is the sequence, or flow, of items in the situational analysis.

1. Background
2. Organization
3. Relationships
4. Key Stakeholders
5. Issue/Problem/Opportunity
6. Impact/Consequences
7. Challenges
8. Previous Efforts

PROJECT INPUTS AND SCOPE

A project has certain requirements that are often labeled, "inputs." These inputs are translated into objectives that involve people, timing, and resources. Listing these objectives is important in order to remove any misunderstanding on the part of all the involved parties. Sometimes, the inputs aren't clearly identified, but it is beneficial to include them and restate them in the proposal.

Staffing levels

The total number of individuals involved in a project is sometimes an issue. A project may require that a maximum or minimum number of people be involved. For example, in a technology project, the staffing level input dictated was that no more than 15 full-time staffers would be involved in the project at any given time. Project teams can also be counted. These teams can be assigned by division, department, function, or even different region.

The participants needed in a project may be divided into demographic categories. For example, an objective may require,

"Forty percent of participants to be females with five years of experience." Some organizations want to ensure that upward mobility exists for all employees, particularly female.

Project scope

Scope establishes the limits and parameters of a project. Scope places boundaries on implementation and on participants or departments and organizations, directly involved, as well as the specific function or content explored. A project's scope might also define the total time for the project or the nature of the work to be done. Defining the scope prevents "scope creep," where a project starts out with a narrow focus of one or two topics or areas, and then mushrooms, requiring additional time, effort, and money.

Audience/Coverage

An important scope category is the participants in the project. This could involve employees in occupations, job groups, and even functional areas. For example, with the current focus on talent management, some organizations implement projects to address critical talent coverage. They do this by defining critical talent and setting objectives for the number of project participants in the critical talent categories.

Another way to address an audience is by status or condition, such as registered voters or persons with HIV. Coverage might also be defined by specific job groups, such as nurses, farmers, professionals, or nonexempt employees. Many organizations are concerned about particular job groups, such as aid workers. For example, as an individual job category, nurses are a very important group. When they are effective, the impact is multiplicative.

Coverage can also focus on specific strategic initiatives. Projects often are aligned with particular strategic objectives, supporting them with implementation issues. Scope might include the total hours and people included in a particular strategic area. This shows current alignment with an important strategy and can be revealing. When particular strategic areas have little or no coverage with projects, action should be taken to devote more resources directly to those areas.

A final way to represent coverage with scope is to focus on particular operational problems. A scope objective might be written as, "All medical staff will be involved in addressing our patient satisfaction."

Location

Projects sometimes require particular locations. For example, in the meetings and events industry, a project might call for a particular type of site, or the preference might be a resort. Location can be dictated by whether the project is internal or external. If there is a required location, it is stated as a scope objective.

Disruption

Disruption of normal work activities almost always presents a concern for project leaders. They often design projects to minimize disruption, which might include a scope objective to ensure that individuals' regular duties are not affected by participation in the project. For example, a requirement in implementation of a Six Sigma project (a quality improvement process) was that completion of the projects to reach green belt and black belt status should not disrupt normal work activities on the job.

Technology

In most cases, technology is an integral part of a project. Sometimes technology should be defined as a scope parameter. For example, an objective might require that parts of the project be conducted virtually using Microsoft Office Live Meeting. Another objective might require that all participants network with each other through tools such as LinkedIn, Facebook, or IBM's Lotus Connection. Technology makes a critical contribution to the success of projects and programs. It should be defined upfront with other appropriate objectives.

Outsourcing/Contracting

An increasing number of organizations outsource part of the project. As an organization moves in this direction, outsourcing objectives might be needed. For example, an objective in the project development stage might require that external contractors develop no more than 50 percent of the project. The project team develops the remainder. Another objective might reflect outsourcing of delivery, detailing the percentage of the project delivered by external services compared to internal sources.

OBJECTIVES AND FORECASTS

Chapter 3 described the different levels of objectives and their power in describing the project. The elements of the objectives form a pyramid, with the most powerful at the top of the pyramid, whereas some elements are contained in and will be involved in every project (see Figure 5.1). All of these levels support the goals or broad objectives of the project. These objectives can be very specific, as described

Figure 5.1 Hierarchy of objectives.

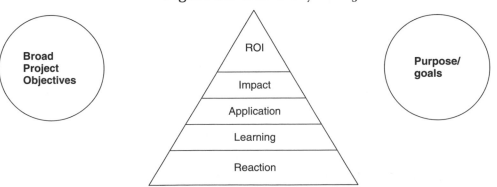

in Chapter 3, and may be written in terms of conditions and criteria. Criteria are a particular accuracy, quality, or time when the objective is achieved. In short, objectives should be delivered in different levels, and stated with as much specificity as possible.

Objectives are similar to a forecast, but there's a difference. A forecast is an objective with precision and an estimation of what will be accomplished. The difference between an objective and a forecast is that an objective states an acceptable value from the stakeholder's perspective. Even when the objective is precise, it is an acceptable amount. For example, in terms of ROI, an objective may be to achieve an ROI of 15 percent, if the client accepts that as an objective. However, the forecast could be a much larger percentage because it's a best estimate of what will actually happen. Thus the forecast is usually greater than the objective. Another way to distinguish the difference is that typically the objectives are not very specific (although they should be), and a forecast is very specific. For comprehensive proposals, a forecast should be implemented.

Forecasting at all the levels described in Chapter 3 is an option and may include the following:

1. A forecast of precise reaction in a variety of categories, such as relevance, important to success, appropriate for the organization, and so forth.
2. A forecast of the amount of learning of project content that is essential for the project to be successful.
3. A forecast of application, indicating the extent to which individuals will be using the project content properly to make it successful.
4. A forecast of the impact measures and of the business measures connected to the project.
5. The forecast of monetary benefits accruing directly from the project (this converts the impact measures to money).
6. A forecast of the costs of the project.

7. A forecast of the ROI for the project.

8. A forecast of the intangible benefits connected to the project.

For some projects including these forecasts is optional. Later chapters will show how to develop these forecasts in terms of inputs for the data, how they can be analyzed, and how they should be reported in the proposal.

PROJECT TIMING/SCHEDULE

Timing indicates when certain tasks will be accomplished, milestones will be reached, or an entire project will be completed. These objectives might dictate when certain individuals become involved in the project or even the timing of payments to the project team. Timing is critical. Without it, accountability might be absent and misunderstandings might prevail.

Duration

Setting objectives for the duration of the project is important for some projects, such as organizing a three-day innovations conference, conducting a one-year literacy program, or upgrading the technology in nine months.

The length of time participants are involved in a project is another timing issue. Some organizations track the total hours per person, targeting a specific amount of time for a particular job or job group. Other organizations track the number of hours involved by various diversity groups, including age, gender, and race.

Delivery

One of the most interesting and mysterious processes is the way in which a project is delivered to an organization. Although strides are being made to transform traditional delivery processes into those that are more technology-based, progress has been slower than most experts have forecasted. An organization attempting to make dramatic shifts in delivery needs to use the latest technological advancements.

Delivery includes not just the use of technology, but also the efficiency with which the project will be implemented throughout the organization. This is particularly important when a project is implemented on a pilot basis and the results are disseminated throughout the organization. When it comes to creating a new system, procedure, or policy, much of the success hinges on how and when it is implemented throughout the organization. Capturing expectations is critical to success.

Project schedule

The schedule of the project details the events from proposal acceptance to the last step in the process, which is usually delivering the final results after the solution has been implemented. This could be shown on any type of project management tool, perhaps even a Gantt chart. A flow chart could be used to show how steps are sequentially followed, the time for each step, and the timing of the entire process.

PROJECT BUDGET/COSTS

The costs of projects are increasing, creating more pressure to know how and why money is spent. To forecast the ROI, the total cost of a project is required, which means calculating indirect as well as direct costs.

Project cost sources must be considered. The three major categories of these sources and some reporting issues are listed in Table 5.2. Project staff expenses usually represent the greatest percentage of costs and are sometimes transferred directly to the client or project sponsor. The second major cost category is participant or user expenses, both direct and indirect. These costs are not identified in many projects, yet

Table 5.2. Project costs.

SOURCE OF COSTS	COST-REPORTING ISSUES
1. Project staff expenses	• Costs are usually accurate. • Variable expenses may be underestimated.
2. Participant/user expenses (direct and indirect)	• Direct expenses are usually not fully loaded. • Indirect expenses are rarely included in the costs.
3. External expenses (equipment and services)	• Sometimes understated. • May lack accountability.

they reflect a significant amount of the total expenditures. The third cost source is payments to external organizations. These include payments directly to hotels and conference centers, equipment suppliers, and services used for the project. As the table shows, some of these cost categories are often understated. Accounting records should track and reflect the costs from these three different sources.

Another key method of developing cost objectives follows the natural project progression. Figure 5.2 shows the typical project cycle, beginning with the initial analysis and assessment and progressing to the evaluation and reporting of results. Costs can be developed for each of these steps.

The specific items to be included in the project costs must be defined. Input from the finance and accounting staff, the project team, and from management might be needed. The recommended cost categories for a fully loaded, conservative approach to estimating costs are:

- Needs analysis and assessment
- Design and development costs

Figure 5.2 Project functions and cost categories.

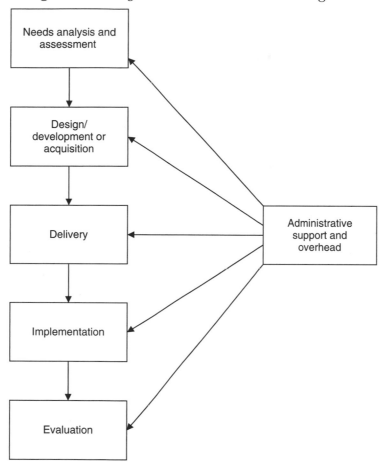

- Acquisition costs (in lieu of development costs, many organizations purchase items such as software)
- Delivery/implementation costs (five categories)
  - o Salaries of project team, facilitators, and coordinators
  - o Program materials and fees
  - o Travel, lodging, and meals
  - o Facilities (external and in-house)
  - o Participants' salaries and benefits

- Evaluation costs
- Overhead costs

METHODOLOGY AND APPROACH

There are two issues connected to having a unique methodology. The first is the expertise you bring to the project. This is often the rationale for starting the consulting practice and growing it into a successful business. The unique methodology must be used and protected throughout the process. The second issue is the approach to consulting—showing that there is a systematic way in which the project is to be conducted and delivered. The systematic process ensures consistency and replication and shows the client exactly what will be done and what steps will be taken to ensure success. All of this is contained in the proposal process and must be delivered according to the proposal's terms.

Systematic process

Apart from the unique advantage offered by a consulting firm and the expertise of the consultant, is the method in which the consulting is delivered. A systematic, step-by-step process should be developed that defines the approach outlined in the proposal. Figure 5.3 shows one approach, a five-phase consulting model offered by Mooney (1999).

Phase 1: The first phase of the process is the initial involvement that leads to firming up the objectives.

Phase 2: Data collection begins in this phase, along with the diagnosis of the situation. This is the heart of the consulting process.

Phase 3: This involves communicating the data to the appropriate individuals to secure acceptance and to drive the decision making for the consulting solution.

Figure 5.3 The five-phase consulting model.

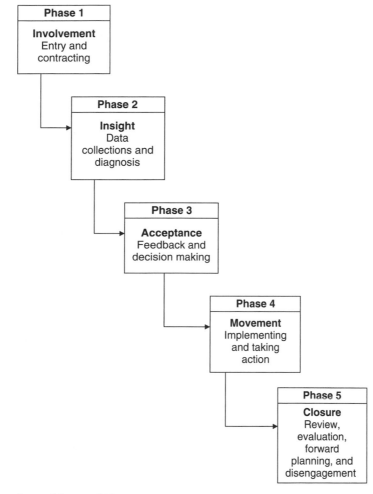

Source: Mooney (1999).

Phase 4: This is the implementation of the consulting solution.

Phase 5: The final phase includes the evaluation described in Chapter 9, along with recommendations and communication of the data described in this chapter.

The important issue is to have a systematic approach to solving the problem or pursuing the project. This approach may be separate from the unique methodology and know-how provided.

Protecting the methodology

Sometimes it's necessary to protect the unique methodology, expertise, or know-how that is brought to the consulting process. This may include specific analytical tools, the structure of the entire project as it relates to how the data are collected, or how decisions are made and conclusions are drawn. Whatever the specific methodology, it is important to ensure that it is protected from unauthorized use.

The first decision to be made is based on the public use of methodology. Some consultants prefer their approach to be proprietary with little discussion or disclosure of the process in the consulting reports. They may require the client to sign a confidentiality agreement with a commitment not to disclose proprietary methods. While this may work for some consultants, it can create frustration and anxiety for clients—leaving them with the impression that the consultant does not trust them to be discreet. Other consultants are very open with their process but request that clients be discreet. Other consultants are very open with their process and will make presentations about it, write about it, discuss it, and display it on their Websites. This is a personal decision.

In our work at the ROI Institute, we use a proprietary process when we conduct ROI studies. The process has been copyrighted in several books and articles and trademarked as well; however, the trademark symbol is rarely used. In a proposal, for example, the symbol is used only once. The clients reading the proposal understand that the processes are copyrighted and trademarked.

The recommended approach is to be as open as possible about the process, while protecting any unauthorized use by obtaining a trademark, sales mark, copyright, or, in some cases, a patent. Part of the protection is to ensure that materials are presented with the appropriate notations and markings. Attempts to protect the methodology should be based on common sense. Copyrights, trademarks, and sales marks can be overused. It should be mentioned early in the report that the process is protected by law, but mentioning it in every instance or on every page is unnecessary. Being aware of what competitors are using and writing about will let you know if others are using the process.

Proposed approach

The proposed approach would use the methodology along with actions and activities to show what approach would be taken in this particular project. Essentially, this shows how things will progress in this setting. It should list actions, activities, methodology, and methods. The actions are defined to achieve the specific objectives, the specific activities that will take place, the unique methodology—along with the rationale for using it—and the particular way the objectives will ultimately be achieved. Regardless of the arrangement of sequencing, the approach section takes the mystery out of how you will accomplish the objectives using your unique methodology.

RESOURCES

If additional resources are required in the project, they are detailed next. The project may require the use of external contractors, resources within the organization, temporary staff, other vendors, or a variety of other possibilities. These resources may or may not be a part of the project. If they are, they should be included in the cost. If they are not, they should be clearly spelled out in terms of responsibilities and the projected cost.

RESPONSIBILITIES

An often overlooked part of the process is clearly defining the responsibilities. The consultant obviously has certain responsibilities for securing data and assisting in the implementation. In complex projects, the responsibilities become quite complex, utilizing different groups as well as individuals in specific roles. In this section, accountabilities need to be underscored.

DELIVERABLES

The specific items delivered to the client should be listed and detailed. This may include a solution or part of the solution, in whatever form it may take. It may include various reports, job aids, procedures, policies, and, in some cases, even software. Table 5.3 shows the variety of possibilities.

EXPERIENCE/UNIQUE ADVANTAGES

It is important to communicate to the client the unique advantage of the proposal and the rationale for using your firm or consulting practice.

Table 5.3. A sample of deliverables.

A working system	A design
New procedure	New equipment
New policy	New standards
Technology implemented	A merged process
Capability	An integrated system
A report	A prototype
Job aid	A problem solved
A facility	A presentation
An instruction guide	An executive summary
Survey results	A successful event

The advantages may hinge on the proprietary methodology, experience with the type of project, or the qualifications offered to achieve it. Advantages may includes the ability to do this quickly, perhaps faster than others, because of the size of the staff, experience of the team, and the priority that will be placed on the project.

This section in the report should detail these particular issues:

1. The leadership position for this kind of work and this project
2. Similar projects you've encountered or worked on previously
3. Descriptions of those projects and the success they've achieved
4. Specific references of individuals who can speak to those projects and their success
5. Any other items that would emphasize the experience with this type of project

QUALIFICATIONS

The qualification section lists the backgrounds of the individuals who are involved in this project. This includes their experience in detailed and biographical sketches, written to show a results-based focus. It should show these individuals' experiences with this type of project. If possible, the actual project team involved should be listed. Problems could be created in some cases if generalized information is presented and the actual consultant's experience is different. The expectations of the client have to be properly managed.

RESULTS GUARANTEE

Consultants should consider providing a guarantee of results. Some consultants are offering complete satisfaction for the project or there is no charge. Others put specific conditions around the guarantee. Still others offer variable pay depending on the success of the project. These options are discussed in Chapter 11.

TERMS AND CONDITIONS

This section includes any condition that has not been set forth under the project schedules, responsibilities, or costs. It may include a summary of these items with an expiration date on the project proposal. If the client decides to wait until a particular time beyond what is specified in the RFP, then the proposal may no longer be viable. Conditions and terms for addressing disputes, difficulties, and problems—including how they will be resolved—should be addressed here. It could also address typical client concerns, such as how communication will be two-way and flowing. Essentially, this is a place to clarify conditions for both parties.

ACCEPTANCE

This final piece of information provides the client with an opportunity to agree and return a particular part of the proposal, which is recognition of acceptance. This makes the acceptance formal, although many clients may prefer to issue an acceptance letter, following some predetermined procedure, guidelines, or compliance requirement. If that is not the case, the acceptance agreement can be used by the client to indicate approval of the project and his or her agreement with all parts of it.

BACK MATTER

The proposal will usually have some additional materials. These could be exhibits showing the unique methodology, appendices showing detailed flow charts on the approach, or details on the project schedules. The resumes and/or qualifications of the project team would also be outlined in the back matter.

FINAL THOUGHTS

As each client and project is unique, this chapter details different sections for a comprehensive proposal process. A simple process would be much shorter and contain only parts of the process. However, for a very comprehensive project, where forecasting would be an important element, these different elements are necessary. Chapter 12 presents a proposal with all of these elements in place. The next chapter focuses on managing the proposal process for success.

6

Managing the Proposal Process

Consulting the map every now and then when you are traveling usually ensures a successful, smooth journey. The same is true about the journey of a proposal: Consulting a map ensures success. While the previous chapters focused on what should be in the proposal developing those documents, this chapter takes a look at the process, often stepping back from the development cycle. Here, it's important to manage the proposal process from the beginning when the project is first considered, all the way through the delivery of the proposal and the follow-up. Concurrent with managing is the issue of planning, the steps, resources, and requirements to organize the process efficiently. The challenge is to win the project on the basis of the quality of the proposal and the value that is projected—not necessarily on the price. Yet, if the proposal is not as effective as it could be, then the only way to win the project is price, which can be an equation for disaster. This chapter will show what's necessary to manage the process to keep it on track.

GATHERING INTELLIGENCE

Before tackling the issues involved in developing a proposal, much information is needed, and gathering intelligence becomes a critical skill. First, if the system is in place and properly working, the RFP will not be a surprise. Information in an effective intelligence gathering process will involve both the topics addressed and the sources of information on the topics.

Intelligence topics

The information needed when you are developing a proposal is listed below. Some of these topics are very sensitive, and, as a result, it may be difficult to uncover the information credibility. Other topics can be developed over time, working with other consultants in the marketplace and through contacts with the client. The information about the client history with the consulting issue is important. Essentially, a proposal developer needs to know how the issue evolved, what caused it to be addressed at this time, the issue's relationship to other projects, and other ongoing activities that might be related to the issue.

Intelligence gathering

- Client history with this issue
- Relationship of this project to other projects
- Other competitors that may be involved
- Whether there is a commitment to another firm
- Competitor relationships to client
- Pricing insights including history with other projects
- Related or supporting documents
- Management commitment to project (from client's organization)
- Funding mechanism
- Proposal and project hot buttons
- Typical success measures used by client
- Concerns and worries about project
- Urgency of project
- Stakeholders involved in the project
- Client perception of our consulting firm

Understanding your competition is crucial. Knowing the competitors who might be involved in the project and the extent of their relationship with the client begins to show the strengths and weaknesses of the competition. Most important is knowing whether the client has any sort of commitment to another consulting firm. Gaining insight into expected pricing would be crucial information. Is there a history of what they're willing to pay? Funding for the project is important. Which department or division is actually providing the funding? This may provide critical insight in terms of what the budget might be, or what budget might be acceptable.

It is also important to understand more about the proposal. Several questions need answers. Are there any particular hot buttons in the proposal that must be addressed in a particular way? What arc the success factors for the project? How will the proposal be judged? What has been done previously? What are the concerns and worries about the project, both from the perspective of the client and the consulting team? Who may have concerns about the project's viability? How urgent is the project? Does it need to be done even quicker than the time frame specified? Would this be an advantage?

Understanding more about the situation may involve other documents. Availability and accessibility become issues. Understanding the key stakeholders, defined later in this chapter, is important. Trying to understand the management commitment to the project is a tricky issue. Without commitment and support, the project will not be successful. The final issue is the perception of the consulting firm. Is there a current relationship? How effective has this bccn? This, at least, should be easily assessed. These and perhaps other issues are topics to explore before proposal development begins. Information may not be available on all of them, but the more information that can be obtained, the better the proposal. Some of this information will be used in detailing the situational analysis described in the previous chapter and the stakeholder analysis described later.

Sources of information

Information sources can vary significantly depending on the situation. The most obvious source would be the client, if the client is willing to provide information. Some of this information may have been obtained routinely over time. An understanding of the pricing, success factors, hot buttons, and similar issues may be readily available from the history of working with the client. If this is not the case, another individual may be able to discuss these issues. Other members of the client team involved may be able to shed some light as well. Those closest to the situation but not constrained about providing information are excellent sources. These sources often come from informal networks with the client.

Sometimes the market will have information through informal networks, like other consultants and professionals involved in the same field. Related documents may be available directly from the client or others familiar with this situation. Previous consultants who have worked with the client may be feasible to provide data, although this may not be the case if they're competing for the project.

This exercise underscores the importance of having an existing relationship before the RFP is actually presented. When this is the case, many of these answers are already known and the consultant is actively involved in the process leading to the proposal.

PROPOSAL PHILOSOPHY

Proposals should be addressed with a certain philosophy in mind consistent not only with what the client desires or needs but with what the consulting firm is willing to offer and present. Having an effective philosophy should provide the consultant with an important edge.

Several key issues should be considered when choosing a philosophy for the proposal that is likely to suit the client.

Adjusting the needs

The first part of the philosophy is to determine how to address the needs outlined in the proposal. Should they be met as described or should they be shifted or changed? In some cases the needs may not be on track, or they may be vague. The challenge is to convince the client that the needs should be more clearly defined, that there is an assumption of a different need, or that the needs should be specified completely differently. These are all possibilities, but it's important to reflect the philosophy of the consulting practice. While it's sometimes best to just do what is requested, an alternative approach is to discuss, explore, negotiate, or even challenge a need that appears to be inconsistent with logic or where additional information suggests a problem.

Results versus activity

As mentioned earlier in this book, there has been a dramatic shift to results-based projects. Traditionally, projects were based on activity: analyzing issues, performing tasks, implementing software, and completing action items. However, since more clients are seeking results, projects need to focus on outcomes. This philosophy, if practiced, should be highlighted throughout the proposal, providing measures of business success, clearly defined objectives, monetary benefits, and forecasts. Making the focus of the project more results-based is the key.

General versus specific

Some would like for the proposal to be brief and vague. The more detail, these consultants argue, the more problems it can create, the more work they have to do, or the more difficult it will be to make changes in the approach. However, most clients desire specifics and details showing exactly how something will be accomplished and when it will be accomplished, by whom, and at what cost. Specifics usually win.

Cost detail

When dealing with the cost of a project, the consultant is often faced with a dilemma: How much of the cost should be detailed? It's tempting to show an overall cost without much breakdown, giving the client an opportunity to compare the total cost with those of competitors. However, providing details of the cost may improve the credibility of the proposal. This involves showing the time it takes to complete a task, the hourly rate of the individuals involved, and the costs of different tasks. With this approach, all cost details that add up to the final cost of the project are included and can be analyzed.

There is a reluctance to show this degree of detail for fear that the client may think parts of the project are overpriced, or might want to cut parts of it. This can usually be addressed with some flexibility in the actual time and costs for each step. When considering these issues, clients typically want more data on costs. They are curious about how costs evolve. Detailed cost presentations usually win out over the less detailed proposal.

Logic versus topics

Should the proposal address the topics outlined in the proposal in the sequence offered or as the entire project unfolds logically? The logic usually wins out. Ideally, the topics should be presented on a logical basis showing how the process evolves to obtain the desired results, using a flow chart or a step-by-step outline. Almost any client would prefer a logic approach showing how things will be accomplished in an orderly sequence.

Create a proposal-development process

Finally, it may be helpful to create and implement a formal proposal-development process. Figure 6.1 outlines one such process—used by a successful proposal-writing team—that goes beyond simply listing the steps in a logical form. It guides users sequentially through the process, prompting them to think through the rationale in each specific step as they work toward the final document. Making regular use of a well-conceived, effective process minimizes the time required to develop proposals, reduces confusion, provides for greater consistency despite variables, and helps consultants create more informative, compelling proposals.

UNDERSTANDING THE STAKEHOLDERS

Knowing which stakeholders are involved in a potential consulting project is critical in the proposal development. Understanding who they are and their concerns can lead to the development of specific items in the proposal. Here are seven different stakeholders that may be involved in a project.

Requester

The requester is a person who initiates the projects—who actually has asked for it. This requester may be the key client. It may be the individual who has had some informal discussions with the consultant. In any case, this is the individual who essentially initiates it.

Decision maker

Although a team may evaluate proposals, there is usually a key decision maker. In simple projects there is only one client involved, and the decision maker is that individual. In more complex projects involving many individuals, the decision maker may not be readily obvious.

Figure 6.1. Proposal development process.

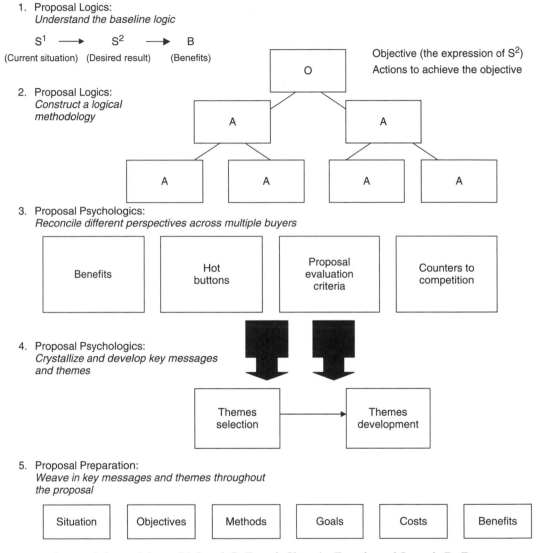

1. Proposal Logics:
   Understand the baseline logic

   $S^1 \longrightarrow S^2 \longrightarrow B$

   (Current situation) (Desired result) (Benefits)

   Objective (the expression of S^2)
   Actions to achieve the objective

2. Proposal Logics:
   Construct a logical methodology

   O
   A   A
   A   A   A   A

3. Proposal Psychologics:
   Reconcile different perspectives across multiple buyers

   | Benefits | Hot buttons | Proposal evaluation criteria | Counters to competition |

4. Proposal Psychologics:
   Crystallize and develop key messages and themes

   Themes selection → Themes development

5. Proposal Preparation:
   Weave in key messages and themes throughout the proposal

   | Situation | Objectives | Methods | Goals | Costs | Benefits |

Source: Adapted from Richard C. Freed, Shervin Freed, and Joseph D. Romano, *Writing Winning Business Proposals: Your Guide to Landing the Client, Making the Sale, Persuading the Boss* (New York: McGraw-Hill, 2003).

Contractor

This is the individual who ensures that the proposal follows the proposal guidelines. The concern is compliance, fairness, objectivity, and consistency. This individual will process the proposal and, following the rules, may decide if a proposal moves forward or not.

Implementer

This is the group or individual who will have to implement the solution from the project. These are the people who have to make it work and must be committed. They must be involved. They must be willing to take whatever steps are necessary to make the project a success. The ultimate success of the project solution rests with the implementer.

Champion

Behind almost every project there is a champion, a person who wants this project in the worst way, the person who is eagerly awaiting the outcomes of the project. The champion may be at any level. At lower levels, it may be a person who located the consultant or discovered the process and wants the requester to request a proposal, the decision maker to make the decision, and the implementer to make it work. This is a very important person who can provide much insight into the project and issues surrounding it.

Senior executive

In almost every setting there is a senior executive who may not necessarily be the decision maker but who is responsible for the ultimate budget for the project. This individual needs to be pleased, either directly or indirectly, with the success of the project. It may be the division head, the department head, chief operating officer, chief information officer, chief marketing officer, or even the CEO in smaller firms.

Detractor

For almost every project there is someone who would prefer not to do it, who may even be opposed to it. At best, this person is completely indifferent to it. At worse, this person will try to kill the project before it gets started or even kill it before the contract is awarded. Knowing this individual is critical so that the proper information can be in the proposal to at least render him or her neutral concerning the project.

Information and actions

Each of these individuals plays an important part in the project. In simple, small-scale projects, many of these roles would be played by one person, but as the complexity of the project grows, the scope of the project increases, and the size of the budget blossoms, all of these stakeholders may be in separate roles. It's necessary to analyze the stakeholders with as much intelligence as possible. Table 6.1 shows a useful form for collecting information about the stakeholders. It provides places for the name and the role of the individuals to be identified, which could simply be their title or responsibility.

Table 6.1. Stakeholder analysis.

STAKEHOLDER NAME	JOB CONCERNS / PERSPECTIVES	ACTIONS NEEDED
Requestor		
Decision maker		
Contractor		
Implementer		
Champion		
Senior executive		
Detractor		

It is important to understand what concerns these individuals will have and what perspective they will bring to the project, including their level of enthusiasm for it. Finally, the most important issue is to see what action is necessary. Is contact needed with each stakeholder? Should something be included in the proposal to address each of these roles? Do some of the roles have to be validated? For example, is the implementer interested in implementing this project and committed to making it work? These may be action items, either conducted formally or informally, to understand more about the proposal process.

MANAGING THE EFFORT

Let's face it; if a proposal is for a large-scale project, involving a tremendous amount of effort and many team members, the process will be chaotic. The concept of a smooth, effortless proposal process is virtually nonexistent. Almost by definition, a large proposal is high stress and involves long hours and often much anxiety. The key to minimizing stress and anxiety is to front-load it into the early part of the process, if possible.

Figure 6.2 shows the recommended breakdown from one group of proposal experts. In this case, 25 percent of the effort is absolutely needed from the time the RFP is received and the kickoff meeting is held. When this part of the process is sufficiently addressed, it can minimize later problems. If there are going to be long work hours and late-night meetings, try to plan these for early in the cycle and prevent the usual chaos and stress that occurs at the end of the cycle.

As this figure shows, drafting a proposal is 50 percent of the total effort. This figure also shows the importance of having reviews and revisions near the end of the process, devoting 25 percent of the time to this process. Doing this is vital and is described later in the chapter.

Figure 6.2. The 25-50-25 proposal process.

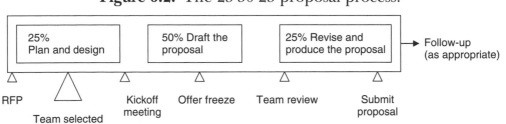

Source: Adapted from David C. Pugh and Terry R. Bacon, *Powerful Proposals: How to Give Your Business the Winning Edge* (New York: Amacom, 2005).

The Proposal team

Selecting the proper proposal team is very important, as this is a group that will make or break the proposal. For small projects from small consulting firms, this team may be limited to one or two people with the necessary resources that can be applied. Contrast this with large-scale projects, where the proposal team may involve hundreds of people. Obviously, the larger the team, the more difficult it is to manage. However, a variety of viewpoints are needed, so a variety of perspectives must be considered in the process. Potential proposal team members are listed below:

Potential proposal team members include:
- Partners/executives
- Proposal managers
- Project leaders
- Subject matter experts
- Functional managers
- Support staff
- Analysts
- Field representatives
- Audience experts

- Communication experts
- Marketing experts
- Project managers
- Review teams

At the top of the list are the partners and executives in the organization developing the proposal. They may not have an active role in the process, but need to be informed and briefed on the proposal and its development.

The individual responsible for the proposal, the proposal manager, is usually selected first as the person who is going to manage the entire proposal process. For some organizations, this is a full-time responsibility, with expertise in the proposal management process.

Should the proposal be accepted, who is going to lead the project? Sometimes the project leader is the proposal manager, if the firm is organized with that strategy in mind. But for some organizations, it's another person who is skilled at delivering and managing the project, but not as skilled at managing the proposal process. If it's not known who will manage the proposal process, at least a potential project leader needs to be a part of the proposal team.

Critical to the process is the subject matter experts, who understand the nature of the project and opportunity for success more than anyone else. They are often internal to the organization, but in some cases, could be external with a contract to work on this particular process. The functional managers represent different functions in the organization, such as IT, design, logistics, and accounting.

The support staff is the administrative team that provides coordination and administrative support for a smoothly running project.

The analysts are those who crunch the numbers and are involved early in the process, gathering data for intelligence, developing the situation analyses and stakeholder analyses. They are necessary to continue through the project.

The field representatives are those individuals who understand the ultimate user or participant in this project. They understand the issues in the context or location where the project will be completed. They sense the environmental, social, structural, and relationship issues that will make the project successful. Tied closely with this group are audience experts, the people who understand the recipients, users, and participants who will benefit from the project. They may not be part of the organization and can bring a perspective that no one else can.

Next are a few experts who may or may not be included in the functional category. Communication experts make sure the messages are consistent, simple, and understandable. A marketing expert keeps underscoring the client focus that's needed, ensuring that the value of the proposition is always clear throughout the process and that themes are covered consistently. A project manager is someone who's familiar with the project management tools and guides the project through timelines and keeps it on track. Finally the review team, which is not involved in the development of the proposal, is charged with a review process that is described later in the chapter.

Offer freeze

Another important issue highlighted in Figure 6.2 is the "offer freeze." This is an important issue that, when neglected, can cause serious problems in the proposal process. When should the pricing for the project be determined? If we wait until the proposal is fully developed, the prices may be inflated because the experts only add more cost because of overdesign—just to be safe. The project could be lost because of overpricing. Many experts suggest the firm price should occur early in the proposal development process. With many of the decisions made in planning and early design, based on the intelligence gathering, stakeholder analysis, and the RFP itself, pricing may be set as either acceptable or competitive. At this time, the proposal team can quickly come to the conclusion of what is needed to secure the project, and then that price should be frozen. This offer freeze allows the team to work toward that price instead of adding to it.

Kickoff meeting

Another event on the schedule is the kickoff meeting, which involves the proposal team and is designed to discuss the project and to motivate the team to develop a winning proposal. Although the proposal team is invited to the meeting, this is a great opportunity to bring others who are not involved directly for support. For example, an often-overlooked group is the spouses of the project team, who may perceive that the project may take long hours (as they almost always do). For the spouses to see the importance of the project, what's involved, the necessity for the long hours, and even a glimpse of the rewards that may follow, is a great opportunity to get this important group committed and supportive. In addition, it may be helpful to include the administrative team that will support the group in a variety of ways.

THEMES

Themes are helpful to make the proposal more attractive to the client and the decision-making team. The theme represents the specific messages that are highlighted, underscored, and presented throughout the project that express the nature of the project proposal to satisfy the client needs.

Figure 6.3 shows where the themes typically originate. The first important issue is the hot buttons. Examining the RFP, understanding the audience, conducting the stakeholder analysis, gathering all the intelligence, and detailing the situations will uncover particular hot buttons from the perspective of the buyer. Key words, such as

Figure 6.3. Proposal themes.

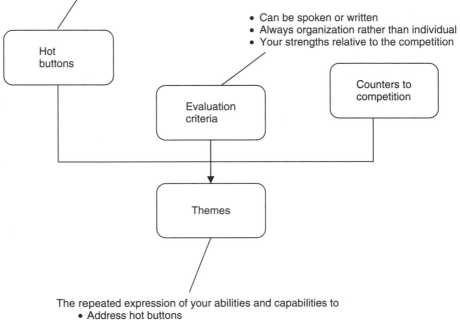

- Affect how the project will be performed
- Are individualized and spoken rather than written (e.g., in an RFP)

- Can be spoken or written
- Always organization rather than individual
- Your strengths relative to the competition

Hot buttons

Evaluation criteria

Counters to competition

Themes

The repeated expression of your abilities and capabilities to
- Address hot buttons
- Meet evaluation criteria
- Counter the competition, based on those criteria

Source: Adapted from Richard C. Freed, Shervin Freed, and Joseph D. Romano, *Writing Winning Business Proposals: Your Guide to Landing the Client, Making the Sale, Persuading the Boss* (New York: McGraw-Hill, 2003).

value, ROI, cost-benefit analysis, value proposition, results, and *success* are very critical in most projects. Other hot button terms, such as *seamless, fully integrated,* and *sustainable,* describe how the project will work.

Themes can also be extracted from the evaluation section of the RFP. Almost every project will detail how it should be evaluated, and this provides cues to discuss the results and how to meet the evaluation criteria.

For some, hot button issues are the involvement of others or minimizing any disruption of the organization. These hot buttons clearly become important themes to address and fully integrate into the process.

Another important issue to consider is the relationship to competitors. Knowing the competitors involved is crucial, and distinguishing your proposal from others is essential. Using the themes, comparisons should be highlighted consistently, accurately, and constantly throughout the proposal.

PRESENTATION STYLE

The appearance, wording, and message of the presentation are significant issues for discussion. The style of the proposal involves several elements, described in this section.

Mock-up

At times, doing a mock-up of the proposal is helpful to show the table of contents, different sections, charts, figures, exhibits, and flow without the actual wording. This is an excellent way to see the big picture before the writing is started. From here, the writing begins.

Simple, business style

As for writing style, simple and straightforward is best, and although it's tempting to have long sentences, complicated expressions, and even technical jargon, this approach should be used only if the reader prefers it. Put simply, it's best to keep the proposal very understandable, readable, and business-focused. A key client in an executive or managerial role often approves the proposal and that person prefers a simple, easy-to-read proposal. Keep it user-friendly and consider a predetermined reading level, which is checked with Microsoft Word or another software package.

Charts and visuals

The proposal should include charts that are easy to understand—without a lot of words—have compelling messages, and provide essential information for a quick summary of a concept or further explanation of the proposition. Charts should be consistent in their style, formatting, and presentation, so they flow seamlessly together, as if prepared by one individual.

Video clips, CDs, photographs, and other presentation tools are appearing more frequently. These visuals increase understanding and are recommended if they are allowed. A video could describe a successful project, interview a satisfied client, describe a previous a design, or present a briefing on the methodology and approach. This may be a way to animate parts of the proposal process.

Selling, but not overselling

When selling, remember the themes that are developed in order to meet the customer needs and win the proposal. Selling must be subtle, responding to the issues, but not overselling. The client (i.e., the buyer) realizes that all proposals are selling documents, but if it becomes too commercial, "too much sizzle and not enough steak," it can easily turn off the buyer.

Address results and deliverables

The uniqueness of the process presented in this book is the focus on results, which should be the highlight of the proposal. Results often appear not only in meeting the evaluation criteria, outlined in the original RFP, but speaking to forecasted value in reminding the audience of the forecast and the forecasted values.

Also there should be a continued focus on deliverables. The reader is always thinking: "What's in it for me?" "What are we going to get from this?" "What will they provide?" "What will they leave behind?"

Don't let the deliverables be a mystery. While a section in the proposal discusses deliverables, it is appropriate to discuss them in different parts of the proposal.

Draft

The proposal lives through many drafts, and at times, many different individuals write the proposal, which proves a challenge for consistency. Simple things may be ignored, such as first person versus third person perspectives, reading levels, and flow. Resolving these in the first draft is important.

After the draft is spell-checked and grammar-checked, it's ready for the editing process, which may be provided by a professional writer, the communications member on the team, or even an external editor. The goal in editing is for a smooth and fine-tuned document that is in sync with the spirit and concept of the proposal process and the value added. An editor must be constantly thinking about the themes and be results-focused throughout the process. A polished draft is then ready for the review team.

GRANT PROPOSALS

Sometimes proposals respond to grant opportunities. In some ways, developing a proposal for a grant for a nonprofit or government agency is no different than a proposal made to any other type of organization. However, in some ways they are different, and the difference must be considered in the proposal process.

Great source of funding

The amount of money granted to consultants from states, federal governments, nonprofits, and nongovernment organizations is growing significantly. In some cases governments have been trying to reduce the number of employees, thus creating contracting opportunities for consultants to provide the same or similar services. In fact, using consultants in the government is the norm, when compared to the private sector. After you've mastered the procedures and the process has been fine-tuned, responding to grant requests may be an efficient way to obtain new business. Relationships, of course, are still important, and many of the issues are the same.

The differences

In the opinion of most consultants, several differences make grant writing more difficult. First, there are more formal requirements. Rarely will an opportunity be provided by handshake agreements. Also the process is much more structured, following more detailed procedures. Consequently, it is perceived to be more time-consuming and difficult for some consultants, requiring a much more detailed proposal. For grants, the qualifications are more critical and the budgets often tighter, which may mean lower fees for the consultants. Also grants usually require an evaluation of the project—although an evaluation is recommended for all projects.

Major components

In the box that follows you will see the major components of a proposal to a state or federal agency (Hall and Howlett, 2003). The sections are similar to the components presented in the comprehensive approach in Chapter 5, but five key differences are often found:

1. A statement of assurance or compliance is required to ensure that the consultant is able to provide the services and that there are no conflicts of interests.
2. An abstract is often presented and is similar to the executive summary.
3. The sustainability is important because there are so many government contracts, with one often immediately following

the other. This essentially shows how the consulting solution will be sustained over a period of time.

4. Evaluation indicates how it will be evaluated as well as the types of data that will be collected.
5. The qualifications and credentials of those who are part of the consulting team are emphasized.

Major components of proposals to state and federal agencies (element/information usually provided and the approximate length)

Title Page: *one page*

Title of project, name and contact information of the project director, name and address of submitting organization, name of the program and agency to which the proposal is being sent, inclusive dates of the project, total budget and amount requested in this proposal, signatures of persons authorizing submission.

Signed Assurances: *length varies*

All government sources will describe what assurance or compliance statements are required for their programs.

Abstract: *a half page*

A self-contained, ready-for-publication description of the project, covering purpose/outcomes/objectives, need and significance, procedures, evaluation, dissemination. This should stress the end products and benefits of the project if funded. Normally this is 200 to 250 words long. It will be used verbatim by the program manager to describe your effort.

Statement of Purpose: *one and a half pages*

Specific description of the expected outcomes, goals, and objectives to be achieved through this project.

Continued

Statement of Need: *one page*

Well-documented description of the problem to be addressed, the need, and why it is important. Should establish significance, timeliness, generalizability, and contribution to other work. Credible sources should be used for all statistics supporting and explaining the needs.

Procedures: *three pages*

A plan of action for how the purposes will be achieved and why this approach is the most effective. Discuss how it is different from or complementary to similar efforts by others. Stress collaborations, if possible. Describe how the results will be disseminated to others.

Sustainability: *a half page*

Government funders want to know how these activities will be supported after this grant ends. Some agencies ask that this be discussed as part of the procedures or in the budget. Others want it to be a separate component. Be specific about your plans for future funding, including other grantors, individual donors, and earned income.

Evaluation: *two pages*

Details the means by which the applicant and funding source will know what the project has accomplished. Should describe the questions to be asked, the methods to be used in gathering and analyzing the data, and how the information will be used and reported. Many government sources are now requiring that this section be formatted as outcome-based evaluation.

Qualifications/Personnel: *two and a half pages*

Provides an overview of the mission, history, programs, and relevant experience of the sponsoring organization, and documents why it is

Continued

ideally suited to undertake this work. Describes specific consultants and staff who will work on the project, their qualifications, their duties, and, if not covered by the budget, the percentage of time they format or template. This section should also discuss any cooperating organizations and give evidence of their willingness to participate.

Budget: *two pages*

The cost of the project for each year of its operation should be displayed by major line items (government sources usually have detailed budget forms). Itemize what is being provided by the sponsoring organization, what is being requested from the government, and what will be contributed by other sources. There is increased interest among government sources in supporting projects that are also funded by private foundations and/or corporations. A plan of action for any additional fund-raising should be provided. You may also want to use footnotes or a budget narrative to explain how various costs were computed.

Attachments: *length varies*

Nonprofits should attach their 501(c)(3) letter unless told in the guidelines that this is not necessary. All organizations should include the names and affiliations of their boards. The program guidelines will describe what other attachments are desired, such as an audited financial report of the organization. Letters of support or agreements to participate should be provided from any organizations or groups whose involvement is essential to the project's success. In some cases, it is useful to get a letter of support from your congressional delegation or, if applying to the state, from key legislators. Ask the program officer if this would be appropriate. Be very careful to follow the funder's guidelines about what can go into attachments.

The public sector can be a very important target for proposals, and the concepts and processes in this book would apply to all audiences or businesses, both public and private, and the private sector of funding agencies or organizations. Currently, there's a tremendous amount of interest from privately funded grants that show the value of the project in terms typically requested by businesses. That is, they are thinking about cost-benefit analysis, monetary benefits, and ROI. In sum, forecasting value is becoming an important issue.

TEAM REVIEW

A review process is needed to ensure that the proposal represents the best thinking of the firm. Some consulting firms think that their "secret weapon" or competitive advantage is a product of this team review process. It can be powerful, it takes time, and it must be managed properly.

Why a review?

To reflect on the advantages of the review, it's helpful to examine four very important reasons for doing this.

1. A review creates a much better proposal, because with the best thinking of the entire team, your proposal will be more on target, consistent, creative, compelling, and results-driven.
2. A review increases the chance of winning, because the review team identifies additional points, issues, and sometimes, the clincher—the issue that made the difference.
3. The review process beats the competition. As the competition becomes more intense, it's necessary to have the thinking of the entire group, not just the proposal writers and proposal team. Taking time to do this can help create a unique image.
4. The proposal team learns something from the process. It makes the team much better, and makes the next proposal

much better. After all, this is the opportunity to tap the best thinking in the entire firm, outside of the proposal-writing members of the team.

The green team

Some organizations have different names for this kind of team: "The Pink Team," "The Red Team," or "The Green Team." "The Green Team" popularized by Edward deBono in *The Six Thinking Hats* (1999) is the name most commonly used. According to deBono, different colored hats are used to reflect ways and styles of thinking. By focusing on one particular aspect at a time, confusion is often reduced when there are multiple issues, tasks, and objectives involved. DeBono's work suggests that team members all wear a particular hat at a particular time. In essence, you can figuratively put on different hats and have a different response to the proposal. When every person is wearing the same hat, they are united in that same perspective. Their egos also are protected because they are in that same mode of thinking and role. Thus it encourages more discussion than normal. Two colors of hats come into play here. The first is the black hat, which is the negative hat and usually worn by proposal team members as they develop the proposal. Wearing this hat, they are ultimately trying to minimize the risk of the project through the proposal process.

According to deBono, the green hat represents new ideas, new concepts, and new perceptions. It encourages the deliberate creation of new ideas, alternatives, and scenarios. Green is deBono's color for this hat because "green is the color of fertility and growth and plants that grow from tiny seeds." Green is the symbolic color for the thinking hat specifically concerned with creativity, new ideas, and new ways of looking at things, escaping from the old ideas in order to find better ones.

DeBono suggests why green-hat thinking is so difficult:

For most people...creative thinking is difficult because it is contrary to the natural habits of recognition, judgment, and criticism.... The brain is designed to set up patterns, to use them and to condemn anything that does not "fit" these patterns. Most thinkers like to be secure. They like to be right.

Creativity involves provocation, exploration, and risk taking.... You cannot order yourself (or others) to have a new idea, but you can order yourself (and others) to spend time trying to have a new idea. The green hat provides a formal way of doing this.

How it works

By definition, the review team is a group of individuals who are not directly involved in the proposal nor involved in the direct selling to the customer. The green team can be representatives from marketing, IT, logistics, and other areas described in the makeup of the team. But the team could also be a group of important experts in the firm, who do not have very much at stake, but can offer valuable advice.

The goal itself is to gain the knowledge of the rest of the firm. Figure 6.4 shows the levels of knowledge. First we have, "we know what we know," which is what the proposal team knows as they develop the proposal. Then, there's "what we don't know," which is outside of the proposal team and may come from the green team. The next level, "know what our organization knows" is a chance to bring in the rest of the firm's knowledge, so that the proposal represents the entire firm's best thinking. The green team can accomplish this.

Figure 6.4. Levels of knowledge.

Source: Adapted from Richard C. Freed, Shervin Freed, and Joseph D. Romano, *Writing Winning Business Proposals: Your Guide to Landing the Client, Making the Sale, Persuading the Boss* (New York: McGraw-Hill, 2003).

The process must be managed with minimum resources and effort, as well as structure. It often involves a process, such as this:

1. The proposal is presented, and the team listens.
2. The team members pose questions to clarify.
3. The team members point out strengths.
4. The team members point out weaknesses.
5. After discussion, the team members come to a conclusion about strengths and weaknesses.
6. They examine potential actions to improve the situation, to resolve weaknesses, and to build on strengths.

This process can be accomplished in about an hour or more, and hopefully, it leaves the proposal team with matter to edit and consider. The proposal team must also consider the timing, resources, and the feasibility of doing what is suggested. The benefit of this exercise is that the proposal developers have the best thinking available throughout this process.

PROBLEMS AND ISSUES WITH PROPOSALS

Several problems or issues with a client may surface during the proposal process that deserve additional attention. Here are the most important issues.

Proposal conference

The client may ask for a meeting to discuss the proposal when a live presentation was not required. While this is an excellent opportunity to present the proposal and clarify issues, it's also a signal that the process went astray, something wasn't clear, or in some way the proposal is off base.

A conference should be accepted as a welcome opportunity and scheduled as quickly as possible. Insist that the key decision maker attend, and find out who else will be there. It also may be helpful to specifically ask if there are any concerns about the proposal. This can present an opportunity to explore the issue prior to the meeting. Finding out everything you can about the concerns is helpful. It might also be helpful to explore how close they may be to accepting your proposal. Ask bluntly: "If we can work out the differences and adjustments, are you willing to go with us?" This can help you understand how close you may be to actually landing the project.

Ethics

While every attempt is made to uncover information needed for the proposal and gather as much intelligence as possible, this should all be done ethically. Using clandestine ways to determine information and finding unnamed sources to reveal insiders' viewpoints may backfire. All information should be collected ethically, using the same sources that would be available to anyone else who could be responding.

Jargon

Unfortunately, a proposal is an opportune time for some business writers to use terms, concepts, and statements that are not known, vague, or represent the latest jargon. The proposal is not a place for this. Perhaps the best preparation for writing the proposal is to refer to the book, *Why Business People Speak Like Idiots: A Bullfighter's Guide* by Brian Fugere, Chelsea Hardaway, and Jon Warshawsky (Free Press, 2005). This handy book, written by consultants, is a must-have for any consultant's library and explains how so much miscommunication has seeped into the corporate vernacular. Certainly, jargon should be left out of the proposal.

Vagueness

Several times during this chapter the point was made that vagueness should be replaced with specific statements; objectives should be clear and unambiguous, results should be clearly defined, and success measures clearly articulated. Nothing is more dysfunctional than vague proposals. Perhaps more dangerous, vague proposals lead to unmet expectations, false assumptions, and misguided actions. A final step in any proposal would be the review of the document for specificity.

Page-limited proposals

In some cases, the client may require a maximum number of pages. This is often because of the time required to read several proposals. Sometimes this is fixed in the proposal procedures or the compliance regulation. When this is the case, it means that the same topics must be covered but in a shorter presentation. Precise, to-the-point presentations would be helpful, with additional references placed on the consultant's Website.

Scope creep

Scope creep occurs when there are many add-ons suggested by the client, often with the expectation that there will be no additional charge. In the eagerness to secure the contract, the consultant may agree to provide them. Also, add-ons often emerge during the project as issues are uncovered or new issues are raised, and ultimately scope creep—moving the project beyond what was intended—eats away at any profit margin that may have been generated from the consulting project. To avoid scope creep the consultant must say no, diplomatically of course, or offer to do any additional item for an additional amount. You do not have to be as blunt as asking for money for everything you may do, but you may suggest that it can be provided quickly through a separate proposal since it was not in the original contract or RFP. This brings the issue to the attention of the client and provides the client with options. In this way, scope creep can become a revenue enhancement.

The unresponsive client

When the client does not respond by a particular date, there may be good reasons. It may be a sign that something is not working. A courtesy phone call after the due date would certainly be appropriate. If there is still no answer, a second or even third phone call may be appropriate. Beyond that, it may be helpful to send a letter, and e-mail, or maybe even consider a certified letter. It might be helpful to find out from colleagues if there is some particular problem. At some point it may be helpful to just let it go after every effort has been made to make contact. Just to be covered, it might be helpful to send a certified letter after several weeks have passed indicating that unless there is some correspondence or communication by a particular date, you would have to consider the proposal null and void. This would prevent the client from asking for the proposal to be implemented a year later, when things have changed and costs might have to be adjusted.

PRESENTATION STRATEGIES

To be sure, communication skills must be at their best when presenting the proposal. From the title page to the appendix, the writing should be clear, specific, professional, and compelling. It must be logical, systematic, engaging, and content rich. This is a challenge for some of the proposal team, who underestimate the importance of the written word. While there are other ways to present the proposal, the written document will be the most significant.

Proposal presentation

The proposal begins with the cover. It should be uncluttered and direct, usually beginning with the words *proposal from* and then listing the company, the title of the project, followed by the words *submitted by* the consulting firm, and the date.

The executive summary should be a very brief presentation of the entire proposal, highlighting the key points. It should contain the summary items discussed in the simple proposal, using the same logic. Usually a two-page summary for a comprehensive proposal would be enough.

The writing style throughout should be consistent with headings, formatting, and itemizing, using the same bullets and consistent formats for tables and charts. Very clear writing is important. There should be several "hooks" that quickly get to the point to make this proposal stand out. A hook is a one- or two-sentence conclusion and a compelling reason to accept the proposal. They may even be boxed in to make those points clearer. There could be a hook for each section of the proposal.

Delivery of the proposal

Obviously, the proposal must be delivered by the deadline, but not much earlier than that. An earlier delivery may be too soon to reflect adjustments that might be made in the RFP. Ideally, proposals should be delivered in person. This provides a chance to see who else is delivering or involved in the process. In some cases, e-mail delivery is acceptable, but it's important to follow up to make sure that the proposal has been received. Express package services are quite effective, but they must be traceable and with guaranteed delivery dates.

Electronic communications

In some settings, the proposal can be discussed electronically. In simple terms, a telephone conversation may be helpful to underscore the important parts (the hooks) and express appreciation for being a part of the process. Beyond telephones, teleconferencing may be allowable. This approach brings decision makers and the consulting team together in a live teleconference, providing an opportunity to discuss highlights, review issues, and clarify key points. In some cases, the client may accept a Webcast, which essentially follows the format of a live presentation, but is conducted over the Internet.

Face-to-face presentation

Although not available for every situation, live presentations of proposals are appropriate. Some clients require this. A face-to-face meeting is a great opportunity to present the proposal in a professional and compelling way, highlighting the key points and underscoring the hooks. This is the time to have a powerful presentation, though not necessarily a PowerPoint presentation. PowerPoint slides with bullets may not engage the audience, but highlighting certain parts of it, showing examples of work, underscoring the deliverables, and describing the payoff will. Measurable results might hook the decision makers. A compelling story is needed that leads to an obvious action: accepting the proposal.

The live presentation has several distinct advantages and affords several important opportunities for the proposal team. For one, it provides an opportunity to develop or refine a relationship on a personal basis. After all, the chemistry and the relationship with the consultant is a critical issue in the decision-making process. Also, the meeting represents an opportunity to underscore the unique methodology and advantages the consultant offers. You have their attention, and this may be the best time to get them to focus on what you provide and others cannot. Finally, the meeting is an opportunity to present the proposal in quick summary—with details provided in the document—and to clarify any issues. There may be some confusion over parts of it.

Negotiations

In some cases, proposals are not accepted as is, but are brought into a negotiation process. This is particularly useful when the proposal did not address the needs that the client expected. Also, if costs are extremely high, or what is offered exceeds what's needed, the negotiation may be a way to adjust the proposal. To be fair, all individuals are involved in renegotiating their proposal. This process represents both good news and bad news. The good news is that it is an opportunity to clarify changes and make adjustments to fit the needs of the client. The bad news is that others get the same opportunity, and that apparently there were some miscommunications that led to the negotiation.

Whatever approach is taken, the presentation is important to proposal success, and planning it is essential. Suggesting that a live presentation be included might be a significant strategy. It might be the best way to make sure that the proposal is accepted.

WHEN YOU LOSE

Losing a bid—not having a proposal accepted—provides a unique learning experience and an opportunity to build a relationship. Although you'd like to learn in some other way, failing to have your proposal accepted should compel you to shift into trying to understand why. Most clients will explain why it was rejected, and then how you handle the rejection and work with the client in the future can show much in terms of building that relationship and others.

Understanding the reasons for rejection

There can be many reasons for rejection, and many of them are completely out of the hands of the decision maker. Some of the more common reasons are listed below. These and other reasons for not obtaining the proposal provide an opportunity to find out why. Most clients will explain, particularly if it's a reason that is completely out of their control. But even if it is their decision, most clients are prepared to tell you your weaknesses or the parts of the proposal that presented the most concern. This is not a time to argue, but a time to listen and understand.

Common reasons for rejection include:
1. The proposal missed the deadline.
2. The project was delayed or canceled.
3. The funding or budget went away.
4. There is a reorganization that caused the project to be postponed.
5. The proposal guidelines were not followed.
6. The proposal was not clear and compelling in terms of what was being provided.
7. The proposal was not complete in providing detail.
8. A more thorough, compelling, and complete proposal was accepted.

9. The proposal costs were unrealistic in terms of the budget for the project.
10. The quality of the proposal was unacceptable.
11. The proposed approach appeared to be beyond the capability of the consultants.
12. The projected value was missing.

Handling the loss

Taking the rejection personally is a serious mistake. The best response is to thank the client for the opportunity and ask to be considered again for similar projects as they arise in the future. If you are familiar with any of the winning consultants, sending a note of congratulations can be a nice gesture that reflects positively on your character and professionalism. Attempting to challenge the decision or discredit the winning firm can do nothing but destroy your reputation.

A likely scenario is that the client will closely observe bidders who did not win the project to see how they handle the rejection. Attempting to maintain a cordial, friendly, and productive relationship with the client is a valuable character-building exercise and highly recommended. Doing so sets the stage for you to work on strengthening the relationship with that ongoing prospect, and to identify and overcome the shortages and weaknesses in your proposal.

FINAL THOUGHTS

As you may very well know by now, making your way on the road of proposal success cannot be a lone effort. Effectively managing the proposal based on valuable feedback from others and utilizing helpful resources are essential to reaching the goal of an accepted proposal. While the previous chapter focused on the content of the proposal in terms of different elements, this chapter focused on how to manage the process. Both are very critical to success. If not managed properly with best advice and expertise, then the proposal will be subpar. The only way to win, in this case, is with some serious price cutting, which is not a desirable approach. With an effectively managed process, the content can be presented in such a way that tells the proper story and presents the theme and value proposition consistently through the process. This chapter discusses the various issues and processes that can make a significant difference in the success of the proposal, while at the same time, addressing some of the critical issues that can become stumbling blocks to success. The next chapter begins the most critical phase of this book, forecasting.

7

Forecasting Reaction and Learning

Every project leader desires a positive reaction to his or her efforts. Unfortunately, the terms *positive* and *reaction* are vague. Sometimes a specific reaction to the project is desired. A reaction forecast tells us what initial success to expect. Projects can go astray with an adverse reaction. If participants view the project as irrelevant, the likelihood that anything will change is slim. Consequently, defining the desired reaction through a reaction forecast is an important step toward ensuring results that meet stakeholder expectations.

Just as reaction is important, it is also important to forecast learning. Learning defines what individuals involved in the project must know to make the project successful. For some programs, such as competency building, technology implementation, leadership development, and compliance programs, learning is very critical to the process.

At this point, it is helpful to briefly review the difference between forecasts and objectives. In Chapter 4, the concept of learning objectives was introduced at multiple levels. A forecast is, basically, a modified objective. Instead of covering how objectives are developed in this chapter, we will explore how to develop a forecast. The difference is that the amount of the objective is the acceptable level, whereas a forecast represents our best estimate of what will actually happen.

For some, the forecast is much more important because it shows what should realistically occur instead of an acceptable level. We will also find in this chapter that forecasts are very precise, and objectives are typically broader and not as specific. This chapter examines forecasting reaction and learning forecasts, as well as how they are constructed and used.

ARE REACTION AND LEARNING FORECASTS NECESSARY?

Some might argue that reaction and learning are always understood and do not need to be forecast. Of course, we want a favorable reaction and want learning to be present. So why should we bother with this? Here's the rationale for forecasting at both levels.

Reaction is a vague, subjective construct that needs clarification if we want to ensure we obtain the reaction we seek. A forecast provides the basis for this clarification. For example, at times the reaction is based on motivating participants to achieve success with the project. In other situations, the reaction explains why they're there. Sometimes the reaction forecast answers the question, "What's in it for me?" The reaction forecast is there to avoid a negative reaction because the project is controversial. At other times, reaction forecasts show what is necessary and appropriate for the target audience and its role in the organization. Clarity is needed.

Projects can fail if the reaction is unfavorable (that is, the desired reaction is not achieved). An example is a project perceived to be controversial because it changes the way in which the group works by adding extra tasks to the schedule or removing freedoms that the group previously enjoyed. These situations can provoke a negative reaction; therefore, the forecast would be to present the project in a logical, rational way so participants can see that it is necessary. At best, this approach would foster an understanding of the importance of the new approach with participants' willingness to apply necessary actions. At worst, it would prevent participants from sabotaging the success of the project.

Clearly defined reaction forecasts are needed because they represent the first level of project success. The chain of impact begins at this level. While sponsors and clients undervalue reaction, the reaction forecast is important to those people intimately involved in implementing the project. The irony is that in most projects, reaction is captured, but a forecast is not developed.

The rationale for a learning forecast is based on the importance of learning a particular project. As explained in the chain of impact (Chapter 3), it must exist for a project to be successful. The individuals involved in a project (i.e., the users, participants, audience, etc.) must know what to do to make the project successful. If they do not, the project can fail at this level, and in many cases, this happens. People simply don't know what to do or how to do it properly. Fortunately, a learning forecast explains what participants will learn when the project is implemented. If the forecast shows that learning may not occur, this is a red flag, because without the learning, the project will probably be unsuccessful.

In some projects, such as in a compliance project, the definition of success is often learning. A compliance project's success may be defined as everyone must know these items or know how to do something specifically. If that's the definition, then the success of the project rests on learning. However, even in compliance projects success is defined at higher levels to see if they add value to the organization. Consequently, a learning forecast is important to provide the focus to ensure that this learning does occur. Essentially, the forecast is a modified learning objective, which provides direction to the project leader to ensure that project participants have learned what they need to learn.

HOW TO CONSTRUCT REACTION FORECASTS

Developing a reaction forecast is quite straightforward. It's easy to develop, easy to measure, and takes very little time. Keep these concepts in mind when developing a reaction forecast.

Descriptions of perception

By definition, a reaction forecast is based on the perception of those involved in the project. Perception is essentially a measure of how someone reacts to the project. Descriptions of perception vary. The key is to be clear on what perception is needed to ensure that participants are engaged and willing to acquire the knowledge, skills, or information required to make the project successful. Key words that reflect reaction are listed below. Here is an example of how these words are used: "Participants will *perceive* this project to be relevant to their work, as indicated by an average of 4.2 out of 5 on a 5-point scale."

Key words for a reaction forecast include:

- Perceive
- React
- Rate
- Envision
- Interpret
- View
- Deduce
- Deem
- Grade
- Feel
- Regard
- Think
- Consider
- Inclination
- Stance
- Opinion
- Attitude
- Impression

Specificity

A forecast should reflect a certain amount of reaction. If a 2-point scale is used (yes or no, favorable or unfavorable), planning for a percentage of "yes" or "favorable" responses may be the precision that's needed. On a 5-point scale, measuring the percentage rating 4 out of 5 may be appropriate. Sometimes even decimal points are used (that is, 4.2 out of 5), although the incremental parts of a 5-point scale might have no actual meaning from a statistical standpoint. Sometimes a 4-, 6-, 7- or 10-point system is used in the forecast and in measuring success, although a 10-point scale is usually not appropriate for this type of evaluation. Five to 7 points represents enough variance in the scale to provide respondents the choices they need. The best approach, however, is to identify a specific degree of success, regardless of the type of question or scale. This specificity may be based on historical results or obtained from experts (discussed later). In either case, it is important to set the specific desired measure of success and know why you have set it at that level.

The number of reaction forecasts

While the principal issue in developing a forecast is precision, the challenge is to avoid having too many reaction measures in the forecast. After all, in the success value chain, reaction is perhaps the weakest level of feedback, at least from an executive viewpoint. Overkill should be avoided. Identify only the most critical reaction issues, and develop specific targets of success for each measure to make the measure meaningful.

An important consideration in developing a reaction forecast is to obtain data about the content of the project. Too often, feedback data reflect aesthetic issues that may not reflect the substance of the project.

MEASURES FOR A REACTION FORECAST

Many topics serve as targets for a reaction forecast, because so many issues and processes are involved in a typical project. Reaction is important for almost every major issue, step, or process to make sure outcomes are successful. Here are a few typical topics for a reaction forecast.

- **Ready**. Many projects fail because of inadequate preparation by participants or perhaps involvement of the wrong participants. While specific actions could focus on ensuring that the right people are involved, a forecast will define how ready they are for the task.

- **Useful**. Although this might seem apparent, the project must be useful to participants. In far too many situations, it is not perceived as useful.

- **Necessary.** For some projects, it's important for participants to realize the need for the project. This measure might be appropriate for implementation of a new ethics project or a cost-containment project for health care, as participants must see that action is necessary.

- **Appropriate.** A project needs to be appropriate for the situation. Sometimes mismatches occur between the project (a solution) and the problem. Participants need to see that this is the appropriate action to take given the situation at hand.

- **Motivational.** Some projects are designed to motivate employees to improve performance or reach a goal. The participants must be motivated to take action. This is particularly helpful for enabling new technology, reward systems, meetings and events, and leadership development projects.

- **Rewarding.** Some projects need to be rewarding for participants and other key stakeholders. This is particularly true for projects such as a suggestion system where cash rewards are provided for submitting a suggestion; a pay-for-skills project where participants are rewarded with promotion if they learn new skills; or a new compensation system that rewards employees directly for performance. Participants must see these projects as rewarding; otherwise, their involvement may be limited.

- **Practical.** In a world of complex workplace issues, practicality is imperative. Projects should provide a practical application, devoid of unnecessarily theoretical issues.

- **Valuable.** One of the most powerful measures focuses on the value of a project. Participants need to see value, both as it benefits them and as it benefits the organization. Value can be expressed in terms of a good investment by the taxpayer or a good investment of the participants' time.

- **Timely.** Some projects need to be perceived as timely—not too early and not too late. This is particularly important for new technology, new tools, or the development of new products or services.

- **Powerful.** To achieve dramatic improvement or urgent action, a project might need to be perceived as powerful. This is particularly important for breakthrough processes, exciting technology, and new approaches to old problems. Participants need to see this project as making a powerful impact on them and others.

- **Leading Edge.** Some projects are implemented to stay ahead of others—to stay on the leading edge of technology or processes when compared to competitors. This is important when new systems are implemented and new products are developed.

- **Efficient.** All projects need to be implemented efficiently. Those involved need to see excellent organization and precise execution. People do not react favorably to inefficiency.

- **Easy/Difficult.** Project participants need to perceive the effort as both not too easy and not too difficult to accomplish. If it becomes too difficult, participants avoid it or do it improperly, resulting in problems. If it's too easy, they ignore it. There needs to be an appropriate balance between too easy and too difficult.

- **Relevance.** Participants want a project that is relevant to their world. Consequently, it is helpful to explore the relevance of the project to the participants' current or future responsibilities. If it is relevant, it will be used.
- **Importance.** Participants need to see that the content is important to their success. This provides an answer to, "What's in it for me?"
- **Intent to Use.** Asking participants about their intentions to use the project's content (i.e., make it work) can be helpful. The extent of planned use can be captured, along with the expected frequency of use and the anticipated level of effectiveness when using the information, skills, and knowledge. Intent to use usually correlates to actual use.
- **Overall Evaluation.** Almost all organizations capture an overall satisfaction rating, which reflects participants' overall satisfaction with the project. While this might have very little value in terms of understanding the real issues and the project's relationship to future success, comparing one project to another and with the projects over time might be helpful.
- **Content.** Project content includes the equipment, technology, procedures, policies, principles, steps, and situations contained in the project. The content is critical, and participant perception of that content is necessary.
- **Facilities/Environment.** Sometimes, the environment is not conducive to a successful project implementation. Typical issues include the project workspace, the comfort level in the environment, such as temperature, lighting, noise, and other safety issues. A word of caution: If nothing can be done about the environment, then the environment should not be pursued.

- **Project/Team Leader Evaluation.** Perhaps one of the most common uses of reaction data is to evaluate the project. If properly implemented, helpful feedback data that participants provide can be used to make adjustments to increase leader effectiveness. The issues usually involve preparation, presentation, level of involvement, and pacing of the process. Some cautions need to be taken, however. Because facilitator evaluations can be biased either positively or negatively, other evidence might be necessary to provide an overall assessment of project leader performance.

SECURING INPUT FOR THE REACTION FOCUS

The input for the forecast can come from several sources. The sources should have a knowledge of the ultimate participant user or audience the project would be serving—the "usual suspects." Collectively, the following sources should provide quality input to make the forecast as accurate as possible.

Proposal team

Anyone on the proposal team may have knowledge of how the project participants will react to what is being presented. The forecast is what can be achieved by the team, working with project participants. A precise forecast focuses the proposal team and the project delivery team to achieve the forecast. Because there are several experts on the proposal team, they have different insights and this may be helpful to define what will be achieved.

Review team

It might be helpful for the review team to examine the forecast. Because forecasting is such an important part of the proposal, these review team members may be able to provide some new information on the anticipated changes in measures selected for the forecast.

Participants

Considering input directly from the participants—the individuals who will be directly involved in making the project successful—is also helpful. After all, it is their reaction that the team is attempting to forecast. Understanding their perspective is very critical in many projects, but two issues should be examined. First, access to these individuals may be difficult to obtain. Because they are not known during the proposal time frame, this could be difficult. Second, the participants may be biased and perceive the project—whether it's new software, procedure, tool, or process—as extra work. Because it is a change, the project may take them out of their comfort zone, so they reject it. Thus they may not be able to provide credible input for the forecast because of their perceived biases. They also may not have enough understanding of the project to have a valid judgment. While this is a valuable audience, forecasting issues must be addressed very carefully.

Benchmarking data from previous projects

A credible source of data is what has been achieved in other projects. After all, if a similar project has been implemented and reaction has been secured, this data shows what is possible. However, this data would have to be considered within the context of this particular project if there are differences in terms of scope, audience, organization, etc.

HOW TO CONSTRUCT A LEARNING FORECAST

A learning forecast requires more precision than a reaction forecast. The best learning forecasts are clearly written, use action verbs, and are performance-focused. They might contain conditions and criteria.

Action verbs

Learning forecasts usually contain action verbs and are performance-based. Specific action verbs reduce the risk of misinterpretation.

For example, if a new strategy is being launched and it is expected that participants must understand the strategy, a forecast might read, "After completion of this project, participants should understand the strategy." However, this forecast is nonspecific and can lead to misinterpretation. A more precise forecast would be, "After completing this project, participants will identify the five elements of the strategy and name the three pillars of the strategy in less than five minutes." These verbs identify action and leave no doubt as to the forecast's meaning. Here is a list of specific verbs used in learning forecasts.

Action verbs for a learning forecast include:

- Name
- Write
- Prepare
- Describe
- Recite
- Reboot
- Differentiate
- Identify
- Load
- Explain
- Search
- Sort
- Locate
- Stop
- Solve
- Calculate
- Eliminate
- Construct
- Complete
- Start up
- List
- Compare
- Recall
- Contrast
- Determine

Words to avoid are those without clear meaning, such as *know, understand, internalize,* and *appreciate.* These words are open to interpretation and should be avoided in learning forecasts. This is not to suggest that if a learning forecast uses the word *understand* that it is absolutely wrong. However, it probably is not the best choice to convey meaning, and it opens the door to confusion.

Performance

Essentially, performance describes what the participant will be able to do after participating or becoming involved in a project. To be precise, learning forecasts must state what the participants will be able to do based on observable (visual or audible) behavior. The key question to ask is what a person will be doing to demonstrate mastery of the particular forecast. This leads to the precise action verbs listed previously. Consider this example: "Given the detailed client information, write a proposal for the product that meets the client's needs." This statement is performance-driven, as the participant must produce a proposal in one hour, which is a visible action.

The issue of overt and covert forecasts is important when addressing performance. An overt forecast clearly expresses an action item that can be observed or heard, such as the example above. In a covert forecast, the action is internalized, but lacks observable action. For example, in the forecast, "Contrast the differences between consumer and commercial loans," the individual could make the contrast mentally, which would not be visible. This is a covert forecast. To make a covert forecast more usable, a statement is often added to provide a way to make the forecast more observable. For example, the above forecast could be rewritten as, "Contrast the differences between consumer and commercial loans, and write the key differences." The action of writing provides an overt measurement.

Conditions

Following the performance/action verb approach we've discussed is a step toward well-developed learning forecasts; however, more detail might be necessary. Sometimes the parameters or conditions under which a person is expected to perform might need to be detailed. For example, consider the forecast, "At the end of the conference, write a business development plan." The question of condition comes into play here. Are participants supposed to write the plan from memory, or will guidelines or templates be provided? We suspect some example or guideline will be offered. So the new forecast could be, "At the end of the conference, write a business development plan using the template supplied by the project leader." The revised forecast gives more detail on the conditions under which the performance should occur.

Conditions can be written in a variety of ways. Some typical conditions for learning forecasts are listed below. They provide additional detail to define what is expected. For example, instead of having a forecast to calculate ROI for a technology project, the forecast might be reworded as, "Given the total monetary benefits of the project and the total cost of the project, calculate the ROI." In this statement, detail helps communicate expectations. The amount of detail should be adequate for participants to understand clearly what they must do. It must also be clear to all stakeholders.

Typical conditions for learning forecasts include:
- With the aid of software...
- Given a list of materials...
- Given this new procedure...
- Using the template provided...
- Given an environmental database...
- When provided with the new policy...
- Given a properly functioning laptop...
- Without the aid of resources...
- With the aid of a calculator...
- Given the attached job aid...

Conditions can also be included in forecasts at the application and impact levels. The next chapter will focus on these levels.

Criteria

In addition to action verbs and detailed conditions, a third dimension is helpful in developing learning forecasts: stating clearly how well something is to be done. For example, a forecast is, "Be able to list 8 out of 10 elements of the company's sexual harassment policy, given a copy of the policy." The forecast is met when 8 out of 10 of the policy items are listed, given the return copy of the policy. The 8 out of 10 is the expected level of performance or the criterion for success.

Criteria are developed using limitations of speed, accuracy, and quality. In the above example about a company's sexual harassment policy, the focus is on accuracy. We are allowing only two mistakes.

Criteria can be stated in a variety of ways. Sample statements for the accuracy, quality, and speed (time) for learning objectives appear below. Each of these provides a criterion that suggests how accurate the demonstration or competency must be.

Criterion statements for learning forecasts include:
- ...with no more than 2% incorrect entries.
- ...and completed tasks must be accurate to within two minutes of standard.
- ...with productivity increased by 10 percent.
- ...completed within one day.
- ...with no more than two complaints for every 1,000 citizens.
- ...demonstrate all six routines in 10 minutes.
- ...with the provided informative accurate enough so that no more than one repeated request for information is received.
- ...with a rating of four or more (out of five) on performance as judged by an independent observer.

Speed reflects the desired time required to demonstrate a particular performance. For example, consider the objective, "Be able to classify the type of customer complaint in five minutes, given the complete customer complaint report." The five-minute time frame places a speed criterion on the objective. The third type of criterion is quality. When speed and accuracy are not the critical criteria, a quality measure might be needed. Quality focuses on waste, errors, rework, and acceptable standards. For example, in the objective, "Be able to operate the machine with no more than 2 percent waste," the percentage of waste allowed is a quality measure. Quality is similar to accuracy, but the two criteria have distinct differences. Consider the objective, "Be able to make 85 percent of the daily sales calls with success ratings of 4.8 or higher from clients." The 85 percent represents accuracy, while the success ratings reflect the quality of the sales calls.

Criteria may be (and usually are) included in forecasts for application and impact and will be discussed in Chapter 8.

Categories for learning forecasts

Learning forecasts can be categorized in several ways. Although they generally focus on skills and knowledge, there are other elements that can be important. Typically, the objectives are broad and only indicate specific major skills or knowledge areas that should be achieved as the project is implemented. These are sometimes called key learning forecasts.

Learning forecasts focus on knowledge, skills, and attitudes, as well as confidence to apply or implement the project as desired. Sometimes, learning forecasts are expanded to different categories. The typical measures collected at this level are listed below. Obviously, the more detailed the skills, the greater the number of measures. Programs can vary, ranging from one or two simple skills to massive projects that may involve literally hundreds of skills.

Knowledge often includes the assimilation of facts, figures, and concepts. Instead of knowledge, the terms *awareness, understanding,* or *information* may be specific categories. Sometimes, perceptions or attitudes may change based on what a participant has learned. For example, in a diversity project, the participants' attitudes toward having a diverse work group are often changed with the implementation of the project. Sometimes, the desire is to develop a reservoir of knowledge and skills and tap into it when developing capability, capacity, or readiness. When individuals are capable, they are often described as being job ready.

In summary, the typical learning measurement categories are:
- Skills
- Knowledge
- Awareness
- Understanding
- Information
- Perception
- Attitudes
- Capability
- Capacity
- Readiness
- Confidence
- Contacts

When participants use skills for the first time, an appropriate measure might be the confidence that the participants have to use those skills in their job settings. This becomes critical in job situations where skills must be performed accurately and within a certain standard. Sometimes, networking is part of a project, and developing contacts that may be valuable later is important. This may be within, or external to, an organization. For example, a leadership development project may include participants from different functional parts of the organization, and an expected outcome, from a learning perspective, is to know whom to contact at particular times in the future.

SECURING INFORMATION FOR THE LEARNING FORECAST

The challenge in the learning forecast effort is to determine how much learning should occur as a project is implemented. This is a two-part challenge. First, it must be determined what individuals must learn to make the project successful. The second part is to determine how much learning will be achieved in the project implementation. This will require input from several sources.

The proposal team

The proposal team is a group of experts who understand the project very well. They may be the best source of input in terms of what skills and knowledge must be learned and how much learning is needed to make the project successful. Their combined input should determine specific levels of learning that can be achieved.

Review team

The "green review team," discussed in Chapter 6, is another source of data. Here the specific forecast would be offered in draft form, detailing how much learning would occur. These experts, who are not involved in the project directly, may provide unique helpful insight into this issue.

Subject matter experts

Although a subject matter expert may be a member of the proposal team, it may be helpful to have someone who understands the project in terms of tasks, processes, and procedures, which are all targets for the learning forecasts. These experts would use their knowledge to define the kind of learning needed to be successful.

Participants

As with reaction, participants may be a source of input here. The participants are the group of individuals who will be the recipients, the users of the project. They are the audience that will be influenced most by this project. They may have some understanding of what they need to do to make it successful, but may not understand enough or be familiar with issues, particularly if they're new. Also, as described before, access to this group may be limited, and there could be a potential for bias.

FINAL THOUGHTS

At first glance, forecasting reaction and learning may appear unnecessary, as the typical forecasting is stated in terms of impact, cost, and ROI. However, because forecasts can fail if there is an adverse reaction or the participants fail to learn what's necessary to make it successful, forecasts at this level become a very important issue in a proposal. Essentially, the forecast is an objective with a specific amount of predicted reaction or learning that will occur when the project is delivered and is an important part of the value proposition. Chapter 8 focuses on forecasting application and impact.

8

Forecasting Application and Impact

An application forecast defines the actions participants will take after the project is implemented. This is an uncomfortable level for some project leaders, as they might have less control over success in achieving these forecast values. The typical issues in developing application forecasts are addressed in this chapter with examples and exercises. While forecasts of reaction and learning are important, clients and senior executives are more interested in application and impact.

For some stakeholders, impact forecasts are the most important element and represent both tangible and intangible measures. This is a key measure for the individuals who fund projects. This chapter focuses on how to develop impact forecasts, which are based on business measures that are plentiful throughout organizations, including educational institutions, governments, and nonprofits. Data developed at this level are explored along with the issues and examples.

ARE APPLICATION FORECASTS NECESSARY?

Some project leaders would argue that the development and use of application forecasts are necessary. After all, these forecasts provide direction to project participants and clarify expectations about the project in their own work or life situation. A forecast creates the expectation of what will be accomplished within a desired time frame.

However, others might take the stance that application forecasts are not needed. This view comes from two assumptions. First, when learning forecasts are clearly developed and participants master what is needed for project success, it is assumed that they will perform in a way that reflects what they have learned. Second, project leaders have less influence on participants' initial work on the project. There may be no control over these individuals during much of the implementation.

These two assumptions are not necessarily accurate in practice. First, participants do not always do what they have learned when a project is implemented. Many barriers interfere with successful application of almost every project. To drive (or at least influence) application, the forecasts must be established and communicated to participants and maybe their immediate managers. To apply what was learned properly, participants need clear expectations about what they must do. For example, consider the implementation of new software. Participants might learn all the routines, features, and options of the software. In reality, though, they need only learn parts of it to succeed on the job. An application forecast defines how and when they will likely use the software in their work. Also, the forecast sets expectations for participants' managers so they can provide the necessary support.

The second assumption—that project leaders have no influence on participants during project implementation—is inaccurate in today's workplace. Forecasts are developed for all project stakeholders, not simply for the project leader during early stages of the project. While it is true that a project leader will have more control over learning forecasts and less control over application forecasts, he or she can still influence success with the application. With an application forecast, the project leader teaches and leads with application in mind, using the work environment as the context. Using personal experience, the project leader examines barriers and shows how to minimize or overcome them. He or she creates expectations and shows participants how it's done.

At various times, different stakeholders have more or less influence on a particular forecast. As a result, the application forecast becomes an important extension of the learning forecast. It provides direction and guidance and forms the basis for evaluation.

ARE IMPACT FORECASTS NECESSARY?

The chain of impact presented earlier defines the impact measures as the consequence of a project's implementation. These include measures of hard data, such as output, quality, cost, and time, as well as soft data, such as customer satisfaction, employee engagement, and image. A forecast of these measures is particularly important for senior executives and administrators. Some executives lack enthusiasm about a project unless the results reflect key business measures. These impact measures are found in operating reports, scorecards, dashboards, and key performance indicators. It is often the deficiency in performance of one or more impact measures that has led to the creation of the project. This was discussed in Chapter 3 on developing objectives. In terms of power to affect project design, delivery, and success, impact objectives are the most powerful. They provide the focus needed to drive the results that top executives desire.

In practice, many projects do not contain these impact forecasts. This is particularly true in soft projects, such as ethics, leadership development, executive coaching, communication, change management, public relations, and corporate social responsibility. In reality, these types of projects can be connected to a business measure and thus have business impact forecasts connected to them. The challenge is to perform the analysis described in Chapter 4 and develop the forecasts using the techniques in this chapter.

HOW TO CONSTRUCT APPLICATION FORECASTS

The good news is that the development of application forecasts essentially mirrors the development of learning forecasts. Learning forecasts define what participants must learn to make the project successful, while application forecasts define what participants are expected to do with what they have learned.

Components

Application forecasts have their own distinct areas of emphasis. First, they should include an action verb that has clear meaning. (See the list of action verbs in Chapter 7.) Second, a performance statement is connected to the action verb. The performance element must be specific, as in learning forecasts. The statement might be as simple as completing a report or making a phone call or as complex as using comprehensive negotiation skills or using complicated technology.

Third, conditions can exist, but they might not be readily apparent. For example, in a learning session, participants are given requirements or a reference and then are asked to demonstrate what they know. In the job setting, the given requirements are sometimes already on the job and are understood; therefore, the forecast might not always include the given condition. (Refer back to Chapter 7 for typical conditions for learning forecasts, or "givens.")

Fourth, criteria become more important in an application forecast. The criteria—whether speed, accuracy, or quality—are needed because the importance of success with these criteria is critical. Most application forecasts include a time limit, which is sometimes assumed to be understood. For example, participants will learn a particular skill and are expected to apply that skill three weeks later to make the project successful. Having a forecast to use the skill will require a time frame of three weeks. To be more specific and ensure the participants are clear about this expectation, however, the time should be identified in each forecast item. Accuracy is another example. Participants might be required to complete 80 percent of their action items by a certain date. Quality is also important. The application forecast might indicate that a skill or task must be completed with less than a 1 percent error rate or with a minimal success rating from an observer. (See Chapter 7 for sample criteria for learning forecasts.)

Application objectives are critical because they describe the intermediate outputs—outputs occurring between the learning of new tasks and procedures and the impact that this learning will deliver. Application describes how things should be or the state of the workplace as the project is implemented. They provide a basis for the evaluation of on-the-job changes and performance. They emphasize what has occurred on the job as a result of the project.

The list that follows provides a summary of the key issues and questions involved in developing application forecasts. Application forecasts have almost always been included to some degree in projects, but have not always been as specific as they could be or need to be. To be effective, they must clearly define the expected environment in the workplace following the successful project implementation. The best application forecasts:

- Identify behaviors, tasks, and actions that are observable and measurable.
- Are outcome-based, clearly worded, and specific.
- Specify what the project participant will change, or has changed, as a result of the project.
- May have four components:
  - *Action verb*
  - *Performance statement*—what the participant will change or accomplish at a specified time
  - *Condition*—circumstances under which the participant will perform the task, procedures, or action
  - *Criterion*—degree or level of accuracy, quality, or time within which the task or job will be performed.
- May address the following questions
  - What new or improved *knowledge* was applied?
  - What new or improved *skill* was applied?

○ What is the *frequency of skill* application?

○ What new *tasks* will be performed?

○ What new *steps* will be implemented?

○ What new *action items* will be implemented?

○ What new *procedures* will be implemented or changed?

○ What new *guidelines* will be implemented or changed?

○ What new *technology* will be implemented?

○ What new *processes* will be implemented or changed?

The detail on developing application forecasts is presented in the material in the previous chapter on learning forecasts. The basis is the same (action verb, performance statement, a condition, and a criterion). With application forecasts, however, the criterion becomes more important, and the conditions become less important.

Topics for application forecasts

The topics addressed at this level parallel many of those identified in the previous chapters. Therefore, many of the areas detailed there can be mapped into this level. For example, questions about the intent to apply what is learned in the project are logical issues to measure at this time—when the application occurs. However, because of the timing for successful application, additional opportunities to measure success arise.

Forecasts at this level focus on activity or action, not the consequences of those actions (impact). The number of activities to measure at this level can be varied. Table 8.1 shows some coverage areas for application forecasts. While the examples can vary, the action items shown are included in many projects.

HOW TO CONSTRUCT IMPACT FORECASTS

Chapter 4 focused on how objectives are developed working through levels of needs assessment. A business measure reflects a business need.

Table 8.1. Examples of coverage areas for application.

ACTION	EXPLANATION	EXAMPLE
Increase	Increase a particular activity or action.	Increase the frequency of the use of a particular skill.
Decrease	Decrease a particular activity or action.	Decrease the number of times a particular process has to be checked.
Eliminate	Stop or remove a particular task or activity.	Eliminate the formal follow-up meeting and replace it with a virtual meeting.
Maintain	Keep the same level of activity for a particular process.	Continue to monitor the process with the same schedule as previously used.
Create	Design, build, or implement a new procedure, process, or activity.	Create a procedure for resolving the differences between two divisions.
Use	Use a particular process or activity.	Use the new skill in situations for which it was designed to be used.
Perform	Conduct or do a particular task or procedure.	Perform a postaudit review at the end of each activity.
Participate	Become involved in various activities, projects, or programs.	Each associate should submit a suggestion for reducing costs.
Enroll	Sign up for a particular process, program, or project.	Each associate should enroll in the career advancement program.

(*continued*)

Table 8.1. Examples of coverage areas for application *(continued)*.

ACTION	EXPLANATION	EXAMPLE
Respond	React to groups, individuals, or systems.	Each participant in the program should respond to customer inquiries within 15 minutes.
Network	Facilitate relationships with others who are involved or have been affected by the program.	Each program participant should continue networking with contacts on at least a quarterly basis.

Job performance needs and the subsequent analysis ensure that the business measure is connected to the project. When this happens, the business need is clearly defined and is usually the primary driver for selecting or developing the project.

Precise definition

It is important to ensure that the precise definition of the impact measure is offered. Definitions can vary considerably. For example, a broad definition of quality is unusable. Quality may be defined as errors, rework, warranty claims, or low scores on industrywide customer satisfaction surveys. The specific quality measure must be defined, which occurs during the business needs analysis. Consider employee turnover. A forecast for a project might be to reduce employee turnover. The wording here is too vague. The measure must be defined as involuntary turnover, avoidable turnover, regrettable turnover, or some other measure. The definitions are critical so that the specific measure becomes a focus during the project.

A consequence of action

A business impact measure, the basis for the impact forecast, is a consequence of a specific action. Sometimes, there is confusion between application and impact. Application is always action (activity), and impact is the consequence of that action. Consider the forecast to reduce equipment downtime by 20 percent. Some may consider this an application forecast, where participants will simply reduce the amount of time. However, to accomplish the forecast, participants must do something different. What has worked before is not working. Perhaps a new process, new technology, new tool, or even a new skill is needed to reduce the time. Any of these solutions can reduce equipment downtime if implemented properly. The application forecast would be the use of the process, technology, tool, or training. The downtime reduction is the consequence of the use of the technology, process, policy, tool, or training. This distinction should be reviewed routinely to ensure understanding of these two types of forecasts.

CRITERION

As with learning and application forecasts, impact forecasts should include a criterion. The criterion is usually defined as speed, accuracy, or quality and follows the same rules stated in Chapter 7. For example, a forecast for a safety project might be that government-imposed safety fines should decrease from $2.5 million per year to less than $500,000 within one year after project completion. This forecast includes accuracy and time criteria. This degree of specificity is needed to measure success. For some projects, the specificity is at the individual level. For example, a project designed to increase sales in a new-product launch could vary with each individual sales representative. In some territories, the new product has little competition, and the growth number can be set high. In others, where competition is intense, the sales growth number might be much smaller. The overall forecast might be more appropriate. For example, the forecast might be that sales reach a 12 percent increase throughout the entire company with individual forecasts varying by territory.

TOPICS FOR IMPACT FORECASTS

Impact forecasts are measures located throughout the organization and its environment. There are hundreds, if not thousands, of these common indicators. When identifying impact measures, consider the following issues.

Hard versus soft data

To help set the forecast for the desired measures, a distinction is made in two general categories of data: hard data and soft data, as described in Chapter 4. Hard data are the primary measurements of improvement, presented through rational, undisputed facts that are easily collected. They are the most desirable type of data to collect. The ultimate criteria for measuring the effectiveness of management rest on hard data items, such as productivity, profitability, cost control, and quality control. Chapter 4 provided examples of hard data grouped into categories of output, quality, cost, and time.

Hard-data measures are often supplemented with interim assessments of soft data, such as brand awareness, satisfaction, loyalty, and teamwork. Although a program designed to enhance competencies or manage change should have an ultimate impact on hard-data items, measuring soft-data items may be more efficient. While soft data may be more difficult to analyze, they are used when hard data are unavailable. Soft data are more difficult to convert to monetary values than hard data; are subjectively based, in many cases; and are less credible as a performance measurement. Chapter 4 provided a list of typical soft-data items grouped into typical categories.

The preference of hard data in programs does not minimize the value of soft data. Soft data are essential for a complete evaluation of a project; success may rest on soft-data measurements. For example, in an empowerment project at a chemical plant, three key measures of success were identified: employee stress, job satisfaction, and teamwork. All were listed as intangibles.

Most projects have objectives that use a combination of hard- and soft- data items in the evaluation. For example, a project to install new technology in a manufacturing plant had the following impact measures in the forecasts:

- Reduction of production costs
- Improvement in productivity
- Improvement in quality
- Reduction in inventory shortages
- Improvement in production capability
- Increase in technology leadership
- Increase in job satisfaction

These improvements included both hard data (production costs, productivity, and quality) and soft data (capability, technology leadership, and job satisfaction). Most projects include both types of data.

Tangible versus intangible

The confusion about the categories of hard and soft data and the often-reduced value placed on soft data was discussed in Chapter 4. This leads to a critical definition in this book. While the terms *hard data* and *soft data* can be used to discuss impact data, the terms *tangible* and *intangible* can also be used and represent a more accurate depiction. Tangible data are those data that have been converted to monetary value. Intangible data are defined as data purposely not converted to monetary value (i.e., if data cannot be converted to monetary value credibly with a reasonable amount of resources, then they are reported as intangibles). This approach has several advantages. First, it avoids the sometimes-confusing labels of soft and hard. Second, it negates the argument that being soft equates to little or no value. Third, it brings definition to the context of the project. In some organizations or situations, a particular data item may already be converted to money, and the conversion is credible because the measure is already tangible. However, in other organizations, the same measure may not have been converted to money and cannot be converted with a reasonable amount of resources. Therefore, it is left as intangible. Fourth, use of the terms *tangible* and *intangible* provides a rule that enhances the consistency of the evaluation process. Having this rule helps ensure that if two people evaluate the same projects, they will achieve the same or similar results.

Scorecards

Scorecards, such as those used in sporting events, provide important measures fans can review to understand the position of their team. Similar scorecards are used by top executives and administrators and often form the basis for impact objectives. In Robert S. Kaplan and David P. Norton's landmark book, *The Balanced Scorecard* (1996), this concept was brought to the attention of organizations. The authors suggested that data could be organized and reported from four perspectives: financial, customer, business processes, and learning and growth. Regardless of the type of scorecard, top executives and administrators place great emphasis on this concept. In some organizations, the scorecard concept has filtered down to various business units, and each part of the business has been required to develop scorecards.

The scorecard approach is appealing because it provides a quick comparison of key measures and examines the status of the organization. As a management tool, scorecards can be important in shaping and improving or maintaining the performance of the organization through the implementation of preventive programs. Scorecard measures often link to particular projects. In many situations, a scorecard deficiency measure may have prompted the project in the first place.

Measures linked to a specific project

An important issue that often surfaces when considering impact forecasts is the understanding of specific measures that are often driven by specific types of internal projects. While there are no standard answers, Table 8.2 presents a summary of some typical measures for forecasts for specific types of projects usually found in organizations. The measures are quite broad for some projects. For example, a communication project may pay off in a variety of measures, such as improved productivity, enhanced sales, reduced errors, reduced stress, and enhanced employee job satisfaction. For other projects, the measures are quite narrow. Labor-management cooperation projects typically influence grievances, work stoppages, and employee satisfaction. Orientation, or onboarding, projects typically influence measures of early turnover (turnover in the first 90 days of employment), initial job performance, and initial productivity. The measures that are influenced depend on the forecast and the design of the project. Table 8.2 also illustrates the immense number of measures that can be driven or influenced.

A word of caution is needed. Presenting specific measures linked to a typical project may give the impression that these are the only measures influenced. In practice, a particular project can have many outcomes. Table 8.2 shows the most likely measures based on studies the ROI Institute has conducted or reviewed. In the course of the last decade, we have been involved in more than 2,000 studies, and common threads exist among particular projects. Most of these projects represent internal projects, inside an organization.

Relevant measures

Existing performance measures should be thoroughly researched to identify those related to the proposed project. Several performance measures often are related to the same item. For example, the efficiency of a production unit can be measured in several ways:

- The number of units produced per hour.
- The number of on-schedule production units.

Table 8.2. Typical impact measures for projects.

PROJECT	KEY IMPACT MEASUREMENTS
Absenteeism control/ reduction	Absenteeism, customer satisfaction, delays, job satisfaction, productivity, stress
Association meetings	Absenteeism, costs, customer service, job satisfaction, productivity, quality, sales, time, turnover
Business coaching	Costs, customer satisfaction, efficiency, employee satisfaction, productivity/output, quality, time savings
Career development/ career management	Job satisfaction, promotions, recruiting expenses, turnover
Communications projects	Conflicts, errors, job satisfaction, productivity, stress, sales
Compensation plans	Costs, job satisfaction, productivity, quality
Compliance projects	Charges, losses, penalties/fines, settlements
Diversity	Absenteeism, charges, complaints, losses, settlements, turnover
Employee retention projects	Engagement, job satisfaction, promotions, turnover
Engineering/technical conferences	Costs, customer satisfaction, cycle times, downtime, job satisfaction, process time, productivity/output, quality, waste
Ethics projects	Fines, fraud, incidents, penalties, theft
e-Learning	Cost savings, cycle times, error reductions, job satisfaction, productivity improvement, quality improvement
Executive education	Absenteeism, costs, customer service, job satisfaction, productivity, quality, sales, time, turnover

Table 8.2. Typical impact measures for projects *(continued)*.

PROJECT	KEY IMPACT MEASUREMENTS
Franchise/dealer meetings	Cost of sales, customer loyalty, market share, quality, efficiency, sales
Golfing events	Customer loyalty, market share, new accounts, sales, up-selling
Labor-management cooperation	Absenteeism, grievances, job satisfaction, work stoppages
Leadership development	Cost/time savings, development, efficiency, employee satisfaction, engagement, productivity/output, quality
Management development	Absenteeism, costs, customer service, job satisfaction, productivity, quality, sales, time, turnover
Marketing projects	Brand awareness, churn rate, cross-selling, customer loyalty, customer satisfaction, market share, new accounts, sales, up-selling
Medical meetings	Compliance, efficiency, medical costs, patient satisfaction, quality
Orientation, onboarding	Early turnover, performance, productivity, quality of work, training time
Personal productivity/ time management	Job satisfaction, productivity, stress reduction, time
Project management	Budgets, quality improvement, time savings
Quality programs	Costs, cycle times, defects, response times, rework
Retention management	Engagement, job satisfaction, turnover
Safety programs	Accident frequency rates, accident severity rates, first-aid treatments
Sales meetings	Customer loyalty, market share, new accounts, sales

(continued)

Table 8.2. Typical impact measures for projects *(continued)*.

PROJECT	KEY IMPACT MEASUREMENTS
Self-directed teams	Absenteeism, customer satisfaction, job satisfaction, productivity/output, quality, turnover, job engagement
Sexual harassment prevention	Absenteeism, complaints, employee satisfaction, turnover
Six Sigma/lean projects	Costs, cycle times, defects, response times, rework, waste
Software projects	Absenteeism, costs, customer service, job satisfaction, productivity, quality, sales, time, turnover
Stress management	Absenteeism, job satisfaction, medical costs, turnover
Supervisor/team leader programs	Absenteeism, complaints, costs, job satisfaction, productivity, quality, sales, time, turnover
Team building	Absenteeism, costs, customer service, job satisfaction, productivity, quality, sales, time, turnover
Wellness/fitness programs	Absenteeism, accidents, medical costs, turnover, job satisfaction

- The percentage of equipment used.
- The percentage of equipment downtime.
- The labor cost per unit of production.
- The overtime required per unit of production.
- Total unit cost.

Each of these, in its own way, measures the effectiveness or efficiency of the production unit. Related measures should be reviewed to determine those most relevant to the project.

New measures

In a few cases, data needed to measure the success of a project are unavailable, and new data are needed. The project leader must work with the client organization to develop record-keeping systems, if economically feasible. In one organization, the sales reps' delayed responses to customer requests were an issue. This problem was discovered from customer feedback. The feedback data prompted a project to reduce the response time. To help ensure the success of the project, several measures were planned, including measuring the actual time to respond to a customer request. Initially this measure was not available. As the program was implemented, new software was used to measure the time.

When developing new measures, several questions need to be addressed:

- Which department/section/unit will develop the measurement system?
- Who will record and monitor the data?
- Where will it be recorded?
- Will input forms be used?
- Who will report it?

These questions will usually involve other departments or a management decision that extends beyond the scope of the project. Within an organization, the administration, operations, or technology functions will be instrumental in helping determine whether new measures are needed and, if so, how they will be developed. However, this action should be a last resort.

INPUTS FOR APPLICATION AND IMPACT FORECASTING

One of the critical challenges in forecasting is to identify the appropriate expert inputs to develop the forecast for both application and impact. The experts must be credible, and they must clearly understand the actions that people will take to make the project successful (application), and the consequence of those actions (impact). They must also know or have experience within the situation or context of the project.

For the application forecast, the experts are asked to tell how much change will occur as the project is implemented. This action separates the issue from the objective. An objective is an acceptable level of performance, but a forecast is what we expect them to do. It's a best estimate of what will be accomplished.

For the impact forecast, the individuals must estimate the amount of change for a particular business measure if the project is implemented. These experts are responding to the request: "Tell us to what extent this measure will change as a result of this project." Thus, estimating the actual amount of improvement is the forecast.

The proposal team

Obviously, the proposal team will have an understanding of the project as they are developing the proposal, which contains the forecast. However, they may or may not have experience with the situation to make the forecast, but this group is a great beginning point in understanding the amount of movement expected in impact measure.

Clients/Sponsors

Sometimes the sponsor of the project, the actual client for the implementation, may be able to suggest how much the project should accomplish in terms of application and impact. This suggestion may be indicated in the RFP which states that participants must perform in a certain way, take particular steps or actions, and whether or not specific impact measures must change by a certain amount. If this anticipation is not provided already, the sponsor may be an excellent individual to address in the attempt to understanding change in these two major categories.

Participants or prospective participants

The individuals who will use the project are the participants—the users, audience, employees, delegates, citizens, and others who will make the project successful. It's their actions, activities, and behavior changes that compromise the application data. The consequences of these actions drive performance, and in many cases, it's their performance measures that are categorized as impact measures. These individuals may be able to estimate the amount of change in each of these areas with this project. A word of caution is in order because this project may represent change for them, and they may be biased as they think about what they must change in their present activities and share responsibilities.

Subject matter experts

Perhaps the most important input may come from those who are subject matter experts. These individuals understand the context in which the project is implemented. The subject matter experts have experience with these types of projects and applications, and they can examine the project design and the solutions offered and make a list of forecasts of what can be achieved. These may be the most credible inputs if they are experts in this particular area.

External experts

External experts are those who are not necessarily connected with the project, but may be in the audience where the project will be implemented. They are not necessarily the users of the project, but may be capable of providing realistic input into the success of the project. This input may not be available in all situations, but if it is available, it could provide another credible source of input.

Analysts

The analysts are those individuals who have helped analyze the need for the project. They have studied this situation, analyzed the data, and developed what appears to be the solution. (Of course, this is assuming that the project itself is not aimed at finding the solution.) Many projects are based on implementing the solution, which has already been determined; it's a matter of making it work. These analysts who are very familiar with the data, marketplace, audience, and context can provide some very credible input.

Vendors and suppliers

Many projects will involve the use of vendors or suppliers. They may be supplying the software, system, or support. A variety of different resources are sometimes needed to make the project work. If suppliers have previous experience with this type of project, they might be able to forecast the success on this particular project. For example, some projects involve the implementation of a new system, and a technology provider is the developer of the system. Obviously, they know how it works and should work in the organization and their input may be valuable. The problem is that the vendor may be biased if the project success relies on what they do or in their product. They may overstate the success that can be achieved at the application and impact levels.

Advocates

The advocates are those who champion the project, but are not necessarily funding the project. They are the cheerleaders who know what is needed and how it should be helpful. The advocates can sometimes see how the project can work and the impact it will have in the organization, system, and society in the market. They might be able to provide additional insight into how it will work.

Finance and accounting staff

Because the forecast may include an ROI calculation, it may be helpful to secure input from the finance and accounting staff. Depending on the size of the project, the top financial officer, or for smaller projects, a member of their finance and accounting team should provide input. A word of caution is needed, however, as the nature of the finance and accounting team is often very conservative. Also, they are often removed from the context (the field where it would be implemented), and therefore, may not see clearly how it will work.

Credibility

Collectively, these are the inputs for estimating the application and impact forecast. These are very critical and the credibility of the forecast will rest on the credibility of these individuals. For each audience group, there must be an assessment of the credibility of each. Perhaps a credibility rating can be assigned on a 1 to 5 scale, indicating the credibility of the input. With this exercise, an obvious question surfaces: "If an input is not very credible, why should we include it?" It is necessary to have a complete picture of the possibilities. Often, it's politically correct to involve inputs from several sources because an omission may alert a concern, or serve as a prejudgment on the quality of that input. Thus it's better to err on the side of letting all "experts" be involved, but then step back and examine the credibility of each. When a project team knows there"s a particular bias, they indicate the particular bias, such as "suppliers are overly optimistic," or "the actual end user may be more pessimistic because they see additional work."

The forecast from each of these sources will vary significantly. The variety of possibilities influences the quality of the forecast, because of the credibility of the inputs. This topic will be discussed in more detail later.

Collecting the data

Data must be collected from the individuals listed as experts. If the number of individuals is small (for example, one person from each of the expert groups involved), a short interview may suffice. During interviews, it is critical to avoid bias and to ask clear, succinct questions that are not leading. Questions should be framed in a balanced way to capture what may occur, as well as what may not. If groups are involved, using focus groups may be suitable. For large numbers, surveys or questionnaires may be appropriate.

When the groups are diverse and scattered, the Delphi technique may be appropriate. This technique, originally developed by the Rand Corporation in the 1950s, has been used in forecasting and decision making in a variety of disciplines. The Delphi technique was originally devised to help experts achieve better forecasts than they might obtain through traditional group meetings by allowing access to the group without in-person contact. Necessary features of a Delphi procedure are anonymity, continuous iteration, controlled feedback to participants, and a physical summary of responses. Anonymity is achieved by means of a questionnaire that allows group members to express their opinions and judgments privately. Between all iterations of the questionnaire, the facilitator informs the participants of the opinions of their anonymous colleagues. Typically, this feedback is presented as a simple, statistical summary using a mean or median value. The facilitator takes the group judgment as the statistical average in the final round.

In some cases, benchmarking data may be available and can be considered as a source of input for this process. This success of previous studies may provide input essential to the project as well. It may include an extensive search of databases using a variety of search engines. The important point is to understand, as much as possible, what may occur as a result of the project.

FINAL THOUGHTS

This chapter addresses two very important parts of the forecast, application and impact. For application, a project team forecasts the acting and progress of those who must make the project work. This is the action—activities, behaviors, tasks, and processes—that will actually be accomplished. It is important for these actions to occur to make the process successful; without them, it will not work. The forecast is our best judgment of what will be accomplished with this project.

Most critical to the project sponsor and top executives are the one or more impact measures that will change as a result of this project. The measures often reflect the overall goal of the project, such as key performance indicators for certain government officials, agency directors, division presidents, company CEOs, and so forth. For some, this may be the most important data set.

This chapter provided some insight into how to construct these forecasts and secure the data to make them. This continues to build part of the forecasting puzzle, with now four categories of data forecasted. The next chapter will discuss two more very important forecasts: the monetary benefits of the impact measure, which will require converting the impact to money, and the total cost of the project, which goes beyond the actual cost of the proposal and includes all client costs to make this project work. These are necessary to ultimately develop the ROI forecast, which will be covered in Chapter 10.

9

Forecasting Money: Benefits and Costs

Crunching the numbers and revealing the costs are actions that cause some tension between you and your client, but this isn't an excuse to hesitate or present vague promises in your proposal. With clients' eyes on the bottom line, and their ears tuned to your reasoning, this forecast of the benefits and costs could mean the difference between project approval and rejection.

To calculate the ROI, two critical steps are necessary: calculating monetary benefits of the project by converting impact measures to monetary values and tabulating the fully loaded costs of the project. While forecasts at the lower levels are important, converting the positive outcomes into monetary figures and weighing them against the total cost of the project is more valuable from an executive viewpoint. This is the ultimate level of evaluation. This chapter explains how proposal writers are moving beyond simply forecasting business impact to developing monetary values to use in calculating ROI. Many methods are available to convert impact data to money and are presented in this chapter.

This chapter also explores the cost of projects, identifying the specific costs that should be captured and some efficient ways in which they can be developed. This moves the cost beyond the actual cost of the proposal to include the total cost of the project for the client. For example, the cost of the proposal is what will be charged to do the project. It involves the fees and expenses to make it work.

However, the project implementation will often involve more costs because the time and expenses of others are involved. To forecast ROI from the perspective of the client presented in Chapter 10, all of the costs are needed. This requires going beyond a traditional proposal cost to include the cost of the entire project for the client.

Some costs are hidden and not usually counted. The conservative philosophy presented here is to account for all costs, direct and indirect. Several checklists and guidelines are also included.

WHY FORECAST MONETARY BENEFITS?

The answer to this question is not always clearly understood. A project could be labeled a success without converting data to monetary values, just by using business impact data to show the amount of change that should be directly attributed to the project. For example, a change in quality, cycle time, teenage pregnancies, or citizen complaints could represent significant improvements linked directly to a new project. For some projects, this may be sufficient. However, many sponsors need the actual monetary value requiring this extra step of converting data to monetary values.

Value equals money

Although there are many different types of value, money is becoming one of the most important values, as the economic benefits of projects are desired. This is particularly true for executives, sponsors, clients, administrators, and top leaders. They are concerned about the allocation of funds and want to see the contribution of a project in monetary values. Anything short of this value for these key stakeholders would be unsatisfactory.

Money is necessary for ROI

Monetary value is required to develop ROI. As described in Chapter 10, a monetary value is needed to compare the costs to develop the benefit/cost ratio, the ROI (as a percent), and the payback period. The monetary benefits become the other half of the equation and are absolutely essential.

Monetary value is needed to understand problems

In all businesses, costs are necessary for understanding the magnitude of any problem. Consider, for example, the cost of excessive turnover of critical talent. The traditional analysis may not show the full cost of the problem. A variety of estimates and expert inputs may be needed to supplement cost statements to arrive at a particular value. The monetary value is needed in a fully loaded format to understand the problem. The good news is that many organizations have developed a number of standard cost items representing issues that are undesired. For example, Wal-Mart has calculated the cost of having a truck idling one minute at a store waiting to be unloaded. When this is multiplied over the hundreds of deliveries made at a store and spread over five thousand stores, the cost is huge.

STEPS TO CONVERT DATA TO MONEY

Before describing specific techniques to convert both hard and soft data to monetary values, five general steps should be completed for each data item:

1. Focus on a unit of measure

First, define a unit of measure. For output data, the unit of measure is the item produced (one item assembled), service provided (one package shipped), or one more patient served. Time measures might include the time to complete a project, cycle time, or citizen-response time, and the unit is usually expressed in minutes, hours, or days. Quality is a common measure, with a unit being defined as one error, reject, defect, or reworked item. Soft data measures vary, with a unit of improvement representing such things as a citizen compliant, or a one-point change in the customer satisfaction index. Here are some examples of these units:

- One unit produced
- One lost time accident
- One student enrolled
- One grievance
- One package delivered
- One unplanned absence
- One patient served
- One voluntary turnover
- One sale made
- One minute of down-time
- One loan approved
- One minute of wait time
- One project completed
- One day of delay
- One call escalation
- One hour of cycle time
- One FTE employee
- One hour of employee time
- One reject
- One hour of overtime
- One rework
- One customer complaint
- One error
- One person removed from welfare
- One less day of incarceration (prison)

2. Determine the value of each unit

Now, the challenge mounts. Place a value (V) on the unit identified in the first step. For measures of production, quality, cost, and time, the process is relatively easy. Most organizations maintain records or reports that can pinpoint the cost of one unit of production or one defect. Soft data are more difficult to convert to money. For example, the monetary value of one customer complaint or a one-point change in an employee attitude is often difficult to determine. The techniques described in this chapter provide an array of approaches for making this conversion. When more than one value is available, usually the most credible or the lowest value is used in the calculation.

3. Estimate the change in the measure

Estimate the change in the impact measure. The change (Δ) is the forecasted impact, measured as hard or soft data that is directly attributed to the project. The value may represent the performance improvement for an individual, a team, a group of participants, or several groups of participants.

4. Determine an annual amount for the forecasted improvement

Annualize the forecast value to develop a total change in the performance data for at least one year (ΔP). Using annual values has become a standard approach for organizations seeking to capture the proposed benefits of a particular project, although the benefits may not remain constant throughout the entire year. First-year benefits are used, even when the project produces benefits beyond one year (if it is a short-term project). This approach is considered conservative. If it's a long-term project (or solution) a longer period of time is used. More will be discussed about this later.

5. Calculate the annual value of the improvement

Arrive at the total value of improvement by multiplying the annual forecasted improvement (ΔP) by the unit value (V) for the measure. This value for annual project benefits is then compared to the costs of the project, usually with the ROI formula presented in the next chapter.

An example taken from a labor-management cooperation project at a manufacturing plant describes the five-step process of converting data to monetary values. This project was proposed after the initial needs assessment and analysis revealed that a lack of teamwork was causing an excessive number of labor grievances. The estimated number of grievances that should be resolved at Step 2 in a four-step grievance process was selected as the output measure. Table 9.1 shows the steps taken to forecast monetary values, arriving at a total project forecast of $546,000.

Table 9.1. Converting labor grievance data to monetary values. (Setting: labor-management cooperation project in a manufacturing plant.)

Step 1	Define the Unit of Measure
	One grievance reaching Step 2 in the four-step grievance resolution process
Step 2	Determine the Value of Each Unit
	Using internal experts (i.e., the labor relations staff), the cost of an average grievance was estimated at $6,500, when time and direct costs were considered ($V = \$6,500$)
Step 3	Calculate the Forecast Change in Impact Data
	Total grievances per month reaching Step 2 forecasted to decline by 7 ($\Delta = 7$)
Step 4	Determine an Annual Amount for the Forecasted Change
	Using the value of seven grievances per month yields an annual forecasted improvement of 84 ($\Delta P = 84$)
Step 5	Calculate the Forecasted Annual Value of the Improvement
	Annual Value = $\Delta P \times V$
	$= 84 \times \$6,500$
	$= \$546,000$

STANDARD MONETARY VALUES

Most hard-data items are already converted to monetary values and are known as standard values. By definition, a standard value is a monetary value on a unit of measurement that is accepted by key stakeholders. These standards have been developed because these are often the measures that matter in the organization. They are important. They reflect problems, and because of that, efforts have been made to convert them to monetary values to show their impact on the operational and financial well-being of the organization. The best way to understand the magnitude of any problem is to place a monetary value on it.

A variety of process improvement programs—such as reengineering, reinventing the corporation, total quality, transformation, continuous process improvement, Six Sigma, and many others—have had a measurement component where the cost of a particular measure has been developed. A variety of cost controls, cost containment, and cost management systems have been developed such as activity-based costing. These have forced organizations to place costs on activities and, in some cases, relate those costs directly to the revenue or profits of the organization.

Converting output data to money

When a project produces a change in output, the value of the increased output can usually be determined from the organization's accounting or operating records. For organizations operating on a profit basis, this value is typically the marginal profit contribution of an additional unit of production or service provided. For example, a team within a major appliance manufacturer was able to boost the production of small refrigerators after a comprehensive work cell redesign program. The unit of improvement was the profit margin of one refrigerator. For organizations that are performance-driven rather than profit-driven, this value is usually reflected in the savings accumulated when an additional unit of output is realized for the same input. For example, in the visa section of a government office, an additional visa application was processed at no additional cost. Thus an increase in output translated into a cost savings equal to the unit cost of processing a visa application.

The formulas and calculations used to measure this contribution depend on the type of organization and the status of its record keeping. Most organizations have standard values readily available for performance monitoring and setting goals. Managers often use marginal cost statements and sensitivity analyses to pinpoint values associated with changes in output. If the data are not available, the proposal team must initiate or coordinate the development of appropriate values.

The benefit of converting output data to money with this approach is that these calculations are already completed for the most important data items and are reported as standard values. Perhaps no area is more dramatic with the standard values than those in the sales and marketing area. Table 9.2 shows a sampling of measures in the sales and marketing area that are routinely calculated and are considered to be standard values (Farris, Bendle, Pfeifer, and Ribstein 2006). For example, the first two entries go together. The sales cannot be used in an ROI value until they have been converted to profit. Sales are usually affected by the profit percentage to generate the actual value of the improvement. Other profit margins can be developed for a particular unit, a product line, or even a customer. Retention rates and return rates are routinely developed, as is the lifetime value of a customer. Even these days, the market share and loyalty are developed because they all translate directly into additional sales. For the most part—with the exception of workload and inventories—the value is developed through profits. Even market share and customer loyalty are valued based on sales or additional sales obtained from the customer.

Calculating the cost of quality

Quality and the cost of quality are important issues in most manufacturing and service firms. Because many projects are designed to increase quality, the project team may have to place a value on the improvement of certain quality measures. With some quality measures, the task is easy. For example, if quality is measured with the

Table 9.2. Examples of standard values from sales and marketing.

METRIC	DEFINITION	CONVERTING ISSUES
Sales	The sale of the product or service recorded in a variety of different ways: by product, by time period, by customer	This data must be converted to monetary value by applying the profit margin for a particular sales category.
Profit margin (%)	Price minus cost divided by cost for the product, customer, time period	This is the most common way factored to convert sales to data.
Unit margin	Unit price less the unit cost	This shows the value of incremental sales.
Channel margin	Channel profits as a percent of channel selling price	This would be used to show the value of sales through a particular marketing channel.
Retention rate	The ratio of customers retained to the number of customers at risk of leaving	The value is the money saved to retain a new replacement customer.
Churn rate	Churn rate is the complement of the retention rate (the percent of customers leaving compared to the number who are at risk of leaving)	The value is the money saved for acquiring a new customer.
Customer profit	The difference between the revenues earned from and the cost associated with the customer relationship during the specified period	The monetary value added is the additional profit obtained from customers, all going to the bottom line.

Continued

Table 9.2. Examples of standard values from sales and marketing (*continued*).

METRIC	DEFINITION	CONVERTING ISSUES
Customer value, lifetime	The present value of the future cash flows attributed to the customer relationship	This is the bottom line: As customer value increases, it adds directly to the profits. Also as a new customer is added, the incremental value is the customer lifetime average.
Cannibalization rate	The percent of the new product sales taken from existing product lines	This needs to be minimized because it is an adverse effect on existing product with the value added being the loss of profits from the sales loss.
Workload	Hours required to service clients and prospects.	The salaries and commissions and benefits from the time the sales staff spends on the workloads.
Inventories	The total amount of product or brand available for sale in a particular channel	Since the inventories are valued at the cost of carrying the inventory, space, handling, and the time value of money, insufficient inventory is the cost of expediting the new inventory or loss sales because of the inventory outage.

Table 9.2. Examples of standard values from sales and marketing (*continued*).

METRIC	DEFINITION	CONVERTING ISSUES
Market share	The sales revenue as a percent of total market sales	The actual sales are converted to money through the profit margins. This is a measure of competitiveness.
Loyalty	Includes the length of time the customer stays with the organization, the willingness to pay a premium, and the willingness to search	This is the additional profit from the sale or the profit on the premium.

defect rate, the value of the improvement is the cost to repair or replace the product. The most obvious cost of poor quality is the scrap or waste generated by mistakes. Defective products, spoiled raw materials, and discarded paperwork are all the result of poor quality. Scrap and waste translate directly into a monetary value. In a production environment, for example, the cost of a defective product is the total cost incurred up to the point at which the mistake is identified, minus the salvage value. In the service environment, a defective service is the cost incurred up to the point that the deficiency is identified, plus the cost to correct the problem, plus the cost to make the customer happy, plus the loss of customer loyalty.

Employee mistakes and errors can be expensive. The most costly rework occurs when a product or service is delivered and must be returned for correction. The cost of rework includes both labor and direct costs. In some organizations, rework costs can be as much as 35 percent of operating expenses.

Quality costs can be grouped into six major categories (Campanella 1999):

1. *Internal failure* represents costs associated with problems detected prior to product shipment or service delivery. Typical costs are reworking and retesting.

2. *Penalty costs* are fines or penalties received as a result of unacceptable quality.

3. *External failure* refers to problems detected after product shipment or service delivery. Typical items are technical support, complaint investigation, remedial upgrades, and fixes.

4. *Appraisal costs* are the expenses involved in determining the condition of a particular product or service. Typical costs are testing and related activities, such as product-quality audits.

5. *Prevention costs* include efforts undertaken to avoid unacceptable product or service quality. These efforts include service quality administration, inspections, process studies, and improvements.

6. *Customer dissatisfaction* is perhaps the costliest element of inadequate quality. In some cases, serious mistakes result in lost business. Customer dissatisfaction is difficult to quantify, and arriving at a monetary value may be impossible using direct methods. The judgment and expertise of sales, marketing, or quality managers are usually the best resources to draw from when measuring the impact of dissatisfaction. More and more quality experts are measuring customer and client dissatisfaction with market surveys. However, other strategies discussed in this chapter may be more appropriate for the task.

As with output data, the good news is that a tremendous number of quality measures have been converted to standard values. Some of the standard quality measures that are typically converted to actual monetary value are listed below. The typical definition of these measures can vary slightly with the organization, and the magnitude and the costs can vary significantly. The most common method for converting cost is to use internal failure, external failure, appraisal, or penalty costs.

Examples of standard quality measures include:

- Defects
- Failure
- Rework
- Customer complaint
- Variances
- Delay
- Waste
- Missing data
- Processing errors
- Fines
- Date errors
- Penalties
- Incidents
- Inventory shortages
- Accidents
- Unplanned absenteeism
- Grievances
- Involuntary employee turnover
- Downtime, equipment
- Downtime, system
- Risk
- Days sales uncollected
- Repair costs
- Queues

Converting employee time using compensation

Saving time is a common objective for projects. In a team environment, a project may enable the team to complete tasks in less time or with fewer people. A major project could drive a reduction of several hundred employees. On an individual basis, a technology project may be designed to help professional, sales, and managerial employees save time in performing daily tasks. The value of the time saved is an important measure, and determining the monetary value for it is relatively easy.

The most obvious time savings are from reduced labor costs for performing the same amount of work. The monetary savings are found by multiplying the hours saved by the labor cost per hour.

For most calculations, the average wage, with a percent added for employee benefits, will suffice. However, employee time may be worth more. For example, additional costs in maintaining an employee (office space, furniture, telephones, utilities, computers, secretarial support, and other overhead expenses) could be included in calculating the average labor cost. Thus the average wage rate may escalate quickly. In a large-scale employee-reduction effort, calculating additional employee costs may be more appropriate for showing the value. However, for most projects, the conservative approach of using salary plus employee benefits is recommended.

When developing time savings, caution is needed. Savings are only realized when the amount of time saved translates into a cost reduction or a profit contribution. Even if a project produces savings in manager time, a monetary value is not realized unless the manager puts the additional time saved to productive use. Having managers estimate the percentage of time saved that will be used on productive work may be helpful, if followed up by a request for examples of how the time was used. If a team-based project sparks a new process that eliminates several hours of work each day, the actual savings will be based on a reduction in staff or overtime pay. Therefore, an important preliminary step in developing time savings is determining whether the expected savings will be genuine. This will only happen if the time saved is put to productive use.

Finding standard values

As this section has illustrated, standard values are available for all types of hard data and are available in all types of functions and departments. Essentially, every major department can develop standard values that are tracked and monitored in that area. Some of the typical functions in a major organization where standard values would be tracked are listed below. Sometimes, it is a matter of understanding the data set that can be monitored, collected, and published. Thanks to enterprisewide systems software, these functions, including the standard values in some cases, are integrated and available for access by a variety of people. Access may be an issue, and access may need to be addressed or changed to ensure that the data can be obtained.

Standard values are everywhere in organizations such as:
- Finance and Accounting
- Production
- Operations
- Engineering
- Information Technology
- Administration
- Sales and Marketing
- Customer Service and Support
- Procurement
- Logistics
- Compliance
- Research and Development
- Human Resources
- Legal
- Distribution

WHEN STANDARD VALUES ARE NOT AVAILABLE

When standard values are not available, several strategies for converting data to monetary values are available. Some are appropriate for a specific type of data or data category, while others may be used with virtually any type of data. The challenge is to select the strategy that best fits the situation. These strategies are presented next, beginning with the most credible approach.

Using historical costs from records

Sometimes, historical records contain the value of a measure and reflect the cost (or value) of a unit of improvement. This strategy relies on identifying the appropriate existing records and tabulating the actual cost components for the item in question. For example, a large construction firm initiated a project to improve safety. The project improved several safety-related performance measures, ranging from government fines to total workers' compensation costs. By examining the company's records using one year of data, the average cost for each safety measure was developed. This involved the direct costs of medical payments, insurance payments, insurance premiums, investigation services, and lost time payments to employees, as well as payments for legal expenses, fines, and other direct services. Also, the amount of time used to investigate, resolve, and correct any of the issues had to be included—not only the time of the health and safety staff, but the time of other staff members as well. In addition, the cost of lost productivity, the disruption of services, lower morale, and dissatisfaction are also estimated to obtain a fully loaded cost. Corresponding costs for each item are then developed. This example shows the difficulty in working with systems and databases to find a value for a particular data item.

Sorting through databases, cost statements, financial records, and a variety of activity reports takes a tremendous amount of time, time that may not be available for the proposal team. Keeping this part of the process in perspective is helpful. Resources must be conserved. In some cases, data are not available to show all the costs for a particular item. While some direct costs are associated with a measure, the indirect or invisible costs have to be estimated. Finding the values for a particular cost item becomes a sometimes-insurmountable task. Because of these limitations, the calculated values may be suspect unless care is taken to ensure that they are accurate.

Using input from experts

When faced with converting data items for which historical cost data are not available, using input from experts on the process might be an option. Internal experts provide the cost (or value) of one unit of improvement. Individuals with knowledge of the situation and the respect of management must be willing to provide estimates—as well as the assumptions made in arriving at the estimates. Most experts have their own methodology for developing these values. So when you are requesting their input, explaining the full scope of what is needed and providing as many specifics as possible is critical.

Internally, experts are not difficult to find. Sometimes, it is the department where the data originated or the department that was involved in collecting the data. For example, the quality department generates quality measures, the IT department generates IT data, the sales department generates sales data, etc.

In some cases, the expert is the individual who sends the report. The report is sent either electronically or entered into a database, and the origins are usually known. The person sending the report may be the expert, or at least can lead to the expert. Sometimes, an individual's job title can indicate whether he or she is a possible expert. Internally, for almost every data item generated, someone is considered an expert about that data.

Externally, the experts—consultants, professionals, or suppliers in a particular area—can be found in some obvious places. For example, the workers' compensation insurance carrier could estimate the costs of accidents or the labor attorney providing legal services to defend the company in grievance transactions could estimate the cost of a grievance.

The credibility of the expert is the critical issue when using this method. This individual must be knowledgeable of the processes for this measure and, ideally, work with it routinely. Also, this person must be unbiased. Experts have to be neutral in terms of the measure's value. They should not have a personal or professional interest in this value.

Using values from external databases

For some soft data, using cost (or value) estimates based on the work and research of others may be appropriate. This technique taps external databases that contain studies and research programs focusing on the cost of data items. Fortunately, many databases include cost studies of many data items related to programs, and most are accessible through the Internet. Data are available on the cost of turnover, absenteeism, grievances, accidents, and even customer satisfaction. The difficulty is in finding a database with studies or research appropriate to the current program. Ideally, the data should come from a similar setting in the same industry, but that is not always possible. Sometimes, data on all industries or organizations are sufficient, perhaps with some adjustments to suit the program at hand.

For some, the Web holds the most promise for finding monetary values for data not readily available from standard values and experts. Tremendous progress has been made—and continues to be made—in Web searches to develop monetary values.

Linking with other measures

When standard values, records, experts, and external studies are not available, a feasible approach might be to find a relationship between the measure in question and some other measure that may be easily converted to a monetary value. This involves identifying existing relationships, if possible, that show a strong correlation between one measure and another with a standard value.

For example, a classical relationship, depicted in Figure 9.1, shows a correlation between increasing job satisfaction and employee turnover. In a project designed to improve job satisfaction, a value is

Figure 9.1. Relationship between job satisfaction and voluntary employee turnover.

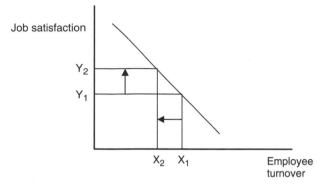

needed for changes in the job satisfaction index. A predetermined relationship showing the correlation between improvements in job satisfaction and reductions in turnover can link the changes directly to turnover. Using standard data or external studies, the cost of turnover can easily be developed, as described earlier. Therefore, a change in job satisfaction is converted to a monetary value or, at least, an approximate value. It is not always exact because of the potential for error and other factors, but the estimate is sufficient for converting the data to monetary values.

Sometimes finding a correlation between a customer satisfaction measure and another measure that can easily be converted to a monetary value is possible. If the relationship cannot be found, it may be best to leave it as an intangible.

Using estimates from participants

In some cases, project participants should estimate the value of improvement. This technique is appropriate when participants are capable of providing estimates of the cost (or value) of the unit of measure improved with the project. When using this approach, participants should be provided with clear instructions, along with examples of the type of information needed. The advantage of this approach is that the individuals who are closest to the improvement are often capable of providing the most reliable estimates of its value.

Using estimates from the management team

Sometimes, participants may be unavailable or incapable of placing a value on the improvement. Their work may be so far removed from the value of the process that they cannot reliably provide estimates. In these cases, the team leaders, supervisors, or managers of participants may be capable of providing estimates. Therefore, they may be asked to provide a value for a unit of improvement linked to the project.

In some cases, senior management provides estimates of the value of data. With this approach, senior managers involved in the project are asked to place a value on the improvement based on their perception of its worth. This approach is used when it is difficult to calculate the value or when other sources of estimation are unavailable or unreliable.

Using proposal team estimates

The final strategy for converting data to monetary values is using proposal team estimates. Using all the available information and experience, the team members most familiar with the situation provide estimates of the value.

CONSIDER THE SHORT-TERM/LONG-TERM ISSUE

When data are converted to monetary values, usually one year of data is included in the analysis for short-term projects. Some programs would be considered long term. The issue of whether it is short term or long term is defined in the context of the time it takes to implement the project. Some projects literally take years to implement with even one particular group. In general, it is appropriate to consider a project short term when the project time is a month or less. When the lag between implementing the program and the subsequent consequences is relatively short, a short-term approach is appropriate. However, in long-term projects, no set time is used, but the time value should be set in the proposal and fully explained. Input should be secured from all stakeholders, including the sponsor, champion, and project leader. After some discussion, the estimates of the time factor should be very conservative and should perhaps be reviewed by a finance and accounting representative.

FUNDAMENTAL COST ISSUES

The first step in forecasting costs is to define and discuss several issues related to a cost-estimate system. The cost presented here moves beyond the classic proposal costs (the client's direct costs) and the client's additional costs to support and help to implement the project (both direct and indirect cost).

Forecast costs, even if they are not requested

For some projects, the pressure of needing to show all the costs in detail may not be necessary. However, because of the reasons explained in this chapter, knowing all these costs is important. In the future, there will be more requests for these. Also estimating these costs brings a discipline and focus to all costs involved in a project. Then the decision can be made later as to how and when to use the costs and whether to push the project evaluation to the ROI level.

Costs will not be precise

Although the costs need to be realistic, they do not have to be absolutely precise. They are estimates. Some costs, particularly those in the indirect category, will not be known exactly, and even in the follow-up evaluation. In some situations, the estimates have already been developed as activity-based costs or have become standard costs. If they have not, estimates from credible sources will suffice, keeping in mind the resources required for this analysis. Spending an excessive amount of time trying to find a better estimate is a misuse of resources.

Fully loaded costs

When using a conservative approach to forecasting ROI, costs should be fully loaded. This includes the costs beyond the proposal costs. With this approach, all costs that can be identified and linked to a project implementation are included. The philosophy is simple: For the total project costs, "When in doubt, put it in" (i.e., if it is questionable whether a cost should be included, including it is recommended, even if the cost guidelines for the organization do not require it). When an ROI forecast is calculated and reported to target audiences, the process should withstand even the closest scrutiny in terms of its credibility. The only way to meet this test is to ensure that all costs are included. Of course, from a realistic viewpoint, if the controller or chief financial officer insists on not using certain costs, then leaving them out or reporting them as an alternate scenario is best.

Reporting costs without benefits

Communicating the costs of a project without presenting the benefits is dangerous. Unfortunately, many project teams have fallen into this trap for years. Because costs can easily be estimated, they are presented to the client in many ingenious ways, such as cost per day and cost per participant. While these may be helpful for efficiency comparisons, presenting them without benefits may be troublesome. When most executives review their project costs, a logical question comes to mind: What benefit was received from the project? This is a typical management reaction, particularly when costs are perceived to be very high.

For example, in one organization, all the costs associated with a major transformation project were tabulated and reported to the senior management team to let them know the total investment in the project. The total figure exceeded the perceived value of the project, and the executive group's immediate reaction was to request a summary of (monetary and nonmonetary) benefits projected in the complete transformation. Because of this, some proposal teams have developed a policy of not communicating cost data unless the benefits can be captured and presented along with the costs. Even if the benefits are subjective and intangible, they are included with the cost data. This helps maintain a balance between the two issues.

COST ESTIMATION ISSUES

The most important task is to define which costs are included in project costs. This task involves decisions that will be made by the proposal team and are usually approved by the client. If appropriate, the client's finance and accounting staff may need to approve the list.

Prorated versus direct costs

Usually, all costs related to a project are captured and expensed to that project. However, some costs are prorated over a longer period of time. Equipment purchases, software development and acquisitions, and the construction of facilities are all significant costs with a useful life that may extend beyond the specific project. Consequently, a portion of these costs should be prorated to the project. For example, if some equipment is purchased that can be used in four other projects, then one-fifth of the costs are prorated to this project. If there is a question about the specific approach to use in the proration formula, the finance and accounting staff should be consulted.

Employee benefits factor

The project participant time is not in the traditional proposal costs. They are employed by (or connected to) the client. Participant time is valuable, and when time is required on a project, the costs must be fully loaded, representing total compensation, including employee benefits. This means that the employee benefits factor should be included. This number is usually well known in the organization and is used in other costing formulas. It represents the cost of all employee benefits expressed as a percentage of payroll. In some organizations this value is as high as 50 to 60 percent. In others, it may be as low as 25 to 30 percent. The average in the United States is 38 percent (Annual Employee Benefits Report 2009).

TYPICAL COSTS CATEGORIES

Table 9.3 shows the typical cost categories that should be included in developing the loaded costs for both the client and the project proposal. These costs are normally a part of a project, built into the proposal, and basically indicate what the client is paying for to have the complete project. However, the client also has many expenses related to the project and are listed as "other client costs." In reality, most of the costs in each category are present for both groups. The only difference is that the salaries and benefits for the project team are not part of the client costs. Also the salaries and benefits for the participant time is not part of the typical project proposal because the participants are connected to the client. The use of the facilities is typically not included in the project proposal cost nor is the administration support and overhead in the client organization.

Table 9.3. Project cost categories.

COST ITEM	PROPOSAL PROJECT COSTS	OTHER CLIENT COSTS
1. Initial analysis and assessment	✓	✓
2. Development of project solutions	✓	✓
3. Acquisition of project solutions	✓	✓
4. Application and implementation		
Salaries/benefits for project team time	✓	✓
Salaries/benefits for coordination time	✓	✓
Salaries/benefits for participant time		✓
Project materials	✓	✓
Hardware/software	✓	✓
Travel/lodging/meals	✓	✓
Use of facilities		✓
Capital expenditures	✓	✓
5. Maintenance and monitoring	✓	✓
6. Administrative support and overhead		✓
7. Evaluation and reporting	✓	✓

Initial analysis and assessment

One of the most underestimated items is the cost of conducting the initial analysis and assessment. In a comprehensive project, this involves data collection, problem solving, assessment, and analysis. In some projects, this cost is near zero because the project is implemented without an appropriate assessment. However, as more project sponsors place increased attention on needs assessment and analysis, this item will become a significant cost in the future. All costs associated with the analysis and assessment should be captured to the fullest extent possible. These costs include time, direct expenses, and internal services and supplies used in the analysis and may involve both the client and project team.

Development of solutions

One of the more significant items is the cost of designing and developing the project. These costs include time in both the design and development and the purchase of supplies, technology, and other materials directly related to the solution. As with needs assessment costs, design and development costs are usually fully charged to the project and client.

Acquisition costs

In lieu of development costs, some project leaders purchase solutions from other sources to use directly or in a modified format. The acquisition costs for these solutions include the purchase price, support materials, and licensing agreements. Some projects have both acquisition costs and development costs.

Application and implementation costs

Usually, the largest cost segment in a project is associated with implementation and delivery. Eight major categories are suggested, although other categories are possible.

- Salaries and benefits for project team time (This is a proposal cost.)
- Salaries and benefits for coordinators and organizers (This is both a proposal cost and a client expense.)
- Participants' salaries and benefits (Client expenses only)
- Program materials (Both)
- Hardware/software (Could be both)
- Travel, lodging, and meals (Both)

- Facilities, even in-house meetings (Client expenses only)
- Capital expenditures (Could be both)

Maintenance and monitoring

Maintenance and monitoring involves routine expenses to maintain and operate the project. These could involve both client and the project team. These represent ongoing expenses that allow the project to be fully implemented. These may involve team members and additional expenses, and they may be significant for some projects.

Support and overhead

Another charge is the cost of support and overhead, the additional costs of the project not directly related to the particular project. The overhead category represents any project cost not considered in the above calculations. Typical items include the cost of administrative/clerical support, telecommunication expenses, office expenses, salaries of client managers, executive time, and other fixed costs. This is an estimate allocated in some convenient way possibly based on the number of project days, then estimating the overhead and support needed each day. This becomes a standard value to use in calculations.

Evaluation and reporting

The total evaluation cost should be included in the project costs to complete the fully loaded cost. Evaluation costs include the cost of developing the evaluation plan, designing instruments, collecting data, analyzing data, preparing a report, and communicating the results. Cost categories include time, materials, purchased instruments, surveys, and external services. Costs could be for both client and project team.

FINAL THOUGHTS

In this chapter the discussion of forecasting moved from the application impact to the monetary value. This chapter addressed the clients' monetary concerns. In the area of the benefits to the project, the impact measures are converted to monetary value. Several methods are available to give this conversion an easy-to-use or easy-to-find basis. Next the costs of the project are calculated. Here, the costs must be fully loaded to include not only the cost that's in the proposal for the delivered project but also the cost in the client organization. This provides a fully loaded cost profile that gives the client a better understanding of what the project is going to cost. These two values come together to calculate a forecasted ROI, which is discussed in the next chapter.

10

Forecasting ROI and Intangibles

Looking into a crystal ball certainly isn't the norm for a business pro-posal, but if you could tell your client the future, what would you say? This final forecasting chapter is perhaps the most important one, as it shows how to forecast the ROI, the financial return on investment. For some executives, project sponsors, donors, funders, and key clients, this is the most essential data set. It's the ultimate level of accountability: comparing the project benefits in monetary terms to the estimated cost of the project.

This chapter also covers the treatment of intangibles, which are those measures that cannot be converted to monetary value. These occur either because the conversion process is not credible or would cost too much to convert to money credibly. These data sets, although not in financial terms, are still very important data sets. The key is to ensure that they are connected to the project, and forecast to the extent to which the project will influence the intangibles. When combined, financial ROI and intangibles are probably the top two measures for projects.

WHY FORECAST ROI?

Although ROI calculations based on postproject data provide the most accurate analysis, it is important to know the forecast before the project is initiated. Several critical issues drive the need for an ROI forecast before the project is pursued.

Expensive projects

In addition to reducing uncertainty, forecasting may be appropriate for costly projects. In these cases, implementation is not practical until the project has been analyzed to determine the potential ROI. For example, if the project involves a significant amount of effort in design, development, and implementation, a client may not want to expend the resources—not even for a pilot test—unless some assurance of a positive ROI can be given. In another example, an expensive equipment purchase may be necessary to launch a process or system. An ROI may be necessary prior to purchase, to ensure that the monetary value of the project outcomes outweighs the cost of equipment and implementation. While there may be trade-offs of deploying a lower-profile, lower-cost pilot, the preproject ROI is still important, and may prompt some clients to stand firm until an ROI forecast is produced.

High risks and uncertainty

Project sponsors want to remove as much uncertainty as possible from the project and act on the best data available. This concern sometimes necessitates a forecast ROI, even before any resources are expended to design and implement it. Some projects are high-risk opportunities or solutions. In addition to being expensive, they may represent critical initiatives that can make or break an organization. Or the situation may be one where failure would be disastrous, and there is only one chance to get it right. In these cases, the decision maker must have the best data possible, and the best data possible often include a forecast ROI.

For example, one large restaurant chain developed an unfortunate reputation for racial insensitivity and discrimination. The fallout brought many lawsuits and caused a public relations nightmare. The company undertook a major project to transform the organization—changing its image, attitudes, and actions. Because of the project's high stakes and critical nature, company executives requested a forecast before pursuing the project. They needed to know not only whether this major project would be worthwhile financially, but also what specifically would change, and how the project would work. This request required a comprehensive forecast involving various levels of data, up to and including the ROI.

Strategic advantage

Perhaps one of the most important reasons to develop a forecast is for the strategic advantage. The purpose of this book is to show how to make the business case in unmistakable terms, and that often leads to impact and ROI forecasted upfront before the project is initiated. Making ROI and forecasting a significant and routine part of the proposal process will provide a strategic advantage and set the consultant or consulting organization apart from others. Only a few organizations are willing to take this extra step, while at the same time, executives are requiring and demanding it be done. In sum, it's best to be proactive and learn how to forecast before it becomes a requirement.

Postproject comparison

An important reason for forecasting ROI is to see how well the forecast holds up under the scrutiny of postproject analysis. An ROI forecast will stimulate interest in a postproject analysis. In an ideal world, a forecast ROI would have a defined relationship with the actual ROI—or at least one would lead to the other, after adjustments. The forecast is often an inexpensive process because it involves estimates and assumptions. If the forecast becomes a reliable predictor of the postproject analysis, then the forecast ROI might substitute for the actual ROI calculation in the future. This could save money on the use of postproject analysis.

Compliance

By policy, more than ever, organizations are requiring a forecast ROI before they undertake major projects. For example, one organization requires any project with a budget exceeding $500,000 to have a forecast ROI before it grants project approval. Some government units have enacted legislation that requires project forecasts. With increasing frequency, formal policy and legal structures are reasons to develop ROI forecasts.

Collectively, these reasons are leading more organizations to develop ROI forecasts so their sponsors will have an estimate of projects' expected payoff.

BASIC ROI ISSUES

Before presenting the formulas for calculating the ROI, a few basic issues are described and explored. An adequate understanding of these issues is necessary to complete an ROI forecast.

Definition

The term *return on investment* is occasionally misused, sometimes intentionally. In this misuse, a very broad definition for ROI is offered to include any benefit from the project. ROI becomes a vague concept in which even subjective data linked to a project are included in the concept. In this book, the return on investment is more precise and is meant to represent financial value by comparing project costs to benefits. The two most common measures are the benefit/cost ratio (BCR) and the ROI formula. Both are presented.

For many years, project leaders sought to calculate the actual return on investment for projects. If the project is considered an investment, then it is appropriate to place it in the same funding process as other investments, such as the investment in equipment and facilities. Although the other investments may be quite different, executives and administrators often view them in the same way. Developing specific values that reflect the return on the investment is critical for the success of projects. An ROI forecast as part of a project proposal can make it more profitable.

Annualized values: a fundamental concept

All the formulas presented in this chapter use annualized values so that the first-year impact of the project investment can be calculated for short-term projects. Using annualized values is becoming an accepted practice for developing the ROI in many organizations. This approach is a conservative way to develop the ROI, since many short-term projects have added value in the second or third year. For long-term projects, longer time frames are used. For example, in an ROI forecast of a project involving new technology in a retail store chain, a three-year time frame was used. The important issue is to decide on the time frame in the proposal process and be conservative.

BCR/ROI calculations

When forecasting ROI, communicating to the target audience the formula used and the assumptions made in arriving at the value are important. This helps avoid misunderstandings and confusion surrounding how the ROI value was actually developed. Although several approaches are described in this chapter, two stand out as preferred methods: the benefit/cost ratio and the basic ROI formula.

Benefit/Cost Ratio

One of the earliest methods for evaluating projects was the benefit/cost ratio. This method compares the benefits of the project to the costs, using a simple ratio. In formula form, the ratio is:

$$BCR = Project\ Benefits / Project\ Costs$$

In simple terms, the BCR compares the annual economic benefits of the project to the costs of the project. A BCR of 1 means that the benefits equal the costs. A BCR of 2, usually written as 2:1, indicates that for each dollar spent on the project, two dollars are returned in benefits. An example will illustrate the calculation.

A simple, Six Sigma quality improvement project was implemented for a medium-size organization. The expected costs of the project (from the consultant's perspective and the organization's perspective) totaled $235,000. The monetary benefits expected to be derived through improvements in quality measures were $710,000. Thus, the ratio was:

$$BCR = \$710,000 / \$235,000 = 3.02:1$$

For every dollar invested in this project, three dollars in benefits were expected. This avoids the traditional financial measure of ROI calculation. Some project leaders prefer not to use benefits/cost ratio.

ROI Formula

Perhaps the most appropriate formula for evaluating project investments is net project benefits divided by cost. This is the traditional financial ROI and is directly related to the BCR. The ratio is usually expressed as a percentage when the fractional values are multiplied by 100. In formula form, the ROI becomes:

ROI (%) = Net Project Benefits / Project Costs × 100

Net benefits are project benefits minus costs. The ROI value is related to the BCR by a factor of 1. Subtract 1 from the BCR and multiply by 100 to get the ROI percentage. For example, a BCR of 2.45 is the same as an ROI value of 145 percent (1.45 × 100%). This formula is essentially the same as the ROI for capital investments. For example, when a firm builds a new plant or purchases new equipment, the ROI is developed by dividing annual earnings by the investment for projects. The annual earnings are comparable to net benefits (annual benefits minus the cost). The investment is comparable to fully loaded project costs, which represent the investment in the program.

An ROI of 50 percent means that the costs are recovered and an additional 50 percent of the costs are returned as "earnings." An ROI of 150 percent indicates that the costs have been recovered and an additional 1.5 times the costs are returned as "earnings."

Using the Six Sigma quality example presented earlier will illustrate the ROI calculation. The return on investment was:

ROI (%) = ($710,000 – $235,000) / $235,000 × 100 = 202%

For each dollar invested, $2.02 will be returned after the costs of the consulting project have been recovered.

Using the ROI formula essentially places project investments on a level playing field with other investments using the same formula and similar concepts. Key management and financial executives who regularly use ROI with other investments easily understand the ROI calculation.

ROI INSIGHTS

Of all of the measures forecasted in this book, the ROI forecast is the most misused, misunderstood, and emotional element in a project. Project team members have a fear of negative ROI, while sponsors often give the ROI a disproportionate amount of weight in making a decision. The challenge is to be able to keep emotions out of the decision making and continually remind the audience that the ROI forecast is only one of several data measures.

Basis for monetary value

Perhaps it's helpful to review the basis for projecting monetary benefits. They are based on profits or on cost reduction or cost avoidance. Profits can be generated through increased sales or cost savings. In practice, more opportunities for cost savings occur than for profits. Cost savings can be generated when improvement in productivity, quality, efficiency, cycle time, or actual cost reductions occur. The vast majority (85 percent) of the almost 500 studies in which we have been directly involved were based on cost savings achieved with improvements in output, quality, efficiency, time, or direct cost reduction. The others had a payoff based on revenue increases, where the earnings were derived from the profit margin. This situation is important for nonprofits and public sector organizations for which the profit opportunity is often unavailable. Most projects will be connected directly to cost savings; ROI values can still be developed in those settings.

ROI history

Financiers have used the ROI approach for centuries. Still, this technique did not become widespread in industry for evaluating operating performance until the early 1960s (Horngren 1982). Conceptually, ROI has innate appeal because it blends all the major ingredients of profitability in one number; the ROI statistic by itself can be compared with opportunities elsewhere (both inside and outside).

Practically, however, ROI is an imperfect measurement that should be used in conjunction with other performance measurements.

ROI misuse

The chief financial officer (CFO) and the finance and accounting staff should become partners in project implementation where ROI is used. Without their support, involvement, and commitment, using ROI on a wide-scale basis is difficult. Because of this relationship, the same financial terms must be used as those used and expected by the CFO.

Misuse of abbreviations can create confusion. Using the abbreviation ROI for return on intelligence or return on information, the abbreviation ROE for return on expectations or return on event, the abbreviation ROA for return on anticipation, or the abbreviation ROCE for return on client expectations will confuse those who are thinking return on investment, return on equity, return on assets, and return on capital employed, respectively. Use of these abbreviations in the calculation of a payback of a project will do nothing but confuse others and perhaps cause you to lose the support of the finance and accounting staff. Other terms such as return on people, return on objectives, return on resources, return on technology, return on Web, and return on value can often be used with almost no financial equivalents. The bottom line: Spell out exactly what you mean.

ROI is not for every project

ROI should not be used with every project. Creating a credible ROI forecast will take additional resources, and when an ROI forecast is used, it should be followed by a postproject ROI analysis. ROI is appropriate for projects that:

- *Are very important to the organization in meeting its operating goals.* These projects are designed to add value. ROI may be helpful to show that value.

- *Are closely linked to the strategic initiatives.* Anything this important needs a high level of accountability.
- *Are very expensive to implement.* An expensive project, expending large amounts of resources, should be subjected to this level of accountability.
- *Are highly visible and sometimes controversial.* These projects often require this level of accountability to satisfy the critics.
- *Have a large target audience.* If a project is designed for a large number of participants, it may be a candidate for ROI.
- *Command the interest of top executives and administrators.* If top executives are interested in knowing the impact and ROI, the ROI should be pursued.

These are only guidelines and should be considered within the context of the situation, the organization, and the proposal opportunity. Other criteria may also be appropriate. These criteria can be used in a scheme to sort out those most appropriate for this level of accountability.

It is also helpful to consider the projects for which the ROI methodology is not appropriate. ROI is seldom appropriate for projects that:

- Have a very brief duration
- Are very inexpensive
- Are legislated or required by regulation and would be difficult to change anything as a result of the project forecast and evaluation
- Are required by senior management; project will continue regardless of the findings

This is not meant to imply that the ROI methodology cannot be implemented for these types of projects. However, careful use of resources and time will result in forecasting more strategic types of projects.

OTHER ROI MEASURES

In addition to the traditional ROI formula, several other measures can be used under the general heading of return on investment. These measures are designed for evaluating other types of financial measures but sometimes work their way into project evaluations.

Payback period

The payback period is another common method for evaluating capital expenditures. With this approach, the annual cash proceeds (savings) produced by an investment are equated to the original cash outlay required by the investment to arrive at some multiple of cash proceeds equal to the original investment. Measurement is usually in terms of years and months. For example, if the cost savings generated from a program are constant each year, the payback period is determined by dividing the total original cash investment (development costs, expenses, etc.) by the amount of the expected annual or actual savings. The savings represent the net savings after the project expenses are subtracted.

To illustrate this calculation, assume that an initial project cost is $100,000 with a three-year useful life. The annual net savings from the project are expected to be $40,000. Thus, the payback period becomes:

$$\text{Payback Period} = \text{Total Investment}/\text{Annual Savings} =$$
$$\$100,000/\$40,000 = 2.5 \text{ Years}$$

The program will "pay back" the original investment in 2.5 years.

The payback period is simple to use but has the limitation of ignoring the time value of money. It has not enjoyed widespread use in evaluating project investments.

Discounted cash flow

Discounted cash flow is a method of evaluating investment opportunities in which certain values are assigned to the timing of the proceeds from the investment. The assumption, based on interest rates, is that money earned today is more valuable than money earned a year from now.

There are several ways to use the discounted cash flow concept to evaluate a project investment. The most common approach is the net present value of an investment. This approach compares the savings, year by year, with the outflow of cash required by the investment. The expected savings received each year are discounted by selected interest rates. The outflow of cash is also discounted by the same interest rate. If the present value of the savings should exceed the present value of the outlays, after discounting at a common interest rate, the investment is usually considered acceptable by management. The discounted cash flow method has the advantage of ranking investments, but it becomes difficult to calculate.

BASIC STEPS TO FORECAST ROI

Eighteen detailed steps are necessary to develop a credible pre-project ROI forecast using expert input:

1. **Understand the situation**. Individuals providing input to the forecast and conducting the forecast must have a good understanding of the present situation. This is typically a requirement for selecting the experts for inputs.

2. **Predict the present**. The project is sometimes initiated because a particular business impact measure is not doing well. However, these measures often lag the present situation; they may be based on data that are several months old. Also, these measures are based on dynamic influences that may change dramatically and quickly. It may be beneficial to estimate where the measure is now, based on assumptions and current trends.

Although this appears to be a lot of work, it does not constitute a new responsibility for most of the experts, who are often concerned about the present situation. Market share data, for example, are often several months old. Trending market share data and examining other influences driving market share can help organizations understand the current situation.

3. **Observe warnings**. Closely tied to predicting the present is making sure that warning signs are observed. Red flags signal that something is going against the measure in question, causing it to go in an undesired direction or otherwise not move as it should. These often raise concerns that lead to projects. These are early warnings that things may get worse; they must be factored into the situation as forecasts are made.

4. **Describe the new project or solution.** The project must be completely and clearly described to the experts so they fully understand the mechanics of what is to be implemented. The description should include the project scope, the individuals involved, time factors, and whatever else is necessary to express the magnitude of the project and the profile of the solution.

5. **Develop specific objectives.** Ideally objectives should include reaction objectives, learning objectives, application objectives, and impact objectives. Although these may be difficult to define, they are developed as part of the up-front analysis described in Chapter 3. Objectives provide clear direction toward the project's end. The cascading levels represent the anticipated chain of impact that will occur as the project is implemented. The forecast builds on the objectives.

6. **Forecast how participants will react to the project.** In this step, the experts are estimating participants' reaction: Will the participants see the project as relevant, important, useful, necessary, motivational, challenging, etc.? Will other stakeholders

see the project in the same way? The response is important because a negative reaction can cause a project to fail.

7. **Forecast what the participants will learn**. To some extent, every project will involve learning, and the experts will estimate what learning will occur. Using the learning objectives, the experts will define what the participants will learn as they enter the project, identifying specific knowledge, skills, and information the participants must acquire or enhance during the project, all aimed at making the project successful.

8. **Forecast what participants should accomplish in the project**. Building on the application objectives, the experts will identify what will be accomplished as the project is implemented successfully. This step details specific actions, tasks, and processes that will be taken by the individuals. Steps 6, 7, and 8—based on reaction, learning, and application—provide important information that serves as the basis for the next step, estimating improvement in business impact data.

9. **Forecast the improvement in business impact data**. The experts will provide the estimate—in either absolute numbers or percentages—of the monetary change in the business impact measure (ΔP) caused by the project. This is a critical step because the impact data are needed for the financial forecast.

10. **Apply the confidence estimate**. Because the estimate may not be very accurate, an error adjustment is needed. This is developed with a confidence estimate on the value identified in Step 9. The experts are asked to indicate the confidence they have in the previous data. The confidence level is expressed as a percentage, with 0 indicating "no confidence" and 100 percent indicating "certainty." This becomes an error adjustment in the analysis. Essentially, the impact measure, ΔP, is multiplied by the percentage to create a new ΔP.

11. **Convert the business impact data to monetary values**. Using one or more methods described in Chapter 9, the impact data are converted to money. If the impact measure is a desired increase such as productivity, the value represents the gain obtained by having one more unit of the measure. If it is a measure that the organization is trying to reduce—such as downtime, mistakes, or complaints—the value is the cost that the organization incurs as a result of one unit. For example, the cost of one complaint may be $1,200. This value is noted with the letter V.

12. **Develop the estimated annual impact of each measure**. The estimated annual impact is the first-year improvement directly related to the project. In formula form, this is expressed as $\Delta I = \Delta P \times V \times 12$ (where ΔI = annual change in monetary value, ΔP = annual change in performance of the measure, and V = the value of that measure) for a monthly amount. If the measure is weekly, it must be converted to an annual amount with a factor of 52. For example, if two lost-time accidents will be prevented each week, the accidents prevented represent a total of 104.

13. **Factor additional years into the analysis for projects that will have a significant useful life beyond the first year**. For these projects, the factor should reflect the diminished benefit of subsequent years. The client or sponsor of the project should provide some indication of the amount of the reduction and the values developed for the second, third, and successive years. It is important to be conservative by using the smallest numbers possible.

14. **Estimate the fully loaded project costs**. In this step, use all the cost categories described in Chapter 9, and denote the value as C when including it in the ROI equation. Include all direct and indirect costs in the calculation.

15. **Calculate the forecasted ROI**. Use the total projected benefits and the estimated costs in the standard ROI formula. Calculate the forecast ROI as follows:

$$ROI\ (\%) = (\Delta\ I - C)\ /\ C \times 100$$

16. **Use sensitivity analysis to develop several potential ROI values with different levels of improvement (ΔP).** When more than one measure is changing, the analysis may take the form of a spreadsheet showing various output scenarios and the subsequent ROI forecasts. The breakeven point will be identified.

17. **Identify potential intangible benefits that will be connected to the project**. Anticipate intangible benefits using input from these experts about the situation on the basis of assumptions from their experience with similar projects. The intangible benefits are those benefits not converted to monetary values but possessing value nonetheless.

18. **Communicate the ROI forecast with caution**. The target audience must clearly understand that the ROI forecast is based on several assumptions (clearly defined), and that the values are the best possible estimates, adjusted for error.

Essentially, these steps summarize what is in this book when it comes to the forecasting chapters; however, they are all positioned toward the ultimate level in ROI forecast. It's important not to lose sight of the other measures that are forecasted, but they are often easier to develop and are clearly understood. A case study that focuses just on the ROI forecast can help illustrate some the issues described in this chapter.

Case study: Forecasting ROI for a technology project

Global Financial Services (GFS) was in the process of implementing contact management software to enable its sales relationship managers to track routine correspondence and communication with customers.

A needs assessment and initial analysis determined the project was needed. The project would involve further detailing, selecting an appropriate software package, and implementing the software with appropriate job aids, support tools, and training. However, before pursuing the project and purchasing the software, a forecast ROI was needed. In the initial analysis, it was determined that four business impact measures would be influenced by implementation of this project:

1. Increase in sales to existing customers
2. Reduction in customer complaints caused by missed deadlines, late responses, and failure to complete transactions
3. Reduction in response time for customer inquiries and requests
4. Increase in the customer satisfaction composite survey index

Several individuals provided input in examining the potential problem. With comprehensive customer contact management software in place, relationship managers should benefit from quick and effective customer communication and have easy access to customer databases. The software should also provide the functionality to develop calendars and to-do lists. Relationship managers should further benefit from features such as built-in contact management, calendar sharing, and the fact that the software is Internet-ready. To determine the extent to which the four measures would change, input was collected from six sources:

1. Internal software developers with expertise in various software applications
2. Marketing analysts with expertise on sales cycles, customer needs, and customer care issues
3. Relationship managers with expertise on expected changes in the job environment if the software was used regularly
4. The analyst with expertise on the initial need for the software

5. The sponsor with expertise on what could be expected from the project

6. The proposed vendor with expertise based on previous experience with the software

When input is based on estimates, the actual results will usually differ significantly. However, GFS was interested in a forecast based on analysis that, although very limited, would be strengthened with the best easily available expert opinion. Input was adjusted on the basis of the estimates and other information to assess its credibility. After discussing the availability of data and examining the techniques to convert it to monetary values, the following conclusions were reached:

- The increase in sales could be converted to a monetary value as the average margin for sales increase is applied directly.
- The cost of a customer complaint could be based on an internal value currently in use, providing a generally accepted cost.
- Customer response time was not tracked accurately, and the value of this measure was not readily available, making it an intangible benefit.
- No generally accepted value for increasing customer satisfaction was available, so customer satisfaction impact data would be listed as an intangible benefit.

The forecast ROI calculation was developed from combined input based on the variety of estimates. The increase in sales was easily converted to monetary values using the margin rates, and the reduction in customer complaints was easily converted using the discounted value of a customer complaint. The costs for the project could easily be estimated based on input from those who briefly examined the situation. The total costs included development costs, materials, software, equipment, facilitators, facilities, and lost time for learning activities, coordination, and evaluation. This fully loaded projected cost, compared to the benefits, yielded a range of expected ROI values. Table 10.1 shows possible scenarios based on payoffs of

Table 10.1. Expected ROI values for different outputs.

EXPERT	POTENTIAL SALES INCREASE	BASIS	POTENTIAL COMPLAINT REDUCTION (MONTHLY REDUCTION)	BASIS	EXPECTED ROI	CREDIBILITY RATING (5 = HIGHEST, 1 = LOWEST)
Relationship manager	3.5%	Sales opportunity	3	Lower response time	60%	3
Analyst	4%	Customer satisfaction	4	Lower response time	90%	4
Marketing analyst	3%	Missed opportunity	5	Quicker response	120%	4
Project sponsor	5%	Customer services	4	Quicker response	77%	4
Vendor	10%	Customer loyalty	12	Higher priority	180%	2
Internal software developer	2%	Customer relationship	3	Faster response	12%	2

the two measures as assessed by six experts. The ROI values range from a low of 12 percent to a high of 180 percent. The breakeven point could be developed with different scenarios. With these values in hand, the decision to move forward was easy: Even the worst-case scenarios were positive and the best case was expected to yield more than 10 times the ROI of the worst. As this example illustrates, the process must be simple, and must use the most credible resources available to quickly arrive at estimates.

With these estimates, the forecast is ready to be made. In this example, we are representing only the impact, intangible, and ROI forecast. Working from Table 10.1, the logic in this example to develop a forecast is as follows. First, the ROI forecast, which has a range from 12 to 180 percent, represents an average of about 90 percent ROI. When the high and low numbers are removed, the average still results in an 87 percent ROI. In terms of the most credible sources, a range from 77 to 120 percent ROI. This team selected 75 percent ROI for the forecast. This number should be a conservative estimate for the value that should be achieved. Regarding the sales increase, an average of the three most credible ones was used representing a 4 percent increase. For the complaints, which ranged from 4 to 5 per month, 4 was used. Although not for analysis, similar data was collected about the response time, and most agreed that response time could be cut in half. As it turns out, this element was not a tangible measure, but an intangible one. Thus, a 50 percent reduction was used. Regarding the customer satisfaction index, because it was a composite value, it was difficult to pinpoint the actual amount of forecast, so it was left as a general statement of an increase in the composite index. With that in mind, here are the actual forecasted values:

1. An increase of 4 percent in sales to existing customers in six months

2. A reduction of four customer complaints per month caused by missed deadlines, late responses, and failure to complete transactions

3. A 50 percent reduction in response time for customer inquiries and requests

4. An increase in the customer satisfaction composite survey index

5. An ROI of 75 percent, based on one year of improvement

As this example shows, the forecasts are very specific, and the focus is on what can be achieved. Incidentally, an ROI objective for this project would probably be in the range of 10 to 20 percent as a minimum, acceptable number. Here, the forecast is a realistic number of what can be achieved.

FORECASTING ROI WITH REACTION DATA

When a reaction evaluation includes the planned applications of a project, the data can ultimately be used in an ROI forecast. ROI information can be developed with questions concerning how participants plan to implement the project and what results they expect to achieve after they have been exposed to the project. For example, consider a project proposed by a major pharmaceutical company. The firm was considering installing high-speed DSL lines in the homes of each of its pharmaceutical sales representatives on the premise that this would save the reps time that they could otherwise spend with their customers. However, when the project was thoroughly described, the reaction to the proposed project was not positive. The sales reps said they do most of their online work at night when speed is not such an issue, and even if they did save time, they would be unlikely to add another call to their schedule, or even be able to spend more time with customers. Although the project's goals had merit, from the standpoint of forecast monetary value, the project would not add value or improve the original measure.

Perhaps it's helpful to clearly distinguish this forecast from the preproject forecast. In a preproject forecast that is part of the proposal, no reaction data has been collected because the project hasn't been approved and implemented yet. Therefore, the financial ROI is based on a set of assumptions from various experts. In this particular scenario, the project is being implemented, and the participants, those who are involved, now are exposed to it. In the case of soft programs, such as ethics, leadership development, coaching, and business development, the individuals involved have learned what is necessary to make it successful. Thus, their reaction before they actually do anything is very important and powerful, which is the type of data collected here. This reaction can be built into the proposal, which suggests to the client that the forecast ROI would be originally provided on a preproject basis and then will be taken again as the project is being implemented to see the difference. This extra step should provide some assurance that the project will be successful. While this information may not be necessary, or even desired by the client; it's a great way to prevent design flaws early in the process so adjustments can be made. A negative forecast with reaction data would indicate that there are serious problems that need to be rectified before the project continues. However, a very positive forecast at this level needs to be taken with caution, as it may be an overstatement.

Data collection

To forecast ROI at this level, at the beginning of a project participants are asked to state specifically how they plan to use the project and what results they expect to achieve. They are asked to convert their planned accomplishments into monetary values and show the basis for developing the values. Participants can adjust their responses with a confidence factor to make the data more credible. Next, estimates are adjusted for confidence level. When tabulating data, participants multiply the confidence levels by annual monetary values. This produces a conservative estimate for use in data analysis. For example, if a participant estimated the monetary impact for his or her part of the project at $10,000 but was only 50 percent confident in his or her estimate, a $5,000 value would be used in the ROI forecast calculations.

To develop a summary of the expected benefits, discard any data that are incomplete, unusable, extreme, or unrealistic. Then total the individual data items. Finally, as an optional exercise, adjust the total value again by a factor that reflects the unknowns in the environment and the possibility that participants will not achieve the results they anticipate. The project team can estimate this adjustment factor. In one organization, the benefits are divided by two to develop a number to use in the calculation. Finally, calculate the forecast ROI using the net benefits from the project divided by the project costs.

Case study: Forecasting ROI from reaction data

This process can best be described using an actual case. Global Engineering and Construction Company (GEC) designs and builds large commercial projects like plants, paper mills, and municipal water systems. Safety is always a critical matter at GEC and usually commands much management attention. To improve safety performance, a safety improvement project was initiated for project engineers and construction superintendents. The project solution involved policy changes, audits, and training. The project focused on safety leadership, safety planning, safety inspections, safety meetings, accident investigation, safety policies and procedures, safety standards, and workers' compensation. Safety engineers and superintendents (participants) were expected to improve the safety performance of their individual construction projects. All of those issues were fully described in a two-day project overview. A dozen safety performance measures used in the company were discussed and analyzed in the overview. At that time, participants completed a feedback questionnaire that probed specific action items planned as a result of the safety project and provided estimated monetary values of the planned actions. In addition, participants explained the basis for estimates and placed a confidence level on their estimates. Table 10.2 presents data provided by the participants. Only 19 of the 25 participants supplied data. (Experience has shown that approximately 70 to 90 percent of participants will provide usable data on this series of questions.) The estimated cost of the project, including participants' salaries for the time devoted to the project, was $358,900.

The monetary values of the planned improvements were extremely high, reflecting the participants' optimism and enthusiasm at the beginning of an impressive project from which specific actions were planned. As a first step in the analysis, extreme data items were omitted (one of the guiding principles of the methodology). Data such as "millions," "unlimited," and "$4 million" were discarded, and each remaining value was multiplied by the confidence value and totaled. This adjustment is one way of reducing highly subjective estimates. The resulting tabulations yielded a total improvement of $990,125 (rounded to $990,000). The projected ROI, which was based on the feedback questionnaire at the beginning of the project, is

$$ROI = (\$990,000 - \$358,900) / \$358,900 \times 100 = 176\%$$

Although these projected values are subjective, the results were generated by project participants who should be aware of what they could accomplish. A follow-up study would determine the true results delivered by the group.

Table 10.2. Level 1 data for ROI forecast calculations.

PARTICIPANT NO.	ESTIMATED VALUE ($)	BASIS	CONFIDENCE LEVEL	ADJUSTED VALUE ($)
1	80,000	Reduction in lost-time accidents	90%	72,000
2	91,200	OSHA reportable injuries	80%	72,960
3	55,000	Accident reduction	90%	49,500
4	10,000	First-aid visits/visits to doctor	70%	7,000
5	150,000	Reduction in lost-time injuries	95%	142,500
6	Millions	Total accident cost	100%	—
7	74,800	Workers' Compensation	80%	59,840
8	7,500	OSHA citations	75%	5,625
9	50,000	Reduction in accidents	75%	37,500
10	36,000	Workers' Compensation	80%	28,800
11	150,000	Reduction in total accident costs	90%	135,000
12	22,000	OSHA fines/citations	70%	15,400
13	140,000	Accident reductions	80%	112,000
14	4 million	Total cost of safety	95%	—
15	65,000	Total Workers' Compensation	50%	32,500
16	Unlimited	Accidents	100%	—
17	20,000	Visits to doctor	95%	19,000
18	45,000	Injuries	90%	40,500
19	200,000	Lost-time injuries	80%	160,000

Total: 990,125

Use of the data

Caution is required when using the ROI forecast: The calculations are highly subjective and may not reflect the extent to which participants will achieve results. A variety of influences in the work environment and project setting can enhance or inhibit the attainment of performance goals. Having high expectations at the beginning of a project is no guarantee that those expectations will be met. Project disappointments are documented regularly.

Although the process is subjective and possibly unreliable, it does have some usefulness:

1. If the project evaluation must stop at this point, this analysis provides more insight into the value of the project than data from typical reaction input, which reports attitudes and feelings about the project. Sponsors and managers usually find this information more useful than a report stating, "40 percent of project team participants rated the project above average."

2. These data can form a basis for comparing different projects of the same type (e.g., safety projects). If one project forecast results in an ROI of 300 percent and a similar project forecast results in a 30 percent ROI, it would appear that one project might be more effective. The participants in the first project have more confidence in the planned implementation of the project.

3. Collecting these types of data focuses increased attention on project outcomes. Participants will understand that specific action is expected, which produces results for the project. The data collection helps participants plan the implementation of what they are learning. This issue becomes clear to participants as they anticipate results and convert them to monetary values. Even if the forecast is ignored, the exercise is productive because of the important message it sends to participants.

4. The data can be used to secure support for a follow-up evaluation. A skeptical client may challenge the data and this

challenge can be converted into support for a follow-up to see whether the forecast holds true. The only way to know whether these results will materialize is to conduct a post-project evaluation.

5. If a follow-up evaluation of the project is planned, the postproject results can be compared to the ROI forecast. Comparisons of forecast and follow-up data are helpful. If there is a defined relationship between the two, the less expensive forecast can be substituted for the more expensive follow-up. Also, when a follow-up evaluation is planned, participants are usually more conservative with their projected estimates.

The use of ROI forecasting with reaction data is increasing, and some organizations have based many of their ROI forecast calculations on this type of data.

FORECASTING ROI WITH SOFT DATA

Although not as credible as some desire, a forecast can be made on the basis of the improved competencies or skills of the project participants (users, audience). This process uses the concept of utility analysis, which is best described in the experience of a large European bank that was seeking to develop a leadership project for its executives. Bank managers identified the specific competencies they wanted to develop. Before making the eight million euro investment in the program, the senior executive team wanted to know the value it would add. The project team used utility analysis to conduct the forecast. The numbers are rounded off to keep the calculations simple.

First, the team assessed the percentage of executives' jobs covered in the leadership competencies. To keep it simple, assume that this involved 40 percent of their job content. This amount was derived from surveying a sample of the management team. Next the average salary was determined—say, €100,000. Thus, the project could influence 40 percent of €100,000, or €40,000. The managers assessed the team's current level of performance of the competencies using a convenient scale. After reviewing the competencies and the project's objectives, the managers indicated that a 10 percent improvement could be achieved on these competencies by implementing the leadership development project. Thus, the project had a potential of improving the €40,000 portion of their salary by 10 percent, or €4,000. (In essence, it would add €4,000 in value.) Table 10.3 provides a summary of this process. This value is compared to the proposed participant cost for the leadership project to determine the forecast on an individual basis. If the cost of the program is €3,000, the ROI is 33 percent.

Although this example is simple, it shows the concept of forecasting based on improving competencies. It ignores what the managers or executives will accomplish with the competencies, so it is not as credible as an ROI forecast with impact data. Nevertheless, it has value and is described in more detail in other sources.

Table 10.3. Forecasting using improved competencies.

Percent of managers jobs covered by competencies	40%
Average manager's salary	€100,000
Monetary value of covered competencies (40% × €100,000)	€40,000
Percent of anticipated improvement in competencies	10%
Added benefit of improved competencies in monetary terms (€40,000 × 10%)	€4,000 per manager
Cost of program per participant	€3,000 per manager
ROI	33%

WHY INTANGIBLES ARE IMPORTANT

Project results include both tangible and intangible measures. Intangible measures are the benefits or detriments directly linked to a project that cannot or should not be converted to monetary values credibly with minimal resources. The range of intangible measures is almost limitless. Examples of these measures are listed in Table 10.4. Some measures make the list because of the difficulty in measuring them; others because of the difficulty in converting them to money. Others are on the list for both reasons. Being labeled as intangible does not mean that these items can never be measured or converted to monetary values. In one study or another, each item has been monitored and quantified in financial terms. However, in typical

Table 10.4. Common intangibles.

Accountability	Intellectual capital
Alliances	Innovation and creativity
Attention	Job satisfaction
Awards	Leadership
Branding	Loyalty
Capability	Networking
Capacity	Organizational commitment
Clarity	Partnering
Communication	Poverty
Corporate social responsibility	Reputation
Employee attitudes	Stress
Customer service (customer satisfaction)	Team effectiveness
	Timeliness
Engagement	Sustainability
Human Life	Work/life balance
Image	

projects, these measures are considered intangible benefits because of the difficulty in measuring or converting them to monetary values.

Although intangible measures are not new, they are becoming increasingly important. Intangibles secure funding and drive the economy, and organizations are built on them. In every direction we look, intangibles are becoming not only increasingly important, but also critical to organizations. Here's a recap of why they have become so important.

Intangibles are the invisible advantage

When examining the success behind many well-known organizations, intangibles are often found. A highly innovative company develops new and improved products; a government agency reinvents itself; a company with highly involved and engaged employees attracts and keeps talent. An organization shares knowledge with employees, providing a competitive advantage. Still another organization develops strategic partners and alliances. These intangibles do not often appear in cost statements and other record keeping, but they are there, and they make a huge difference.

Trying to identify, measure, and forecast intangibles may be difficult, but the ability to do so exists. Intangibles transform the way organizations work, the way employees are managed, the way products are designed, the way services are sold, and the way customers are treated. The implications are profound, and an organization's strategy must address them. Although invisible, the presence of intangibles is felt and the results are concrete.

Intangibles drive projects

Some projects are implemented because of the intangibles. For example, the need to have increased collaboration, partnering, communication, teamwork, or branding will drive projects. In the public sector, the need to reduce poverty, employ disadvantaged children, and save lives often drives projects. From the outset, the intangibles are the important drivers and become the most important measures. Consequently, more executives include a string of intangibles on their scorecards, key operating reports, key performance indicators, dashboards, and other routine reporting systems. In some cases, the intangibles represent nearly half of all measures that are monitored.

FORECASTING INTANGIBLES

In some projects, intangibles are more important than monetary measures. Consequently, these measures should be monitored and reported as part of the project forecast. In practice, every project, regardless of its nature, scope, and content, will produce intangible measures. The challenge is to identify them effectively and report them appropriately.

Measuring the intangibles

From time to time it is necessary to explore the issue of measuring the difficult to measure. Responses to this exploration usually occur in the form of comments instead of questions. "You can't measure it," is a typical response. This cannot be true, because anything can be measured. What the frustrated observer suggests by the comment is that the intangible is not something you can always count, examine, or see in quantities, such as items produced on an assembly line. In reality, a quantitative value can be assigned to or developed for any intangible. If it exists, it can be measured. Consider human intelligence for example. Although human intelligence is vastly complex and abstract with myriad facets and qualities, IQ scores are assigned to people, and most people seem to accept them. The Software Engineering Institute of Carnegie-Mellon University assigns software organizations a score of 1 to 5 to represent their maturity in software engineering. This score has enormous implications for the organizations' business development capabilities, yet the measure goes practically unchallenged (Alden 2006).

Several approaches are available for measuring intangibles. Intangibles that can be counted include customer complaints, employee complaints, and conflicts. These can be recorded easily, and constitute one of the most acceptable types of measures. Unfortunately, many intangibles are based on attitudes and perceptions that must be measured. The key is in the development of the instrument of measure. The instruments are usually developed around scales of 3, 5, and even 10 points to represent levels of perception. The instruments to measure intangibles consist of three basic varieties.

The first lists the intangible items and asks respondents to agree or disagree on a 5-point scale (where the midpoint represents a neutral opinion). Other instruments define various qualities of the intangible, such as its reputation. A 5-point scale can easily be developed to describe degrees of reputation, ranging from the worst rating—a horrible reputation—to the best rating—an excellent reputation. Still other ratings are expressed as an assessment on a scale of 1 to 10, after respondents review a description of the intangible.

Intangibles can be measured when they connect to a tangible, easier-to-value measure. As shown in Figure 10.1, most hard-to-measure items are linked to an easy-to-measure item. In the classic situation, a soft measure (typically the intangible) is connected to a hard measure (typically the tangible). Although this link can be developed through logical deductions and conclusions, having some empirical evidence through a correlation analysis (as shown in the figure) and developing a significant correlation between the items is the best approach. However, a detailed analysis would have to be conducted to ensure that a causal relationship exists. In other words, just because a correlation is apparent, does not mean that one caused the other.

Figure 10.1 The link between hard-to-measure and easy-to-measure items.

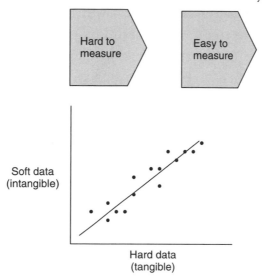

Consequently, additional analysis, other empirical evidence, and supporting data could pinpoint the actual causal effect.

Another instrument for measuring the intangible is the development of an index of different values. These could be a combination of both hard and soft data items that make up a particular index value. An index is a single score representing some complex factor that is constructed by aggregating the values of several different measures. Measures making up the index are sometimes weighted based on their importance to the abstract factor being measured. Some index measures are based strictly on hard data items. For example, the U.S. poverty level is based on a family income amount equal to three times the money needed to feed a family as determined by the U.S. Department of Agriculture, adjusted for inflation using the consumer price index. Sometimes an index is completely intangible, such as the customer satisfaction index developed by the University of Michigan.

Forecasting intangibles

Intangible measures can be uncovered early in the process, during the needs assessment. For example, one technology project has several hard data measures linked to it. Job stress, an intangible measure, is identified with no plans to convert it to a monetary value. From the beginning, this measure is destined to be a nonmonetary, intangible benefit reported along with the ROI results.

Initially, the client or the sponsor may indicate some intangibles that are connected to the project. In some situations, intangibles are the principal reason for the project. In addition to the early identification, the project team members and other experts, who are familiar with the situation, can provide input about the intangibles. These experts, identified in the previous four chapters, can estimate the extent of linkage to these intangibles. A measurement scheme would be devised using one of the measures described here, such as a 1 to 5 scale, and the experts would indicate what percent of the individuals would see this as an intangible and its rating of importance.

It's important to make sure that those who know the situations best are asked to provide input. These results do not have to be flawless, but they do provide data from credible sources that connect this project to an intangible. The exact strength of the connection may not be needed. Just knowing which measures are connected and the relative strength of that connection will be enough for the client. For example, in a project designed to improve the image of a foreign manufacturer in the United States, the experts forecasted that 28 percent of the audience would rate the image as 4 or 5 on a scale of 1 to 5, with 5 being the most favorable.

FORECASTING GUIDELINES

With the forecasting options outlined in this chapter, it may help to follow a few guidelines known to drive the forecasting possibilities within an organization (Bowers 1997). These guidelines are based on experience in forecasting in a variety of projects and programs:

1. **If you forecast, forecast frequently**. Forecasting is an art and a science. Users can build comfort, experience, and history with the process by using it frequently.

2. **Make forecasting an essential part of the proposal strategy**. This chapter began with a list of essential reasons for forecasting ROI, which is increasingly being demanded by many organizations. It can be an effective and useful tool when used properly and in conjunction with other types of forecast data. Some proposal strategies have targets for the use of forecasting (e.g., if a project exceeds a certain cost, it will always require a preproject forecast). Others will target a certain number of projects for a forecast based on the importance of the project. It is important to plan for the forecast and let it be a part of the proposal process, using it regularly.

3. **Forecast different types of data**. Although this chapter focuses on how to develop a forecast ROI using the standard ROI formula, forecasting the value of the other types of data is important as well. A useable, helpful forecast will include predictions about reaction, the extent of learning, and the extent of application and implementation. Chapters 7, 8, and 9 described these data sets, in addition to this chapter.

4. **Secure input from those who know the process best**. As forecasts are developed, it is essential to secure input from individuals who understand the dynamics of the environment and the measures being influenced by the project—go to the experts. This will increase the accuracy of the forecast, and the credibility of the results. In other situations, it may be the analysts who are aware of the major influences in the workplace and the dynamics of those changes.

5. **Long-term forecasts will usually be inaccurate**. Forecasting works better when it covers a short time frame. Most short-term scenarios afford a better grasp of the influences that might drive the measures. In the long term, a variety of new influences, unforeseen now, could enter the process and drastically change the impact measures. If a long-term forecast is needed, it should be updated regularly.

6. **Expect forecasts to be biased**. Forecasts will consist of data coming from those who have an interest in the issue. This is unavoidable. Some will want the forecast to be optimistic; others will have a pessimistic view. Almost all input is biased in one way or another. Every attempt should be made to minimize the bias, adjust for the bias, or adjust for the uncertainty in the process. Still, the audience should recognize the forecast as a biased prediction.

7. **Serious forecasting is hard work**. The value of forecasting often depends on the amount of effort put into the process. High-stake projects or programs need a serious approach, collecting all possible data, examining different scenarios, and making the best prediction available. It is in these situations that mathematical tools can be most valuable.

8. **Review the success of forecasting routinely**. As forecasts are made, it is imperative to revisit the forecast with postproject data to check its accuracy. This can aid in the continuous improvement of the processes. Sources could prove to be more or less credible, specific inputs may be more or less biased, and certain analyses may be more appropriate than others. It is important to constantly improve the methods and approaches for forecasting within the organization.

9. **Assumptions are the most serious error in forecasting**. Of all the variables that can enter the process, assumptions offer

the greatest opportunity for error. It is important for the assumptions to be clearly understood and communicated. When multiple inputs are given, each forecaster should use the same set of assumptions, if possible.

10. **Utility is the most important characteristic of forecasting**. The most important use of forecasting is providing information and input for the decision maker. Forecasting is a tool for those attempting to make decisions about project implementation. It is not a process intended to maximize the output or minimize any particular variable. It will not dramatically change the way a project is implemented. It is a process to provide data for decisions.

FINAL THOUGHTS

The crystal ball isn't cloudy anymore, and your clients are leaning in closer. This chapter proves to be the most intriguing of all the forecasting chapters, as it focuses on the financial ROI and the intangibles. The forecast for the financial ROI is a very precise calculation of the benefit-cost ratio and the financial ROI. The intangibles are those measures that cannot be converted to money credibly with minimum resources. They are still very important, and the forecast details which intangibles will be influenced by the project and to what extent. Obviously, this "calculation" is not as precise as the financial ROI calculation, but taken together, they represent two of the most important data sets that leaders or executive sponsors want to have.

This chapter also concludes the forecasting part of the book. Four chapters are devoted to this process and secure this book as an essential tool for project success. The eight data sets (reaction, learning, application, impact, monetary value, costs, financial ROI, and intangibles) represent powerful information to not only vision where the project is going, but also exhibit a clear, strategic advantage over others who choose not to forecast results. The next chapter focuses on how to guarantee success, as it explains how to take the forecast a step further and place guarantees around the delivery of the results.

11

How to Guarantee Success

Gathering momentum, your proposal through the previous chapters has chugged up a tall hill of client expectations. Your client reels with excitement the whole way, but finally looks down and wonders if perhaps this hill is too high for his or her project. What if you fail? It's a long way down.

Guaranteeing success for your project at this point is the perfect antidote for your client's preproject jitters, but what about yours? The concept of guaranteeing success for a project is, for many, both frightening and extremely rewarding. Many project organizers, consultants, and planners attribute this "frightening" factor to the perceived difficulty of doing this, even when in reality, it is not. It can be achieved and the risks can be controlled. Proposing a guarantee communicates the expected value and promises delivery. These days, with the continued focus on customer service, a guaranteed delivery is the ultimate weapon for all types of projects. This chapter explores how to guarantee success and the conditions that must be in place to make that guarantee. For the most part, no one suggests a promise without conditions, even those successful companies that forge triumphantly by guaranteeing their products. For them, putting some limits on that guarantee is essential.

WHAT'S WRONG WITH THE PRESENT APPROACH?

Presently, a myriad of issues inhibit the success approach to projects. While it's common to see projects taking too long and being over budget, the larger issue is the disappointing success they deliver. From the client's prospective, a project success guarantee is a refreshing thought and a desire they think cannot be fulfilled. From a project proposal team, it may seem like an impossible challenge. Fortunately, some teams are giving this approach a try.

Project failure

Many projects, if not most, deliver disappointing results. If this statement seems exaggerated, consider the projects in which you've been involved and the success of those projects. Were they successful in the eyes of the funder, sponsor, or client? Did they get what they wanted? Some do and others do not. Even those who think they have success are still left wondering about the value and whether there should be more. Unfortunately, in far too many cases, even the expectations are not delivered.

In our experience at the ROI Institute, many projects fail. About 20 to 30 percent of those projects delivered a negative ROI, although the sponsors thought they were successful. Another 30 to 40 percent had a positive ROI, but the client actually wanted more, and the project team could have taken actions to make it more successful. In the remainder of studies—those that are considered successful by all parties—barriers are identified that, if changed, could have made it even more successful.

When we analyze the reasons for lack of success (a more positive way to express project failure), the following usual suspects can be identified, ranked from the most often occurring reason for project failures to the least often:

1. Wrong solution or no need
2. No business alignment
3. Unspecific or missing objectives
4. Lack of focus on results
5. Lack of expectations

6. Lack of support
7. Inadequate measurement and feedback
8. Inadequate project management/controls

The number one reason for project failure is a two-part issue: The wrong solution has been requested for the problem, or the solution is just not needed. The individual requesting the project, whether it's a key executive, agency leader, or others in the organization, thinks this particular solution is needed, but many times, that is not actually the case. In reality, there has been little or no analysis that indicates that this particular solution will solve the problem or address the opportunity at hand. In other cases, the solution is looking for a problem. The "solution" is actually a favorite issue to address, a trend, based on the best-selling book, or another fad that motivates certain projects to be implemented. Yet, these solutions are really not needed or connected to anything that's going to drive success for the organization.

The second reason for project failure is very closely related to the first. No attempt is made to connect the project to specific impact measures that represent the major business needs. Whether it's a private company, public sector, nonprofit, or a nongovernment organization, business measures speak to the outputs, quality, time, incidents, accidents, and thousands of other measures in the system. These are the measures that often need to change or improve to generate success from the project. However, the projects are not always connected to those measures.

The third reason may surprise most individuals: the lack of objectives. Too often, the objectives are vague, nebulous, or missing, particularly at higher levels. Rarely do these projects have a very specific application or impact objectives, although often a business need is driving the project.

Number four on the list is the lack of focus on results throughout the project. It is important for all stakeholders to understand the result desired, the impact that's needed, or perhaps even the ROI that should be generated, if it's appropriate. Too often, they don't know and many ask questions, such as, "Why are we doing this project?" "Will this help the organization?" "How will this help me?" "How will this help anyone?"

Fifth on the list is lack of expectations on the part of the individual who will make it successful. These participants must use the software, apply the skills, or follow the new procedure. In many cases, these are "the worker bees" at the operational or professional level. In some projects, they just don't do what they're supposed to do. In many cases, they haven't been asked to, their expectations haven't clearly been defined, and their role in the project and success hasn't been communicated.

The sixth listed reason for failure is the lack of support from those executives, managers, and leaders whose support is necessary for the project to work. The initial lack of support is often the immediate manager of the participants, the worker bees. These managers can make the difference in success or failure, and, unfortunately, their support is not required, expected, or managed through the process.

Inadequate measurement and feedback through the process is listed as the seventh reason. A dynamic measurement system must exist so that adjustments or changes can be made along the way. Almost every project will go off track at some point, and unless data indicates what must be done to put it back on track, it will not be successful. In far too many cases, the key sponsor does not know about a project failure until everything is over and it's too late to make any adjustments.

Finally, the last reason is inadequate project management or control. Most people think that this is the number one reason for failure because of the tremendous emphasis on all types of project management tools and controls. Unfortunately, though it's on the list, it's not the most critical one, but still serious.

With these failures affecting so many projects, the project team must take action to create changes. The actions described in this book can help.

The blame game

Sadly, when there's a lack of success, people are blamed. Sometimes it's the client or sponsor blaming the project leaders for not delivering the value that they suggested. Others blame the entire firm or organization that delivered the project as being inadequate or incapable of delivering the project. The project leaders (if it's an external provider) blame others in the system, pointing to many of the reasons for failure described above. Still others blame serious flaws that, from the beginning, doomed the project for failure. Sometimes, consultants may be aware beforehand of this disastrous outcome, but didn't want to kill the project because they needed the income. In too many cases, we've heard consultants say that their project is a failure, but they were going to continue with it so that they could complete the billing cycle and obtain all the fees. After all, they are following the schedule of deliverables. Others complain that the wrong individuals were involved in the project, the timing was off, or the technology didn't work. There is more than enough blame to go around. Unfortunately, if we own the project, after winning the proposal, we are responsible for its success.

Miscues, miscommunications, and misfits

This dialogue on project failures and blame leads to some very important conclusions. The first is that many miscommunications occur throughout the process, and these lead to a lack of understanding of the roles, responsibilities, and expectations. Miscues pollute the project along the way, such as not taking action when needed, not challenging when it's necessary, and not knowing precisely what to do. A few misfits on both sides of the project create problems as well.

Sometimes a sponsor wants a particular project completed when it's not needed. Some projects are more politically necessary, ignoring the business needs. Some projects feed the egos of executives. On the project leadership side, some individuals are more interested in getting the fees than delivering the service. To them, project success is defined as racking up the hours and getting paid.

The time and materials mindset

Disappointingly, many projects are priced based on the time invested by consultants and project team members on the project, as well as the number of items that may be in the deliverables section. Time has evolved into the dominant pricing model. Many professions almost always use time and materials as a basis for pricing, such as lawyers, accountants, architects, or maybe professional engineers, for example. Time is easy to measure. The time it takes to complete something can be reasonably judged unless it's an unknown area for the client. This has become a traditional way of how consulting firm revenues grow, and profitability to the partners flourishes. Almost every consulting firm is trying to increase the percent of time billed to clients. The goal is to build more time and at higher fees, and thus, raise the revenues and profits of the firm.

Obviously, while this may be necessary in some projects, it is beginning to diminish in its necessity. It's on the way out, being replaced with flat fees. The ideal way to bill time is to try to forget this "marking" method entirely and move more to delivering value and results instead. See Nathan Koppel and Ashby Jones, "Billable Hour under Attack," *Wall Street Journal*, August 24, 2009, p. A1.

Fear of a promise

Perhaps the greatest reason why the success guarantee concept hasn't worked is a fear of promising it. There's a fear of not being able to deliver, fear of not being able to control, and a fear that this project is really not that valuable. The material in this chapter can speak to the first two. The delivery is addressed in the proposal, particularly in the forecasting, methodology, and approach. The fear of control can be addressed in the conditions placed around the guarantee. Fear of the value that's actually delivered by the service is beyond the scope of this book. If what we're doing is not adding value at the impact level, then it is impossible to guarantee success at that level.

At the ROI Institute, we encountered an interesting example with a coaching firm based in the northeastern United States. The head of the firm reviewed the process described in this book and concluded that there's no way that he would try to forecast success of his project and guarantee results. He said, "I'm afraid I'd never get business because I don't think what I'm doing adds business value, and therefore, something to guarantee the business value would be a disaster for my business. My business would collapse." When we asked whether his service was sold as a way to add business value, his quick answer was, "Yes." However, he was not convinced that it did. Our advice was to either change careers or the process because he was offering a fraudulent service of promising business value but not being capable of delivering it.

THE BENEFITS OF A GUARANTEED PROMISE

Just imagine that we forecast the eight types of data stated in the previous four chapters and add a guarantee to deliver at certain levels, including impact and ROI. Because of that, the forecast and guarantee processes are put in place to ensure that actions occur as planned. The expectations are met. The conditions are met. A bonus is paid because the guarantee is exceeded. If that scenario could occur, what would it mean to you and your projects? Some benefits are rather obvious and others are subtler.

More project successes

No one would disagree with the statement that if the above was a routine process, there would be more project successes. With more successes, clients are more pleased, and the individuals working on the projects are more pleased. The owners of those firms supplying the projects are more pleased. Project successes make all the stakeholders happy. Everyone wants to be connected to a winner.

Less waste

This approach reduces inefficiencies and waste. It helps avoid things that don't matter and irrelevant activities, or perhaps it helps prevent the wrong solution. Time is often wasted on tasks done improperly because no one knows that it's the wrong task. We sometimes focus on a low-value activity instead of high-value activities. When the cost for an ROI calculation is forecasted, these costs have to be managed and controlled, not just by the consulting firm, but by every area where there will be a cost. Otherwise, the guarantee cannot exist. When costs are controlled, a project produces less waste. Multiply waste reductions on a number of projects, and the numbers can be mind-boggling.

Win more projects

From a proposal perspective, having a forecast and a success guarantee will win more projects. This may not occur every time, but the success rate can easily double, as we've heard from colleagues.

Some firms have established their business on guaranteeing success. For example, a New York firm, A.T. Hudson, bases its fees on the percentage of savings generated, which essentially, guarantees success. If there's no success, there's no fee. This is a strategic advantage to win more business and positions your project or proposal apart from others. Even if you don't win the project, you'll receive plenty of questions about your forecasts and guarantee. Also, the term *ROI* always stirs up questions and discussions. If you don't get one particular project, you'll be considered as a candidate in the future because of your focus on results. Ultimately, you win more with this approach than without it.

Reputation and branding

You make a statement by placing forecasts and a success guarantee in the proposal, even if it's in a very difficult area. This action will win points with the sponsor, the ultimate decision maker. Eventually, when forecasting and success guarantees become an important part of what you do, it enhances your reputation and improves your brand of delivering results. Many consulting firms focus on results and have a reputation for delivering results. They measure the results and are very proud of the value they deliver for their clients. However, not all of them actually go to the point of forecasting the value and guaranteeing the success. When they make that extra leap, they enhance their reputation and branding.

Firm success: revenues and profits

If the organization bidding on the project is a profit-making firm, then this approach can generate tremendous increases in revenues and profits, particularly if the success includes an option to be paid more when the project achieves the targets. Some projects deliver incredible value, and the firm has no way of capturing that extra value except by having a more satisfied client. A success guarantee with a bonus option is a way to capture that extra value to add to the revenue stream and ultimately, the profit stream for the partners or owners of the firm.

WHAT MUST CHANGE

The current approach to project value has to change. The number of projects is increasing, expenditures are growing, and yet expectations and delivery are not improving. The changes are not that dramatic, and they involve the several elements outlined here.

Customer service promise

We live in a customer service–oriented economy. We have created standards for customer service that, in turn, yield expectations. If customers aren't satisfied, they complain and demand improvements until they are satisfied. The more progressive, successful companies know this and start with a promise of guaranteeing customer satisfaction. The term *satisfaction guarantee* shows up in almost every type of business, but when it comes to consulting, it's rarely there. Firms are reluctant to guarantee success. They argue, "This is a very soft process. It's hard to define success. After all, most of the reason for lack of success is beyond our control." These are primarily excuses and not defensible reasons for ignoring the satisfaction guarantee.

For almost two decades, our firm has had a satisfaction guarantee provision in our proposals. If a client is not satisfied with the services we've delivered, there's no payment of the invoice or reimbursement for our direct expenses. So far, with almost two decades of service and hundreds of projects, we've never had to destroy an invoice or return funds. A satisfaction guarantee keeps everyone's focus on the needs of the customer, ensuring that these needs are clearly defined, met, and often exceeded. Our philosophy is "underpromise and overdeliver" so that the client is pleasantly surprised instead of persistently dissatisfied. Having this as an arrangement keeps every person focused on customer service, from the support team to the individual consultants on the project. When a contract consultant is used, they clearly understand that client dissatisfaction means that they do not get paid for the project. In short, this profession needs more focus on this type of delivery.

The concept of value

As discussed in Chapter 1, values have different meanings depending on different perspectives; the definition of value is often changing or evolving. The following example describes the problems that occur when a project team focuses on the wrong set of values.

A well-respected leadership development firm proposed to implement a leadership development project involving managers in a publicly owned broadcasting company in Europe. The project deliverables consisted of enrolling almost 4,000 managers in a five-day leadership program and providing a workbook and reference guide during the sessions. Based on the proposal, the measure of success was conducting these programs and providing each person with a copy of the workbook. Senior executives accepted the proposal, but it was not the value that they preferred. They, like many other executives, are concerned about business results. When the project was almost complete, a new CEO of the company asked about the business contribution of the programs. There were no results, because the project team had no plan to deliver anything other than training (and perhaps capture some reaction to the training). In this case, the real "results" left the executives dissatisfied and the firm was banned from doing business with the organization again. The leadership development team was dissolved because of the perception that they had wasted a tremendous amount of money. Yet, even with this consequence, the perspective of the team that delivered the project was that it was successful. After all, they delivered the deliverables. The concept of value has changed. Table 11.1 shows the value chain of impact conducted with every type of project.

As this table describes, there is a chain of impact, which moves from inputs to the ultimate evaluation, ROI. Along the process, various stakeholders react to the project (Level 1). They learn what to do to make it successful (Level 2). They apply or use the project tools, procedures, and processes (Level 3). The consequence is a business impact (Level 4), and when a business impact is converted to money, and compared to the cost of the project; ROI is calculated (Level 5).

Table 11.1. The value chain.*

LEVEL	MEASUREMENT FOCUS	TYPICAL MEASURES
0. Inputs ↓	Inputs into the project including indicators representing the scope of the project	Types of projects Number of projects Number of people Hours of involvement Cost of projects
1. Reaction ↓	Reaction to the project including the perceived value tof the project	Relevance Importance Usefulness Appropriateness Fairness Motivational skills
2. Learning ↓	Learning how to use the project, content, materials, and system, including the confidence to use what was learned	Knowledge Capacity Competencies Confidences Contacts
3. Application ↓	Use of project content, materials, and system in the work environment, including progress with implementation	Extent of use Task completion Frequency of use Actions completed Success with use Barriers to use Enablers to use
4. Impact	The consequences of the use of the project content, materials, and system	Productivity Revenue Quality

Table 11.1. The value chain* *(continued)*.

LEVEL	MEASUREMENT FOCUS	TYPICAL MEASURES
↓	expressed as business impact measures	Time Efficiency Customer satisfaction Employee engagement
5. ROI	Comparison of monetary benefits from project to project costs	Benefit-cost ratio (BCR) ROI (%) Payback period

*Source: Jack J. Phillips and Patricia Pulliam Phillips. *Show Me the Money: How to Determine ROI in People, Projects, and Programs*. San Francisco: Berrett-Koehler Publishers, 2007.

Obviously, from the perspective of the funder, sponsor, or client, they are most interested in application impact and ROI. In the previous example of the failed project in the European broadcasting company, the focus was on inputs (Level 0) with no regard for the outcomes of the project.

Deliver more value

Inherent in the previous section is the suggestion that projects must deliver more value than was promised, and the project must be pushed to higher levels of evaluation, which begins with forecasting. Projects must move from focusing entirely or obsessively on the activity to focusing on results. Table 11.2 contrasts this activity-based approach to a project to the results-based approach. Each point requires the project team to focus constantly on design, development, delivery, implementation, and measurement with higher levels of results, typically impact and occasionally ROI. This shift means that we must focus on the outcomes, not what we put into the process.

Table 11.2. Activity vs. results: A paradigm shift in projects.

ACTIVITY-BASED PROJECTS ARE CHARACTERIZED BY	RESULTS-BASED PROJECTS ARE CHARACTERIZED BY
No need for the project	Project linked to specific business needs
No assessment of performance issues	Assessment of performance effectiveness
No specific measurable objectives	Specific objectives for application and business impact
No effort to prepare project participants to achieve results	Result expectations communicated to participants
No effort to prepare the work environment to support project	Environment prepared to support project
No efforts to build partnerships with key managers who influence the project	Partnerships established with key managers and clients
No measurement of results or ROI	Measurement of results or ROI
Reporting on projects that is input focused	Reporting on projects that is output focused

Investment versus costs

Externally, projects of this nature are regarded as investments. Internally, when a company spends millions of dollars a year on consulting, it's referred to a "consulting cost" or "expense." Few, if any, would describe consulting as an investment. However, if the cost is designed to deliver a return on investment, it becomes an investment on the part of the client and should be presented and described that way. Figure 11.1 shows the cost versus the investment approach

Figure 11.1. Investment versus costs.

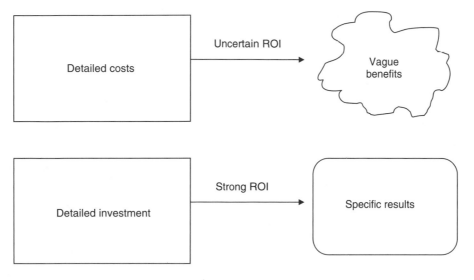

Adapted from Weiss (2008).

to consulting. When efforts are focused on very clearly defined costs, the ROI as an outcome is very vague or nonexistent. With an investment perspective, the cost is considered to be an investment that yields an acceptable ROI, which is known or predicted with credibility. Shifting the mindset from costs to the concept of investment with a return on the investment is an important way to approach a project.

Expanding the deliverables

As described earlier, the deliverables are those pesky things that we list in our proposal, often directly from the RFP, detailing what we must provide at the end of the project. Often, a deliverable is something tangible, such as a report on a person attending a program, the number of people involved in the project, the hours of involvement, a system installed, a procedure in place, etc. For the most part, many of the deliverables are inputs, yet as this chapter has already described, the focus must be on higher levels of data—impact and, possibly, ROI.

Consider the example illustrated in Table 11.3. This project involves the launch of a new automobile in Europe. An external firm with experience in these types of events was selected to launch the new vehicle. The launch involved meeting with a sales representative to present all the features and benefits of the new automobile and to show how to sell it to the customers. The old way this firm approached the deliverables is shown on the left side of the table, detailing the specific inputs into the process. The new way lists deliverables with impact, monetary value, and ROI.

As described in this book, deliverables can be listed for other levels in the evaluation as well. Instead of ensuring the input, the firm showed what would come out of the process, forecasting that 500 cars would be sold was directly attributable to the launch. This approach is unique when considering this type of promotion. Several factors influence the decision to purchase the new auto, such as features of the new car, pricing, and competition. Essentially, sales reps indicated the percent of sales that would be directly related to the

Table 11.3. Expanding the deliverables.

DELIVERABLES (OLD)	DELIVERABLES (NEW)
25 locations covered	500 autos sold in first year attributed to the launch meetings
1,200 sales representatives attended	€ 550,000 in profits generated because of the projects
25 one-day launches conducted	53 percent ROI
7,200 hours of individual content delivered	
Cost €300 per sales representative	

product launch. This translates into a profit of € 550,000 in the first year, and a 53 percent ROI. Obviously, these deliverables are more attention getting, more powerful, and probably would make the difference in getting the project. Is it possible? Yes. To achieve a guaranteed success means that the forecast must be developed as described in the previous four chapters. These forecasts are not that difficult to achieve and involve collecting data from the appropriate expert inputs. They are fundamental to a success guarantee.

The guarantee must be provided in a very clear, understandable way. It should be written as a win-win by describing success at the different forecast levels. With any guarantee, there are conditions necessary for it to be valid. Deviations from the conditions could jeopardize the guarantee, and, in some cases, void the guarantee altogether. The next sections focus on the guarantee and the conditions.

THE GUARANTEE

Writing the guarantee into the proposal, which indicates the specific measures and their amount, is very important. The stakes are high; errors at this point could mean disaster for the project if it were to fail. For example, in the previous situation involving the product launch of automobiles, a number less than 500 would mean that the project missed its forecast. This expectation requires the firm to be very knowledgeable about what they can do, and the impact it will have in the sales. Obtaining that knowledge can come from previous experience, following logical, sequential processes or asking a variety of experts. Here are some possibilities.

Start with the forecast

The obvious starting point is the forecasts, which have been described in the previous four chapters. These forecast amounts are based on what can be achieved, and these can be the guarantee. However, to be safe, project teams often guarantee something less than the forecast. After all, there's error in the forecast, and although ideally, the perceived error has been taken out of the forecast, there is still some uncertainty in the process. Therefore, having a guarantee number less than the forecasted amount would be appropriate.

Review the importance of the measures

It's helpful to review what's most important to a client. A particular client or sponsor has certain data sets that are very important to them. What are their particular hot buttons? What are their critical issues? Here, it's helpful to assist the client to think outside of the box. In their previous types of projects the project pricing was based on time and materials. They have seen inputs (hours) actually being listed as outcomes to the project. Therefore, it might be helpful to review the importance of data from the executive position. Table 11.4 shows the value of different types of data from the viewpoint of executives. In a study conducted by the ROI Institute, the data was taken directly from

Table 11.4. The executive view.

MEASURE	RANK*
Inputs (volume)	6
Efficiency (costs)	7
Reaction	8
Learning	5
Application	4
Impact	1
ROI	2
Intangibles	3

*CEO's ranking of the importance of this measure.

96 CEOs of large companies, where they were asked to rank the importance of certain data sets. From this example, it's clear to see that impact, ROI, and intangibles are the most important data sets. Inputs, efficiencies, reaction, and learning are not so important.

Guaranteeing application

For some projects, guaranteeing certain application data is beneficial and particularly important when an application can be observed or monitored. For example, a project involving the implementation of software, the application is an important issue. In the forecast, 80 percent of the people involved in the project would be using at least 50 percent of the features of the software within six months. The guaranteed amount was 70 percent, or slightly less than the forecast amount. This data is easily measured systematically in the software itself. It's an important measure that should lead to success at the impact level of project times, budgets, and quality.

Guaranteeing impact

For some clients, it's helpful to focus on the impact measure: the consequence. This is perhaps the most important data for project owners and program sponsors, those who want to see improvement in one or more business measures. For example, in a project to reduce the number of teenage pregnancies, the forecast would guarantee a certain decrease in the teenage pregnancy rate in a given area where the project is being implemented. This amount may represent a reduction of annual teenage pregnancies by 5 percent, which would be directly attributable to the project.

Guaranteeing ROI

Perhaps the most impressive and exciting guarantee for a client is the ROI. This is also the guaranteed measure that creates the most anxiety for project leaders and proposal writers. What should that number be? The expression, "I can make ROI be anything I want it to be" suggests that the assumptions alter the ROI very considerably. Consequently, to use ROI as a reliable forecast measure and attach a guarantee to the value, it must follow assumptions that are credible and consistent.

The first set of assumptions involves the costs—not only the cost of the project, which is detailed in the proposal, but the cost of the project itself. The list that follows contains the cost assumptions presented in Chapter 9, where the costs included must have a credible ROI calculation, and, in this case, a credible forecast.

Typical cost assumptions are:
- Needs assessment and analysis
- Development costs
- Equipment/technology costs
- Project materials
- Project management
- Facilities costs
- Travel/lodging/meals
- Consultant costs
- Participants' time (salaries and benefits)
- Administrative/overhead costs
- Operating/maintenance costs
- Evaluation costs

These cost assumptions should be detailed as specifically as possible for the project. After all, a success guarantee is hanging on these assumptions. Here it is more critical to have the costs clearly detailed, because much of the costs of the project are outside of the control of the consulting firm or the organization providing the project. It is important to nail down those other costs or at least make assumptions so that they are clearly stated in the guarantee. Along with the costs are the assumptions made in developing the actual monetary benefits, and ultimately, the ROI calculation. These were described, to a certain extent, in Chapter 9, but are listed again here as guiding principles:

1. When collecting and analyzing data, use only the most credible sources.
2. When analyzing data, select the most conservative alternative for calculations.
3. Estimates of improvement should be adjusted for the potential error of the estimate.
4. Extreme data items and unsupported claims should not be used in ROI calculations.
5. Only the first year of benefits (annual) should be used in the ROI analysis of short-term solutions.
6. Project costs should be fully loaded for ROI analysis.
7. Intangible measures are defined as measures that are purposely not converted to monetary values.

These rules must be followed to ensure that the ROI calculation is first conservative and then consistent. A conservative approach is needed to secure an agreement and get the parties to buy into the final number. Consistency is needed from one project to another so that the ROI values can be compared. These assumptions focus primarily on the conservative nature of using the lowest values in the benefits calculation.

PAYOUT OPTIONS

Now comes the fun part—the payout based on the guarantee, or in some cases, lack of it. Here are the decisions that have to be made regarding how the guarantee amount will work. If the guarantee target is not met, will there be no payment at all? And when the actual amount exceeds the guaranteed target, is a promise arrangement possible? Several options are available.

No success—no charge

When offering a guarantee, the ultimate accountability is that there is no charge if the targets are not met. If success is defined by a specific goal to be achieved, and it's not met, then the client is dissatisfied. Thus a satisfaction guarantee would provide a complete refund or the invoice is canceled.

Although this method seems harsh, it's a concept that has been around for years. For example, we recently encountered a situation at a Marriot Hotel. During our last stay at the hotel, we left a FedEx package to be picked up for delivery the next day. We had checked the pick-up time and left the package two hours before the scheduled pick up. This package was very important because it had a proposal that had to be in the very next day. We checked out the next day and discovered through the FedEx tracking system that the package had never been picked up the day before. When we called the hotel to explain our problem to the general manager, he was very understanding and apologetic. He quickly offered three actions to rectify the situation. First, there would be no charge for our stay. Second, he would pick up the charge of the package as it was missing its deadline. Third, he would write a personal note to the organization receiving the package, stating that the late delivery was entirely his staff's fault. We took him up on all three points and continue to stay at Marriot chain hotels.

This concept of a satisfied customer or there's no payment, is inherent in many types of services and industries, but hasn't moved to the consulting business to a significant extent. Two issues usually stand in the way. The first is that consulting projects often have large amounts—more than a couple of nights' stay in a hotel. The amount can be very staggering to a company with much at stake. Second, there's a concern that much of the success is out of the control of the team delivering the project.

The good news is that a project team can structure the payment to minimize the blow if a large project isn't delivered. More importantly, there are ways to structure the conditions so that the issues that may be out of control would invalidate the service agreement. This is covered in the next section.

No success—no fees

Perhaps an easier variation of this approach would be to donate the team's time for providing the service if the guarantee is not met. In other words, the client would still pay all expenses and external charges to other organizations, although the guarantee is not met. The direct fees of the project team, the work of the firm providing the service, would not be charged to the client. This method is reasonable.

Target met—full payment

When the target is met, a full payment of the fee is owed, as this is the traditional way a consulting project works. When the goal is met, everyone is happy; the firm receives the full fees outlined in the proposal process. This is the desired goal for all parties.

Bonus payment possibilities

Perhaps the greatest upside potential is bonus arrangements that can come out of the consulting project when the success exceeds the guaranteed amount. Figure 11.2 shows the payouts from one example. In this case, the payment is based on the ROI achieved six months after the program is implemented. The first amount is a 5 percent ROI. If that number is not achieved, there is no charge at all. If the ROI is less than 12 percent but greater than 5 percent, there is full payment. If the project exceeds the 12 percent ROI and reaches 20 percent, a fourth of the additional net monetary benefits of the project is paid as a bonus. Therefore, if 20 percent ROI is

Figure 11.2. An example of payout formulas.

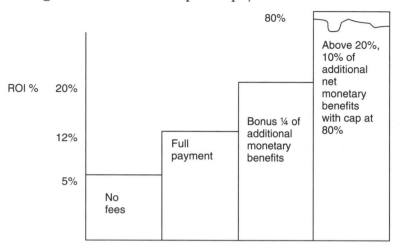

achieved, this is equivalent to a fourth of the difference between 12 and 20 percent, or 8 percent, or a 2 percent ROI. Above the 20 percent, 10 percent of the additional net monetary benefits is paid with a cap at 80 percent. Thus if 80 percent is achieved, the 10 percent of the amount exceeding 20 percent is achieved. For a project costing $1 million, a 20 percent ROI will result in full payment, plus a $20,000 bonus. If an 80 percent ROI is achieved, the bonus is $60,000. If there were no cap and the project achieved a 700 percent ROI, the bonus would be $680,000.

The important issue is that a bonus be constructed so that it is fair for all parties—a win-win agreement. It should be simple enough so that it is easy to understand and calculate, as well as reward superior performance, which is the basis of beating the target.

Shared profits

Another approach is to consider a profit-sharing arrangement for a project. With this arrangement, after a threshold of a guaranteed measure is achieved, the project fee is covered in full, and a profit-sharing arrangement is in place for any of the remaining benefits above that. Profit sharing can be established in a 50/50 arrangement, but often is more conservative with the firm providing the project taking a smaller amount, such as 75 percent for the funding firm, and 25 percent for the providing firm. There are variations of profit sharing, but the concept is appropriate.

Timing

Several timing issues must be considered when calculating the actual ROI on a postproject basis and calculating the financial payout. The first is the timing for data collection. In every project, there's a time when impact occurs. In many projects, it can be as early as three weeks (for new technology), several months, or four years for complex change management. For example, if a software program is implemented to increase sales from the sales team, it may take a month for the software to be put in place, another month for it to be fully utilized, and then two more months for it to generate the impact. Thus three months from the end of the project is the time to collect the impact data.

The next time period is how long the benefits stream would exist. This is one of the guiding principles mentioned earlier and is the conservative—the key word—life of a project. For many projects, one year of impact data is appropriate. For others, it may be two years, and still others, three, four, or five years. The longest the ROI Institute has observed on any project is seven years. The key is to use the conservative input.

CONDITIONS

The most critical part of this chapter is the conditions on which the guarantee is made. Conditions must be addressed properly to make the guarantee work. Almost anyone offering a guarantee will quickly say, "But it's out of my control." "I can't control all of the factors," or "Success is not in my hands." Certain factors often do influence the success of a project. Almost all of these are outside of the influence of the project team; in fact, most of the reasons for project failure are not the project team itself, but other factors. These are factors that are either inherent or dysfunctional in the beginning of a project or caused by those who fail to do what is necessary to make the project successful. Here are some of the key conditions.

Analyze the cause for failure

The starting point for determining which conditions to address is to consider the reasons for failure. Here, the project team asks the questions, "What can make this project go wrong?" "What can occur that can make this project not work?" The team can quickly generate a list of possibilities, and with additional thought and discussion, the number can grow to 15 items, which can make a difference.

The second part of the exercise is to ask "How can we describe this as a condition?" For example, a classic reason for failure is lack of management support. How can we determine if management support is there? A precise indicator or measure is needed to decide if that condition has been met. The concept is very straightforward: Certain conditions that must exist for the guarantee to be valid are identified. If those conditions are not met, the guarantee is void.

Some common sense has to be used in situations such as a project that has 15 conditions and only one of them is not met; here the guarantee can continue. It may be that the conditions are used only if the success is not there. If success is generated, then the conditions are not necessarily considered in the analysis. However, the conditions are there for the protection for the project team for factors that are out of their control. This protection is the only fair approach for the firm providing the project.

The right solution

Too often a project RFP is written asking for bids to implement a solution. This solution has already been determined by the organization and the proposal focuses on implementation of that solution. However, if that's not the right solution, then obviously, success will not materialize for this project. The condition that needs to be addressed first is this issue: "Is it the right solution?" The realization of having the wrong solution often occurs or becomes obvious in the implementation. The particular measure of this condition may be that the project team members are surveyed earlier, and they all have indicated that this is not what is necessary. Perhaps another measure is that when it's implemented and didn't work, and the survey asks why it didn't work, and one of the options to check is "It's the wrong solution." Fortunately, some projects are based on the project team actually finding the solution. In these cases, this condition for success cannot be used because it is part of the project.

The right people

Many times, a project is not successful because the wrong people are involved. The individuals who are there to make it work must be available and participating in the project. For software implementation, it's the people who use the software. For a quality project, it's the people whose quality measures improve. For a project designed to prevent a particular disease in an area, it's the people who must implement the prevention for the disease. The point is that these individuals are the "worker bees," those who must make the project successful by their involvement. Otherwise, the guarantee could be void.

The right timing

Some projects fail because they are too late, too early, or somehow missed the timing. Most projects must be implemented on a particular schedule that is agreed to previously. If that timing is missed, then the guarantee may be voided. The measures are the specific dates that are critical to project success. These are listed in the guarantee section of the proposal.

The appropriate costs

Appropriate timing is a huge issue because of the many costs outside of the project costs that could determine the success of the project. For example, the involvement of all the participants represents a tremendous cost for their time and expenses. These are usually not part of the project cost, and therefore, they must be considered in the cost schedule for the ROI calculation.

An example is a project involving the organization of a business development conference for a group of salespeople. This project includes the design, development, and planning of the conference. Project costs are clearly listed in the proposal. However, there are additional costs of individuals traveling to the conference, and their time away from their normal work as well as even more costs. These have to be considered in the overall project. However, these costs are completely out of the control of the project team and thus, must be spelled out in the proposal. The ROI forecast calculation must include all of these costs, so the amount that's estimated is agreed to as a calculation, and if exceeded, then the guarantee is void.

The right expectations

Expectations are for the project participants and other key stakeholders. Expectations drive results, and when participants have a clear direction as to where they are going through the expectations, they often step up to the challenge and deliver. Certain expectations must be created before and during the project. Expectations are created through meetings, memos, interviews, role descriptions, and project descriptions. Absent these expectations, the project success guarantee could be void.

Responsibilities fulfilled

Sometimes project participants and other key stakeholders don't meet their responsibilities, and the project is a failure. Two very important issues should be addressed. The first issue is the responsibilities of the client, the individual who sponsored the project, and the client team. They must take the same action to make the project successful. They must provide access, facilities, and support. They set the stage for success, and if they don't, the success guarantee could be void. This condition for success is measured by simply listing all responsibilities on the part of the client, knowing that deviating from any of these may be enough to make the success guarantee void. Obviously, the project team must use common sense because it may be just the key actions that make a difference.

The second issue is the responsibilities of others, such as vendors, suppliers, or contract labor involved in the project. For example, if technology is used, a delay, a quality problem, or a technical glitch could be a factor in project success, which can also void the success guarantee.

Opportunities to use

Project participants must be able to use what's implemented. A classic problem is that when the system is put in place, the people who must use it don't have the connection or the computer to make it work. They must have the opportunity to use and be allowed to use what is being provided. Otherwise, the success guarantee could be void. What must be provided is listed.

Supportive management

Another vital issue is how well this project is supported by an appropriate manager. When management perceives this project as not important or necessary, then the project participants involved do not take it seriously either. Management support can be defined in very specific ways, and if that support is not there, then the success guarantee could be void. One of the easiest ways to understand this support is to survey the participants involved and ask them to rank the level of management support (e.g., on a five-point scale). If management support is below a certain level, then the success guarantee is void.

All or part

The list of conditions must include those conditions that are definitely guarantee killers, those that can void the guarantee. The consulting company (or the firm implementing the project) must use judgment and common sense here. While they must be spelled out and addressed, too much detail or rigidity makes it appear that the success guarantee may never be met. After all, there is no perfect implementation; there are always glitches along the way. A common sense approach suggests that the success guarantee still works, even if some of these conditions are not met. However, a culmination of several missed conditions could be significant enough to void the success guarantee.

The following list gives an example of the conditions that could be included in a project for designing, developing, and planning a business development conference. The conditions for the success guarantee to be valid have their own page in the proposal. Usually proposal items are referenced in the conditions.

Conditions for a success guarantee for a business development conference are:
Attendance: The project is based on 600 individuals attending.
Audience: At least 95 percent of the attendees are sales

representatives, and at least 55 percent of the sales representatives are in attendance.

Timing: This conference will be conducted in February, as planned.

Prior Communication: The participants must have the objectives of the conference at four levels (reaction, learning, application, impact) sent to them prior to the conference. Also, the expectation for action plans should be communicated to them in advance as well as their specific role in achieving results.

Speakers: All speakers will attend as planned, and each speaker will address application and impact objectives in their sessions.

Costs: The costs are fully loaded and detailed in the proposal as complete project costs. The assumptions for those costs are included, and the ROI is based on the cost assumptions. These are the costs that will be used to calculate the ROI.

Review Action Plans: Action plans must be reviewed in the session at the end of the conference. Sample action plans will be distributed, and at least 15 minutes of discussion will be allocated to the process.

Tactics for Response Rate: Use 10 of the 12 techniques.

District Manager Support: Sales representatives will be asked three questions related to district manager support. This is on a one to five scale and a composite of the three must be at least four out of the five for management support to be adequate.

Support Material: Materials must be planted, distributed, and explained at the conference.

Product Launch: The new product associated with this conference must be launched just prior to the conference.

Keeping this project sensible and recognizing the value of this gesture is important. By proposing a success guarantee, your proposal is set apart from the others. The process of guaranteeing success, along with clear communication and agreements within client discussions, will have immense value in terms of reputation and branding for future projects. In sum, make sure you don't kill the process with exhaustive fine print and overdone details.

FINAL THOUGHTS

This chapter attempts to address what few have done before, detailing what's necessary to guarantee the success of projects. This chapter follows the four chapters involving forecasts, because the forecast of value, along with eight categories of data, is an excellent basis to develop a success guarantee. Using the most important measures, guarantee amounts are established, often using a number below the actual forecast. The success guarantee is developed with expert input. The conditions under which the success guarantee is paid are detailed also with expert input. These conditions are perhaps the most important part because they identify those factors that are out of the control of the project team. With this approach, the project team and clients all have the opportunity to have a win-win arrangement and complete satisfaction. The next chapter focuses on a case study, showing how the processes in this book are addressed.

12

Federal Information Agency: Project Proposal

SITUATION ANALYSIS

The Federal Information Agency (FIA) provides various types of information to other government agencies and businesses as well as state and local organizations, agencies, and interested groups. Operating through a network across the United States, the work is performed by several hundred communication specialists with backgrounds in systems, computer science, electrical engineering, and information science. Almost all the specialists have bachelor's degrees in one of these fields. The headquarters and operation center is in the Washington, D.C. area, where about 1,500 of these specialists are employed.

The FIA has recently experienced two problems that have senior agency officials concerned. The first problem is an unacceptable rate of employee turnover for this group of specialists—averaging 38 percent in the past year alone. This has placed a strain on the agency to recruit and train replacements. An analysis of exit interviews indicated that employees leave primarily for higher salaries. Because the FIA is somewhat constrained in providing competitive salaries, it has become extremely difficult to compete with the private sector for salaries and benefits. Although salary increases and adjustments in pay levels will be necessary to lower turnover, the FIA is exploring other options in the interim.

The second problem concerns the need to continuously update the technical skills of the staff. While the vast majority of the 1,500 specialists have degrees in various fields, only a few have master's degrees in their specialty. In this field, formal education is quickly outdated. The annual feedback survey with employees reflected a strong interest in an internal master's degree program in information science.

Consequently, the FIA is exploring the implementation of an in-house master's degree in information science to be implemented at no cost to the participating employee and conducted on the agency's time during routine work hours. Designed to address both employee turnover and skill updates, the program would typically take three years for participants to complete. A reputable university with outstanding faculty must offer the program. The faculty must be willing and able to secure a top-secret security clearance.

PROPOSED APPROACH

The proposed approach is principally taken from the RFP, which indicated how the program should work and be managed throughout the process. However, we have included our recommendations for some additional issues to make the project even more successful.

Regional State University should be selected for the master's program because of its reputation and the match of their curriculum to FIA needs. The proposed program allows participants to take one or two courses per semester. A two-course-per-semester schedule (with one course in the summer session) will take three years to complete. Both morning and afternoon classes are available, each representing

Table 12.1. Master of science in information science (typical 3-year schedule).

	YEAR 1	YEAR 2	YEAR 3
Fall	2 Courses – 6 hours	2 Courses – 6 hours	2 Courses – 6 hours
Spring	2 Courses – 6 hours	2 Courses – 6 hours	2 Courses – 6 hours
Summer	1 Course – 3 hours	1 Course – 3 hours	1 Course – 3 hours
		Graduate Project – 3 hours	Graduate Project – 3 hours

Graduate project: 6 hours (3 hours year 2; 3 hours year 3)
Total semester hours: 48

three hours per week of class time. Participants will be discouraged from taking more than two courses per term. Although a thesis option is normally available, the FIA would require a graduate project for six hours of credit as a substitute for the thesis. Under this arrangement, a professor will supervise the project. Designed to add value to the FIA, the project would be applied to the agency's problems and issues and would not be as rigorous as the thesis. Participants will register for three hours in the second and third year of the program.

Classes will be usually offered live with professors visiting the agency's center. Occasionally, classes will be offered through video-conferencing or independent study. Participants will be asked to prepare for classroom activities on their own time but will be allowed to attend classes on the agency's time. A typical three-year schedule is shown in Table 12.1.

MASTER OF SCIENCE IN INFORMATION SCIENCE

With senior management approval, the curriculum can be ready in six months. The program will represent a mix of courses normally offered in the program and others specially selected for FIA staff. Two new courses will be designed by university faculty to be included in the curriculum. These two courses represent a slight modification of existing courses and are tailored to the communication requirements of the agency. Appendix A presents a description of the courses. (Note: The contents of the appendixes in this example of a proposal are not provided.) Elective courses are not allowed for two reasons. First, it would complicate the offering to a certain extent, requiring additional courses, facilities, and professors—essentially adding cost to the program. Second, the FIA wanted a prescribed, customized curriculum that would add value to the agency, while still meeting the requirements of the university.

Selection criteria

An important issue involves the selection of employees to attend the program. Most employees who voluntarily left the agency resigned within the first four years and were often considered to be high potential employees. With this in mind, the following criteria are suggested for identifying and selecting the employees to enroll in the program:

1. A candidate should have at least one year of service prior to beginning classes.
2. A candidate must meet the normal requirements to be accepted into the graduate school at the university.
3. A candidate must be willing to sign a commitment to continue employment with the agency for two years beyond program completion.
4. A candidate's immediate manager must nominate the employee for consideration.
5. A candidate must be considered "high potential" as rated by the immediate manager.

The management team should receive information on the program and be kept informed of its development and progress prior to actual launch. Management briefings should be conducted to describe the program. The selection should be based on objective criteria, following the suggested guidelines. At the same time, managers should be asked to provide feedback as to the level of interest and specific issues surrounding the nomination of candidates.

A limit of 100 participants entering the program each year is recommended, at least initially, based on the needs of the FIA.

Program administration

Because of the magnitude of the anticipated enrollment, the FIA should appoint a full-time program administrator who will be responsible for organizing and coordinating the program. The duties will include registration of the participants, correspondence and communication with the university and participants, facilities and logistics (including materials and books), and resolving problems as they occur. The FIA will absorb the total cost of the coordinator. The university will assign an individual to serve as liaison with the agency.

The drivers for evaluation

Internally in the FIA, this program was selected for a comprehensive ROI evaluation to show its impact on the agency using a four-year time frame. Several influences created the need for this detailed level of accountability:

1. Senior administrators have requested detailed evaluations for certain programs considered to be strategic, highly visible, and designed to add value to the agency.
2. This program was perceived to be very expensive, demanding a higher level of accountability, including return on investment.
3. Because retention is such a critical issue for this agency, it was important to determine if this solution was the appropriate one. A detailed measurement and evaluation should reflect the success of the program.

4. The passage of federal legislation and other initiatives in the United States aimed at bringing more accountability for taxpayers' funds has created a shift in increased public-sector accountability.

Consequently, the FIA team planned a detailed evaluation of this program beyond the traditional program evaluation processes. Along with tracking costs, the monetary payoff would be developed, including the return on investment in the program. Because this is a very complex and comprehensive solution, other important measures would be monitored to present an overall, balanced approach to the measurement.

Recognizing the shift toward public sector accountability, the human resources staff has developed the necessary skills to conduct an ROI analysis. A small group of human resource staff members are certified in the ROI methodology. The ROI process is a comprehensive measurement and evaluation process that develops six types of data and always includes a method to isolate the effects of the program (Phillips and Phillips 2007). Because of the focus on the program's success, including the planned calculation of ROI, this proposal forecasts the impact and ROI. This forecast is an excellent prerequisite to the calculation of the ROI planned by the FIA team.

OBJECTIVES OF THE PROGRAM

From the various meetings, memos, and documents related to the proposal, the objectives evolved. The objectives were linked to the original analysis. The following is a comprehensive set of objectives for the program. The participants should:

1. Have a positive reaction to the program's content, quality, and administration.
2. Achieve an above-average grade point average for the program (3.0 out of a possible 4.0).
3. Understand their role in making the program successful.

4. Use the knowledge and skills learned in the program directly on the job.
5. Develop and apply innovative projects to add operational value to the agency.

The program should:

1. Have a very high completion rate with at least 80 percent of the participants obtaining their degrees.
2. Reduce avoidable turnover to no more than 10 percent for the target audience.
3. Enhance job satisfaction, commitment to the organization, and career development.
4. Upgrade technology and capability of the agency.
5. Generate operational results through direct value-added projects.
6. Improve recruiting success as more job applicants apply to future opportunities.
7. Generate a return on investment of at least 25 percent when benefits are spread over a four-year period.

These objectives will frame the direction and focus of the program and become important information to develop the data collection plan and ROI analysis plan necessary for the ROI postanalysis.

FORECASTING

To forecast the success of the project from a balanced perspective, a variety of types of data had to be estimated. During the initial analysis and proposal development, meetings were conducted with FIA administrators to obtain their estimates. The administrators were willing to provide estimates about the program and detail the extent of knowledge and skill enhancement and the successes that would be achieved on the job. Estimates were taken at four distinct levels:

1. Reaction to individual courses and the program, including the administrative and coordination issues.

2. Learning that will be achieved from the individual courses and the information about the program.
3. Application and implementation of the program as learning is applied on the job and the program is coordinated effectively.
4. Changes in business measures in the agency, directly related to the program (i.e., employee turnover).

In addition to these data items, program costs were estimated so that the return on investment could be calculated.

Reaction forecast

A few issues involving reaction were estimated from prospective participants and administrators. Perceived value, anticipated difficulty of the courses, and usefulness of the program on the job, were estimated in initial meetings along with other issues. At the end of each semester, a brief scannable questionnaire will be collected to measure reaction to the program. Table 12.2 shows the various items for the questionnaire and the estimated average rating. The forecast is to have a composite of at least four out of five for this program.

Next, reaction measures were estimated for courses, as the participants will evaluate the course material, instructor, delivery style, and learning environment.

Two opportunities to collect reaction data will occur at the end of each semester. For each course, the instructor will obtain direct feedback using standard instrumentation. Table 12.3 shows the estimated faculty evaluation for this program. The questions are slightly modified versions of what RSU normally collects for its instructors. In addition to providing feedback to various RSU department heads, this information will be provided to the program administrator as well as the major sponsor for this project. This constant data flow is an attempt to make adjustments if the faculty is perceived to be unresponsive and ineffective in delivering the desired courses.

Table 12.2. Reaction forecast (Measures of reaction to the program).

ISSUE	AVERAGE RATING*
Value of program†	4.6
Difficulty of program	4.0
Usefulness of program	4.4
Quality of faculty	4.1
Quality of program administration†	4.2
Appropriateness of course materials	4.1
Intent to use course material	4.3
Amount of new information†	4.4
Recommendation to others	4.7

*On a 1 to 5 scale, with 5 = exceptional
†Part of success guarantee

Table 12.3. Anticipated reaction to the faculty—faculty evaluation.

ISSUE	ESTIMATED RATING
Knowledge of Topic	4.12
Preparation for Classes	4.3
Delivery/Presentation	4.1
Level of Involvement	4.1
Learning Environment	4.2
Responsiveness to Participants	4.3
Ability to Relate to Agency Needs	4.3

*On a 1 to 5 scale, with 5 = exceptional

As Table 12.3 shows, on a scale from one to five, the estimates are positive. At several different times, adjustments will be made in an attempt to improve these two areas. The ratings presented in Table 12.3 are for the three-year project for the 100 participants who initially began the program.

Learning forecast

The initial meeting with the administrators provided an opportunity to collect information about their understanding of how the program works and their role in making the program successful. Most of the learning will take place in individual courses. The faculty member will assign grades based on formal and informal testing and assessment. These grades reflect individual learning, skills, and knowledge. Professors will use a variety of testing methodology, such as special projects, demonstrations, discussion questions, case studies, simulations, and objective tests. The overall grade point average will provide an ongoing assessment of the degree to which the participants are learning the content of the courses. Table 12.4 shows the estimated cumulative grade point average through the three-year period ending with an average of 3.26.

Application forecast

The application of the program was estimated. At the end of each year, a questionnaire will be distributed in which the participants indicate the success of the program in three areas:

1. The opportunities to use the skills and knowledge learned in the program.

Table 12.4. Learning measures: cumulative grade point averages.

YEAR	GRADE POINT AVERAGE*
1	3.3
2	3.3
3	3.2
Cumulative Grade Point Average	3.26

*Out of a possible 4.0

2. The extent to which the skills have actually been used on the job.

3. The effectiveness in the use of the skills.

In addition, several questions will focus on the progress with (and barriers to) the implementation of the program. At this level of analysis, it is important to determine if the program material is being used on the job. Program statistics will be collected, including drop-out and completion rates of the participants. The list that follows shows the categories of data for the questionnaire. Nine areas will be explored with the focus on the extent to which the participants will be utilizing the skills and knowledge learned. The analysis will also explore improvements and accomplishments over and above the individual project improvement. Barriers and enablers to implementation will be detailed in addition to input on the management support for the program along with recommendations for improvement.

Topics for annual questionnaire include:
- Course sequencing/availability
- Use of skills/knowledge
- Linkage with impact measures
- Improvements/accomplishments
- Project selection and application
- Barriers to implementation
- Enablers to implementation
- Management support for program
- Recommendations for improvement

Table 12.5 presents application estimates for knowledge and skills, showing four specific areas and the estimate for each. While these estimates reveal probable success, there was some concern about the frequency of use and opportunity to use skills. The input scale for these items is adjusted to job context. For example, in the frequency of skills, the range of potential responses is adjusted to reflect anticipated responses and, consequently, in some cases it may

Table 12.5. Application estimates: use of knowledge and skills.

ISSUE	ESTIMATED RATING*
Opportunity to use skills/knowledge	3.8
Appropriateness of skills/knowledge	4.2
Frequency of use of skills/knowledge	3.9
Effectiveness of use of skills/knowledge	4.4

*On a 1 to 5 scale, with 5 = exceptional

miss the mark. Some skills are infrequently used because of the nature of the skill and the opportunity to use them.

Business impact of turnover reduction

The primary value of the program should stem from annual voluntary turnover reduction of the target group. Turnover rates of the participants will be compared to the turnover rates of a similar group. Table 12.6 shows the estimated annualized, voluntary turnover rates for two groups. The first group is the program participants, indicating that of the 100 initial participants, 30 are forecasted to leave the program (10 percent, 10 percent, 10 percent), and 10 should leave in the first year following completion, for a total of 40 in the four-year time span. For the similar comparison group, 100 individuals will be identified and the numbers will be replenished as turnover occurred. As the numbers show, essentially the entire comparison group will leave the agency by the end of the third year. This comparison underscores the cumulative effect of an excessive turnover rate. Using the comparison group as the expected turnover rate yields a total expected turnover of 152 in the four-year period (38 percent per year). The estimated, however, is 40 for the same period.

Table 12.6. Turnover data (annualized avoidable turnover).

	1 YEAR PRIOR TO PROGRAM	1ST YEAR, SEPT. TO AUG.	2ND YEAR, SEPT. TO AUG.	3RD YEAR, SEPT. TO AUG.	1 YEAR POSTPROGRAM
Program participants	38%	10%(10)	10%(10)	10%(10)	10%(10)
Similar group	38%	38%	38%	38%	38%

Four-year expected turnover statistics = 152

Four-year actual turnover statistics = 40

Thus, the difference in the two groups (152 – 40) equals 112 turnover statistics prevented with this program.

Converting data to monetary values

The method used to convert data to monetary values was varied as well. For voluntary turnover, external studies were used to pinpoint the approximate value. From various databases, studies in similar job categories had revealed that the cost of turnover for these specialized job groups was somewhere between two and three times the average annual salary. This was considerably higher than the HR staff at the FIA anticipated. As a compromise, a value of 1.75 times the annual salary was used in the forecast. The average annual pay is $47,800.

While this value is probably lower than the actual fully loaded cost of turnover, it is conservative to assign this value. It is much better to use a conservative estimate for this value than to calculate the fully loaded cost for turnover. Most retention specialists would agree that 175 percent of annual pay is conservative for a fully loaded cost of turnover for information specialists.

The total estimated value of the turnover improvement is 112 × $47,800 × 1.75 = $9,368,800. This is a significant, yet conservative, value for the turnover reduction.

Business impact of graduate projects

An important part of the program is a graduate work-study project required to complete the master's degree. The project will involve at least two semesters of work and provide six hours of credit. It will be supervised be a faculty member and approved by the participants' immediate manager. The project must add value to the agency in some way as well as improve agency capability, operations, or technology. At the same time, it should be rigorous enough to meet the requirements of the university. In a sense, this acts as a master's thesis, although the participants are enrolled in a nonthesis option. Through this project, the participants will apply what they learn. The project will be identified during the first year, approved and implemented during the second year, and completed in the third year.

This project provides an excellent opportunity for participants to support the agency and add value to agency operations. As part of the project, participants will develop an action plan detailing how their project will be utilized on the job. The action plan, built into the graduate project, will provide the timetable and detail for application of the project. A part of the action plan is a detail of the monetary contribution to the agency (or forecast of the contribution). This is required as part of the project and will ultimately become evidence of contribution of the project. Follow-up on the action plan will provide the monetary amount of contribution from the graduate project. Table 12.7 shows the summary of the estimated data from the projects. Eighty-five students should graduate from the program and all with approved and implemented projects. Of that number, 70 should actually provide data on their project. Of that

Table 12.7. Estimated monetary values from project.

Number of Projects Approved and Implemented	85
Number of Projects Reporting Completion	70
Number of Projects Reporting Monetary Values	60
Number of Projects with Usable Monetary Values	55
Average Value of Project (Before Adjustments)	$50,000
Total Value	$1,500,000

number, 60 should be able to convert the project to a monetary value. The participants will be asked to estimate the amount of improvement that was directly related to the project (%), recognizing that other factors may influence the results. The values will be reported as adjusted values in the table. It is estimated that only 55 students will have usable values, as unsupported claims and unrealistic values will be omitted from the analysis. For example, the highest value will be eliminated because of the shock value of this number and the possibility of exaggeration. The total estimated value should be $1,500,000.

Forecasted costs

The estimated cost of the program reflects a fully loaded cost profile, which includes all direct and indirect costs. The costs proposed by RSU and anticipated by the FIA were both included. One of the major costs was the tuition for the participants. The university will charge the customary tuition, plus $100 per semester course per participant to offset the additional travel, faculty expense, books, and handouts. The tuition per semester hour will be $200 ($600 per three-hour course).

A full-time administrator at the FIA is needed, with an estimated base salary of $37,000 a year, with a 45 percent employee benefits upload factor. The administrator should have expenses of approximately $15,000 per year. Salaries for the participants represent another significant cost category. The average salary of the job categories of the employees involved in the program is estimated to be $47,800, with a 45 percent employee benefits factor. Salaries usually increase approximately 4 percent per year. Participants will attend class a total of 18 hours for each semester hour of credit. Thus, a three-hour course represented 54 hours of off-the-job time in the classroom. The total hours needed for one participant to complete the program is 756 hours (14×54).

Classroom facilities were another cost category. For the 100 participants, four different courses will be offered each semester and each course will be repeated at a different time slot. With a class size of 25, eight separate semester courses will be presented each regular semester. Half that schedule will be offered in the summer. Although the classrooms used for this program are normally used for other training and education programs offered at the agency, the cost for providing the facilities is included. (Because of the unusual demand, an additional conference room will be constructed to provide ample meeting space.) The estimate for the average cost of all meeting rooms was $40 per hour of use.

The cost for the initial assessment is also included in the cost profile. This charge, estimated to be approximately $5,000, included the turnover analysis and was prorated for the first three years. FIA's development costs for the program were estimated to be approximately $10,000 and were prorated for three years. Management time involved in the program will be minimal, but is estimated to be approximately $9,000 over the three-year period. This will consist of meetings and memos regarding the program. Finally, the evaluation costs, representing the cost to actually track the success of the program and report the results to management, are estimated to be $10,000.

Table 12.8. Total fully loaded costs of the M.S. program for 100 participants.

	YEAR 1	YEAR 2	YEAR 3	TOTAL
Initial analysis (prorated)	$1,667	$1,667	$1,666	$5,000
Development (prorated)	3,333	3,333	3,334	10,000
Tuition, regular	300,000	342,000	273,000	915,000
Tuition, premium	50,000	57,000	45,500	152,500
Salaries/benefits (participants)	899,697	888,900	708,426	2,497,023
Salaries/benefits (program administrator)	53,650	55,796	58,028	167,474
Program coordination	15,000	15,000	15,000	45,000
Facilities	43,200	43,200	34,560	120,960
Management time	3,000	3,000	3,000	9,000
Evaluation	3,333	3,333	3,334	10,000
Total	$1,372,880	$1,413,229	$1,145,848	$3,931,957

Table 12.8 shows the total cost of the project from the perspective of both RSU and the FIA. The tuition portion of the table is the cost for RSU. Essentially, tuition and tuition premium is the project cost from the RSU perspective; however, it is not the major part of the cost of the project. The rest of the costs in Table 12.8 are from the FIA perspective, and it's necessary to calculate the ROI forecast. A more detailed calculation of those costs are presented in Appendix D. (Note: Again, the contents of the appendixes in this example are not provided.)

Intangibles

The intangible benefits should be a significant part of this program. It is anticipated that the program would have an impact on a variety of other business measures as well, including the following:

1. Enhanced agency capability
2. Technology upgrade
3. Job satisfaction
4. Employee commitment
5. Recruiting success
6. Career enhancement

A measure will be listed as an intangible if at least 25 percent of either group perceived it as linked to the program. Thus, the intangibles were not included in the monetary analysis, but were considered to be important and included in the final report.

BCR and ROI forecast calculations

The benefits/cost ratio (BCR) is the total monetary benefits divided by the total program costs. For turnover reduction, the BCR calculation becomes:

$$BCR = \frac{\text{Monetary Benefits}}{\text{Total Program Costs}} = \frac{\$9,328,800}{\$3,931,957} = 2.38$$

The ROI calculation for the turnover reduction is the net program benefit divided by the cost. In formula form it becomes:

$$ROI = \frac{\text{Monetary Benefits} - \text{Total Program Costs}}{\text{Total Program Costs}} = \frac{\$5,436,843}{\$3,931,957} \times 100 = 138\%$$

The BCR for the value obtained on turnover reduction and project completion yields the following:

$$BCR = \frac{\$9{,}368{,}800 + \$1{,}500{,}000}{\$3{,}931{,}957} = \frac{\$10{,}868{,}800}{\$3{,}931{,}957} = 2.76$$

The ROI, using program benefits for the two improvements, is as follows:

$$ROI = \frac{\$10{,}868{,}800 - \$3{,}931{,}957}{\$3{,}931{,}957} \times 100 = 176\%$$

PROJECT TIMING AND SCHEDULE

The scheduling for this project is simple. The program can begin within the next fall semester if the project is approved by February 1. RSU will accept 100 students, but expect more to apply. Given RSU's previous history with accepting applicants, it is recommended that at least 200 high-potential employees be identified, because some may not meet the school's requirements for the master's degree. One hundred students will be in the first cohort following two courses per semester, including the summer sessions. The program will continue with this same schedule until the first group is completed in three years. The second cohort will begin the next fall. Essentially, 100 students will be accepted each fall. In the third year of the first program, there will be a total of up to 300 students involved in the program at the same time.

RESPONSIBILITIES

To ensure that the program operates efficiently and according to schedule, each party must meet certain responsibilities. FIA's senior leadership must support the program and encourage individuals to become involved, make excellent grades, and complete the program. The immediate managers of participants must be willing to have their participants away from work a few hours each week. Although the participants will perform their homework after working hours or in the evenings, they will have to be excused from a few routine responsibilities for the duration of the program.

A full-time administrator for the program is needed at the FIA. This person is responsible for the logistics and coordination with the students and will serve as an essential contact from RSU. The program coordinator must ensure that all of the necessary scheduling, logistics, classrooms, communications, activities, books and other materials are secured and organized properly.

The faculty must ensure that their teaching is at the highest level, customizing their lectures to the context of the FIA and willing to go the extra step to ensure that students learn and are properly encouraged and supported. They must also be willing to obtain a top-secret security clearance to work with students in classified work at the FIA. The administration at RSU will ensure that appropriate faculty is made available to this program, including the requirement that the senior, most experienced faculty will be used. Also, RSU administrators will keep the FIA posted on any issues, concerns about the program, and any changes or adjustments that must be made for it to work efficiently and smoothly.

Finally, the participants must enter this program with the determination to complete all the requirements for the degree, including attending classes regularly and making the effort to complete a graduate project. It is only through the spirit of exceptional corporation, coordination, commitment, and support that this program will achieve its objectives and meet the forecast.

DELIVERABLES

The deliverables for this project are very straightforward. They are:

1. Faculty will teach courses on a predetermined schedule.
2. RSU will offer courses consistent with the schedule.
3. Periodic updates and progress will be reported.
4. RSU will assist as necessary to develop the impact study, including the final ROI calculation after four years.
5. A briefing after four years will be conducted to discuss the forecast versus results.

COSTS

The costs for this project were presented earlier, when the ROI forecast was made. In Table 12.8, the tuition and tuition premium listings show the cost for the project from RSU's perspective. These charges will be for the duration of the first four cohorts. The costs per student basis is fixed for at least 100 students in each cohort. If the number of students changes, the other costs may change as well. These would be negotiated at that time.

EXPERIENCE AND QUALIFICATIONS

Fortunately, RSU boasts much experience with this type of project. At least a dozen other tailored, in-house programs have been implemented to meet a particular client's needs. A list of these programs and appropriate reference contacts are contained in Appendix B (not included in our discussion). In each case, the client's needs were met, and the client regarded the program as meeting their requirements. Success of the graduates was rated as better than expected.

The qualifications of the faculty are outstanding. Each faculty member assigned to this program is either at the associate or full professor level. They all have at least five years teaching experience and relevant business experience. The resumes of the faculty for this program are contained in Appendix C (not included).

RESULTS GUARANTEE

While not common in these types of proposals, guaranteeing success is on everyone's wish list. This project represents a huge investment for the FIA, roughly $4 million for each cohort. With this investment, failure is simply not an option. Consequently, all the parties will focus on achieving the desired results. With that approach, RSU will guarantee results in five key areas that focus on the quality, success, and outcomes of this project:

1. A grade point average of 3.0 would be achieved in the first cohort.
2. The faculty ratings will be 4 out of 5 on the faculty evaluation.
3. RSU will receive a rating of 4 out of 5 on three critical areas marked on Table 12.2.
4. Employee turnover will decrease to 10 percent for the group involved in the program.
5. The graduate projects will average at least $50,000 in savings per project, before adjustments.
6. The ROI will be 176% based on improvements in turnover and the value of the graduate projects.

The success guarantee should be relatively easy to obtain, and the largest payoff item, employee turnover, should be achieved easily as well. By carefully selecting students for their program who are high-potential employees, excellent grades and complete projects are almost certain. At the same time, having each employee sign a service agreement to cover the three years during and two years after the program almost ensures that those in the program will remain at the organization during the four-year period. With a penalty of repayment, the service agreement secures for the FIA an individual's cost for this program, if a student leaves during this five-year period.

Therefore, the 10 percent target should easily be obtained, thus reducing the risk of not meeting the success guarantee.

If the guarantee is not met, the penalties would be negotiated. As a minimum, if the ROI figure is not met and is actually less than 0 percent, then RSU has agreed to refund the tuition for those 100 participants. This is a difficult decision for a state university, but the RSU administrators were motivated and thought that this gesture would give them the edge of being selected for this particular program. If the program continued even if the ROI goal was not met, then the rebate on the tuition would be taken out of future tuition payments.

Conditions

For this success guarantee to be upheld, the following conditions must be met for the first four years of the first cohort (three years in class, one year after class):

1. The FIA will follow its guidelines for selecting high-potential employees for participants in this program.
2. The participants will be allowed to attend class, with no more than a total of 3 percent absenteeism.
3. The managers of participants will be active in selecting a graduate project.
4. The focus of the project will be on adding value or saving costs for the FIA.
5. The FIA will provide a top-quality administrator for the program.
6. The faculty will be given ultimate approval authority on projects.
7. The program will begin at its current target level of 100 students.
8. Participants sign a five-year service agreement.

EXHIBITS

The following appendices would be part of the project proposal.
Appendix A: Course Description
Appendix B: Similar Programs with References
Appendix C: Faculty Resumes
Appendix D: Detailed Cost Schedules

AUTHORS' THOUGHTS

This case study demonstrates the power of forecasting with a project that would normally be pursued without it. This project is a significant expenditure where the value may not be obvious until about four years into the program. At that point, the investment would be around $16 million. Thus, for this project, a forecast ROI is a very logical strategy. The success of the program hinges on several factors, and a forecast of all measures provides some indication of how this project will be accepted and utilized.

This case study also shows the power of guaranteeing results. The conditions are not very restrictive, but the guarantees are straightforward. As a follow-up note to the reader, this project was, in fact, accepted and the forecast after four years was exceeded.

◆ ◆ ◆

Epilogue

This book explores what may be a new territory for most consultants and project managers by focusing on these key issues:

1. The success factors of winning proposals
2. How to develop proposals that are effective, efficient, timely, and on-target
3. How to set objectives for proposals at a variety of levels
4. How to forecast values for up to as many as eight categories of data, including the financial ROI
5. How to develop a success guarantee to drive complete customer satisfaction

Whether you are a consultant or project manager, winning the project is the fundamental goal. This book shows how to win more projects by focusing on value—value that's important to the client, and particularly, value that shows impact, ROI, and ultimate customer satisfaction. Following the processes outlined in this book should easily double the number of project approvals and create extremely satisfied customers, as the value is forecasted and delivered throughout the project. We call the process a results-based approach to proposal writing. Not only will this approach create a strategic advantage, but it also will prepare you for the future, where this approach is becoming a requirement. If you have issues, suggestions, comments, and queries, please don't hesitate to contact us.

ROI Institute
P.O. Box 380637
Birmingham, AL 35238-0637
205.678.8101 phone
www.roiinstitute.net

References

Chapter 1

Colvin, Geoffrey, "The FedEx Edge," *Fortune.* April 3, 2006, 49.

Nickson, David, and Suzy Siddons, *Project Disasters and How to Survive Them.* London: Kogan Page, 2005.

Obama, Barak. "Inaugural Address." Inauguration of the President of the United States. Washington D.C., January 20, 2009.

Pfeffer, Jeffrey, and Robert I. Sutton, *Hard Facts, Dangerous Half-Truths and Total Nonsense: Profiting from Evidence-Based Management.* Boston: Harvard Business School, 2006.

Phillips, Jack J., and Patricia Pulliam Phillips. *Show Me the Money: How to Determine ROI in People, Projects, and Programs.* San Francisco, Berrett-Koehler Publishers, 2007.

Chapter 2

Holtz, Herman. *Proven Proposal Strategies to Win More Business.* 2nd edition. Chicago: Upstart Publishing, 2008.

Chapter 5

Freed, Richard C., Shervin Freed, and Joseph D. Romano. *Writing Winning Business Proposals: Your Guide to Landing the Client, Making the Sale, Persuading the Boss.* New York: McGraw-Hill, 2003.

Mooney, Paul. *The Effective Consultant: How to Develop the High Performance Organization.* Dublin: Oak Tree Press, 1999.

Chapter 6

DeBono, Edward. *The Six Thinking Hats.* 2nd edition. New York: Back Bay Books, 1999.

Freed, Richard C., Shervin Freed, and Joseph D. Romano. *Writing Winning Business Proposals: Your Guide to Landing the Client, Making the Sale, Persuading the Boss.* New York: McGraw-Hill, 2003.

Hall, Mary, and Susan Howlett. *Getting Funded: The Complete Guide to Writing Grant Proposals.* 4th ed. Portland, OR: Portland University Extended Studies, Continuing Education Press, 2003.

Pugh, David C., and Terry R. Bacon. *Powerful Proposals: How to Give Your Business the Winning Edge.* New York: Amacom, 2005.

Chapter 8

Kaplan, Robert S., and David P. Norton. *Translating Strategy into Action: The Balanced Scorecard.* Cambridge, MA: Harvard Business School Press, 1996.

Chapter 9

"Annual Employee Benefits Report," *Nation's Business,* January 2009.

Campanella, Jack, ed. *Principles of Quality Costs,* 3rd ed. Milwaukee: American Society for Quality, 1999.

Farris, Paul W., Neil T. Bendle, Phillip R. Pfeifer, and David J. Ribstein. *Marketing Metrics: 50+ Metrics Every Executive Should Master.* Upper Saddle River, NJ: Wharton School Publishing, 2006.

Chapter 10

Alden, Jay. "Measuring the 'Unmeasurable,'" *Performance Improvement,* May/June 2006, p. 7.

Bowers, David A. *Forecasting for Control and Profit.* Menlo Park, CA: Crisp Publications, 1997.

Horngren, C. T. <u>*Cost Accounting,*</u> 5th edition. Englewood Cliffs: NJ: Prentice-Hall, 1982.

Koppel, Nathan, and Ashby Jones. "Billable Hour under Attack." *Wall Street Journal,* August 24, 2009, p. A1.

Chapter 11

Phillips, Jack J., and Patricia Pulliam Phillips. *Show Me the Money: How to Determine ROI in People, Projects, and Programs.* San Francisco: Berrett-Koehler Publishers, 2007.

Weiss, Alan. *Value-Based Fees: How to Charge—and Get—What You're Worth.* Hoboken, NJ: Pfeiffer, 2008.

Chapter 12

Phillips, Jack J., and Patricia Pulliam Phillips. *Show Me The Money: How to Determine ROI in People, Projects, and Programs.* San Francisco, CA: Berrett-Koehler Publishers, 2007.

Index

Note: Boldface numbers indicate an illustration; *t* indicates a table.